Praise for Bob Delaney and *Surviving the Shadows*

"Filled with examples of courage, wisdom, and innovation, *Surviving the Shadows* is a must-read for anyone in the military, anyone associated with the military, or anyone protected by the military."

—Nate Self, Army Ranger, Captain (ret.), Decorated Iraq and Afghanistan War hero, author of *Two Wars: One Hero's Fight on Two Fronts— Abroad and Within*; featured on a 2006 *Dateline NBC* segment entitled "Rescue on Roberts Ridge"

"The news Bob Delaney brings to those who are challenged by PTSD, and those of us who care for them, is poignant, up-to-date, well earned, and maybe lifesaving: You are not alone; sharing yourself with others can transform your very existence."

—James S. Gordon, MD, author of *Unstuck: Your Guide to the Seven- Stage Journey Out of Depression*, Founder and Director of The Center for Mind-Body Medicine, Chairman of the White House Commission on Complementary and Alternative Medicine Policy

"Anyone who has confronted personal trauma, whether in law enforcement, on the battlefield, or in their everyday lives, can find hope and comfort from what this book tells us about understanding and coping with PTSD."

—Former U.S. Senator Sam Nunn

"Bob Delaney provides an excellent perspective on Post-Traumatic Stress in *Surviving the Shadows*. This book highlights the need for peer-to-peer therapy in the fight against PTSD."

—Joseph Pistone, former FBI agent, author, the real-life Donnie Brasco

"[With PTSD], you get this depression that develops, and you can either give up or you can keep going. And if somebody says something to you that strikes home, something that you can relate to, it can help you understand things better and move forward knowing that you're not alone. Giving a little hope is what it's all about."

—The late Clarence Clemons, legendary saxman for Bruce Springsteen's E Street Band, in the "Are You Robert?" chapter of *Surviving the Shadows*

"Bob Delaney's focus on peer-to-peer counseling is definitely a value-added adjunct to more formalized treatment modalities, and Dave Scheiber's writing brings the many stories in this book to life."

—Lawrence M. Riddles, MD, Fellow of the American College of Surgeons, Fellow of the American College of Physician Executives, Colonel, USAF, Medical Corps, United States Air Force

"Now, more than ever, it is time to remove the stigma surrounding PTSD and mental diseases. My hope is that anyone suffering can relate to any of the stories in this book and seek out the help they need in order to put their inner demons to rest."

—Joe Pantoliano, known as Joey Pants, actor, activist, and author, Founder of No Kidding, Me Too!, a foundation to combat the stigma of mental illness

"PTSD is not something to be embarrassed about and hidden, but rather a real condition that needs specific treatment and requires a tricky pathway for recovery—peer-to-peer conversations are critical components to a successful readjustment."

—William E. Estill, Professor of Communications, Norwich University, the nation's oldest military academy, Executive Producer of acclaimed documentaries *The War At Home, Vermont Fallen*, and *Our American Journey—VIETNAM*

"Bob Delaney and Dave Scheiber provide sorely needed insights into Post-Traumatic Stress Disorder (PTSD) and a highly informative and very moving tribute to the individuals who are battling with its effects."

—Terry Monkaba, Executive Director, Williams Syndrome Association

"Trauma is painful, and so is Post-Traumatic Stress Disorder. If you, or somebody you love, suffers from it, you'll find *Surviving the Shadows* a source of comfort, inspiration, and wisdom."

—Peter Carlson, author of *K Blows Top: A Cold War Comic Interlude, Starring Nikita Khrushchev, America's Most Unlikely Tourist* and *Roughneck: The Life and Times of Big Bill Haywood*, former award-winning writer and columnist for the *Washington Post*, now an editor at *American History* magazine

"Every law enforcement officer, soldier, or individual who has walked through the darkness of his or her own traumatic experience will benefit from a read of *Surviving the Shadows*."

—Bernard E. Beidel, CEAP (Community Emergency Assistance Program), Director, Office of Employee Assistance, U.S. House of Representatives, United States Capitol Police

"After 31 years of policing in four California cities and losing 26 of my law enforcement comrades to the job, Bob Delaney has found a unique way of helping others fill the void from the traumatic losses that take a bite out of our soul."

—Chief James Hyde, Antioch Police Department, MA, Clinical Psychology, Cofounder, West Coast Post-trauma Retreat, Cofounder, California National Guard's Soldier Peer-to-Peer Program

"Bob Delaney's work in the area of Post-Traumatic Stress Disorder is saving lives. *Surviving the Shadows* is a valuable tool that will help bring many broken lives 'out of the shadows' of despair and into the light of renewed hope and focus."

—Gus M. Bilirakis, member of Congress

"Bob Delaney was very effective in addressing our personnel after we suffered the tragedy of having three of our officers murdered in a 10-month period. His perspective as a former law enforcement officer who suffered through PTSD was eye-opening and comforting for our men and women."

—Jane E. Castor, Chief of Police, City of Tampa Police Department

"I personally supervised and directly observed law enforcement undercover agents who had been deployed for lengthy periods. Today, armed with Bob's wisdom I am better equipped to be sensitive and render support to friends and acquaintances who struggle to emerge from their 'shadows.'"

—Ray Maria, former Supervisory FBI Special Agent, former Acting Inspector General, U.S. Department of Labor

"*Surviving the Shadows* brings to light this crucial issue in the world today. I see Bob running up and down all levels of military command to touch leaders, warriors, Vets, Wounded Heroes, and their families— helping in the mission to acknowledge the reality and impact of PTSD until the battle is won."

—Brig. General Arthur F. "Chip" Diehl (ret. Air Force), former Deputy Director of Engagement, Plans and Policy Directorate, Headquarters U.S. Central Command, MacDill Air Force Base, Tampa, Florida

"I often wonder why during 'My War,' World War II, one heard less about PTSD? Perhaps it was kept quiet by the media? Or suppressed by the sufferers. Certainly nerves in our present civilisation seem so much more exposed, nearer the surface than in 1939–45. I hope you will continue with success in the excellent work you do."

—Excerpted from a letter to Bob Delaney from Sir Alistair Horne, British historian and author of 22 books, the latest entitled *Kissinger: 1973, the Crucial Year*

"Bob Delaney is the real deal. He has been there and is all too aware of the negative impact of PTSD. *Surviving the Shadows* is one more way that he is giving back to the often unnoticed and underappreciated public safety and military personnel who regularly put themselves in harm's way—physically and emotionally."

—Robert J. Louden, PhD, Professor, Criminal Justice, Georgian Court University, NYPD Det. Commander and Chief Hostage Negotiator (ret.)

"We have had other speakers address the staff, but none have been as moving as Bob Delaney was. After reading *Surviving the Shadows*, I felt revived and re-motivated in spirit and dedication. The message Bob shares is very inspirational and he and coauthor Dave Scheiber write in a way that touches the heart."

—Lloyd O. Pierson, President/CEO, United States African Development Foundation

"Once again, Bob Delaney and Dave Scheiber form a winning team—this time blowing the whistle on a grave threat to the health of Americans, inspiring our sympathy and calling us to action."

—Roy Peter Clark, Senior Scholar, the Poynter Institute, author of *Writing Tools* and *The Glamour of Grammar*

"*Surviving the Shadows* is a must-read for all those who serve their city, county, state, or country. Post-Traumatic Stress for too long has been treated like a secret—this book helps to remove that stigma and provides education, awareness, and hope."

—Don O'Leary, New York City Fire Department Captain (ret.)

"As a Security Inspector for the Witness Protection Program, I had the privilege of working with Bob Delaney. Bob not only dealt with his PTSD but is actively helping others do the same. This book will increase awareness and provide a better understanding of a disorder that has risen to epidemic proportions."

—Flavio "Flip" Lorenzoni, Witness Security Inspector, Chief Deputy of the U.S. Marshals Office, New York

"Bob's passion and drive to help those suffering as a result of these emotionally powerful events is truly admirable. Bob breaks the mindset that PTSD is a sign of weakness, and enforces the fact PTSD is a sign of being a human who has experienced something horrible."

—Tim W. Dietz, MA, Retired Fire Captain/Paramedic, author of *Scenes of Compassion: A Responder's Guide for Dealing with Emergency Scene Emotional Crisis*, CEO, Behavioral Wellness Resources, Lake Oswego, Oregon

"Bob Delaney's book, *Surviving the Shadows*, clearly defined PTSD, cumulative stress, and suicidal ideation. His book helps erase the stigma of reaching out for help, stresses the importance of trauma management, and provides an understanding for America's Finest, both law enforcement and military."

—Donna G. Schulz, Law Enforcement Coordination Manager, U.S. Attorney's Office, Middle District of Florida

SURVIVING
the
SHADOWS

A Journey of Hope into Post-Traumatic Stress

BOB DELANEY
WITH DAVE SCHEIBER

Foreword by General Robert W. Cone, United States Army

This book is not intended as a substitute for medical advice from a qualified physician. The intent of this book is to provide accurate general information in regard to the subject matter covered. If medical advice or other expert help is needed, the services of an appropriate medical professional should be sought.

Published by Sourcebooks, Inc.
P.O. Box 4410, Naperville, Illinois 60567-4410
(630) 961-3900
Fax: (630) 961-2168
www.sourcebooks.com

Library of Congress Cataloging-in-Publication Data

Delaney, Bob
  Surviving the shadows : a journey of hope into post-traumatic stress / Bob Delaney with Dave Scheiber ; foreword by Robert W. Cone.
    p. cm.
  1. Post-traumatic stress disorder—Case studies. 2. Post-traumatic stress disorder—Treatment. I. Scheiber, Dave. II. Title.
  RC552.P67D455 2011
  616.85'21—dc23

2011019547

Printed and bound in the United States of America.
VP 10 9 8 7 6 5 4 3 2 1

Todd—
Great working with
you at "CFO"

This book is dedicated to all those who serve others—
the men and women of the military, law enforcement, fire
departments, and emergency service first responder units
and their families. By the nature of the work they do,
they are at a higher risk to experience traumatic events
and suffer visible and invisible wounds.
Thank you for all you do to make our world a better place.

—Bob Delaney, August 2011

Stay Safe!

Bob Delaney

You are the
Best—

CONTENTS

Foreword

After nearly ten years of conflict in Iraq and Afghanistan, America's brave service members continue to bear the many burdens of war. Among these ongoing burdens are Post-Traumatic Stress (PTS) and Post-Traumatic Stress Disorder (PTSD). The persistent exposure to the traumatic experiences of war and other incidents such as the November 5, 2009, shooting at Fort Hood, Texas, has caused cases of PTSD to rise. Unfortunately, identifying those affected, in order to provide them the treatment they deserve, is a significant challenge. We face a continuing dilemma in that the barriers of individual denial or the stigmas associated with admitting behavioral health issues often mask the conditions.

Fortunately, those suffering from PTSD have been given a champion in this cause—Bob Delaney.

As a victim of the disorder, Bob helped us—and continues to help us—in breaking through those barriers. I met Bob shortly after November 5, when he came to Fort Hood to meet with soldiers, civilians, and family members and to share his personal experience with PTS from his time as an undercover agent infiltrating the Mafia. His passion for helping others and his personal courage have affected countless victims of PTSD across the nation and overseas.

In my thirty-one years of service, I have come to know that the best thing about the Army is that it is made up of individuals who embody the ideal of service to the nation and to one another. Bob embodies that ideal as well. I am truly grateful to him for his dedication to those who serve. He is a servant in the truest sense of the word. His commitment to the PTSD cause and his genuine care for the military around the world are a testament to his character.

In *Surviving the Shadows*, Bob not only helps individual victims of PTSD find their way out of the shadows but brings this disorder out of the shadows as well. By telling the stories of other survivors and educating us on the latest medical treatments, *Surviving the Shadows* provides PTSD sufferers, their families, and their friends a source of hope.

General Robert W. Cone

United States Army

CHAPTER ONE

Post-Trauma Pathways

"Don't let life discourage you; everyone who got to where they are had to begin where they were."

—Richard Evans

I t is impossible to walk the long halls of the Al-Faw Palace in Baghdad without reflecting on the extreme pain and suffering that the man who lived within the marble walls perpetrated.

The sprawling structure rises from placid blue waters that give no hint of the unfathomable terror that festered here under the reign of Saddam Hussein. The surrounding waters not only once served as a protective moat for the compound but also, in accordance with Saddam's beliefs, hid the sin inside from the eyes of Allah.

When I arrived at the palace in the summer of 2010, memories of that evil lingered—along with faded stains of blood in rooms where Hussein's henchmen tortured, beyond imagination, those whom they deemed enemies of the regime. But this is where the top U.S. Army command was operating, under the name Camp Victory, orchestrating the battlefield and urban combat strategy for our brave men and women in the armed forces.

I had come on a goodwill tour to the heart of the desert war zone to meet with U.S. troops and officers, just as I had done one year earlier when I'd been embedded with ground forces in Mosul. My personal mission—work that has become the guiding force in my life—was to reach out to people grappling with an unseen enemy from within, Post-Traumatic Stress Disorder (PTSD).

I knew the ravages of this condition firsthand from my undercover duty in the 1970s for the New Jersey State Police, before my second career as a referee in the National Basketball Association. And for nearly twenty-five years, I've never stopped speaking with and counseling members of law enforcement, the military, and others who have endured psychological trauma in their lives.

That is what brought me into a room that August morning in an upper chamber of the palace, the headquarters of General Ray Odierno, top commander of U.S. forces in Iraq—an imposing six-foot-five presence who shares my Jersey roots. The meeting included military staff and Deputy Commander General Robert Cone, who became known to the nation as the commander of Fort Hood during the tragic massacre in 2009.

In less than a week, Vice President Joseph Biden and Secretary of Defense Robert Gates would meet with General Odierno and announce the historic drawdown of U.S. troops in a phase dubbed "Operation New Dawn."

Yet now I was seated beside General Odierno in a place where he had hosted countless Iraqi leaders and world dignitaries. With General Cone flanking me, we focused on a subject that would outlive the war itself. After some brief introductions, General Odierno turned and asked me to describe my work with Post-Traumatic Stress Disorder. I proceeded to share many details and ideas with him—chief among them a principle that lies at the heart of my approach and beliefs in combating PTSD: peer-to-peer therapy.

Although I recognize all the important medical treatments available, I view peer-to-peer therapy as the first line of defense in dealing with Post-Traumatic Stress Disorder: cops need to speak to cops, firefighters to firefighters, soldiers to soldiers, combat spouses to combat spouses, and accident victims to accident victims.

The generals listened intently and expressed their complete agreement. As we talked, I was struck by the irony that we were discussing ways to fight a disorder in the very confines of a tyrant who had caused untold cases of it. And I came away more certain than ever that we should take the same preventative approach to this issue as we did with drugs and tobacco years ago: awareness and education need to become our focus so that we do not wait for Post-Traumatic Stress to become Post-Traumatic Stress *Disorder*.

That is where peer-to-peer therapy comes into play. It is a pillar of the work I share when speaking before audiences on Post-Traumatic Stress Disorder. Many of the same experiences and philosophies that I share in those presentations entwine the journey of the men and women—from *all* walks of life—whose courageous and uplifting stories you will learn about in these pages.

Anyone who has suffered from PTSD—whether it has been brought on by a car accident, horrific moments in combat, domestic abuse, being the victim of a crime, surviving a natural or man-made disaster, enduring bullying in school, or even living a double life inside the Mafia—needs to become aware of the triggers that can bring manifestations of old traumas rushing back. That's one of the insidious aspects and defining traits of a condition that has risen to epidemic proportions today.

If you're reading these words, whether standing inside a bookstore, sitting comfortably at home, or settling in for a flight, chances are that something has drawn you to the subject of Post-Traumatic Stress Disorder and a desire to learn more about it. You may have experienced its effects. Maybe a family member or friend is dealing with it, or maybe you have simply encountered the topic in news reports. Whatever the reason, you are about to gain a deeper, more personal knowledge of a subject that is only beginning to be fully understood—especially as it relates to the disorder's ripple effect in our society.

PTSD has shown up in news reports and dialogues about fighting forces in Iraq and Afghanistan with disturbing frequency in recent years. Hundreds of troops are committing suicide each year—with the Army reporting an all-time-high number of thirty-two confirmed or suspected suicides for a single month in June 2010. Twenty-two of those deaths involved soldiers who had seen combat, and ten had been deployed between two and four times.

According to an exhaustive, five-hundred-page 2008 study by the Rand Corporation, "The Invisible Wounds of War," approximately 18.5 percent of U.S. service members returning from

Afghanistan and Iraq have experienced PTSD or major depression. Of the 1.64 million troops deployed at the time of the study, that percentage equates to three hundred thousand returning veterans suffering from PTSD or depression. About half of those veterans in need of treatment seek it, the study found, but "only slightly more than half who receive treatment get minimally adequate care." A persistent problem, according to Rand, was a fear among veterans that seeking mental health care would damage their career prospects or cause coworkers to lose trust in them.

The crisis may even be more widespread than previously believed. A CBS News report in 2011 cited an estimate by Chairman of the Joint Chiefs, Admiral Michael Mullen, drawn from Veterans Administration data, that some 800,000 troops suffer from the condition.

But PTSD is hardly limited to the military. On a broader scale, the National Institute of Mental Health (NIMH) in Bethesda, Maryland, reports that 7.7 million Americans eighteen years and older suffer from the condition.

It's human nature to grow numb to an onslaught of television news coverage—from the unsettling statistics about troops returning from combat to reports of devastating floods and earthquakes. But that makes it all the more important that we look beneath the terminology to understand the meaning of Post-Traumatic Stress Disorder.

• • •

So before we go any further, let's establish what Post-Traumatic Stress Disorder is. PTSD became a recognized diagnosis in 1980, but it was a well-documented mental and emotional condition afflicting vast numbers of people for years prior to receiving official medical status. It was known by the name "shell shock" during and after World War I and "battle fatigue" in World War II, often going undiagnosed or sometimes resulting in a Section 8 discharge when a soldier was deemed mentally unfit to serve. But today we know so much more.

The NIMH offers an excellent description of the condition:

> Post-Traumatic Stress Disorder, PTSD, is an anxiety disorder that can develop after exposure to a terrifying event or ordeal in which grave physical harm occurred or was threatened. Traumatic events that may trigger PTSD include violent personal assaults, natural or human-caused disasters, accidents, or military combat…When in danger, it's natural to feel afraid. This fear triggers many split-second changes in the body to prepare to defend against the danger or to avoid it. This "fight-or-flight" response is a healthy reaction meant to protect a person from harm. But in PTSD, this reaction is changed or damaged. People who have PTSD may feel stressed or frightened even when they're no longer in danger…have persistent frightening thoughts and memories of their ordeal and feel emotionally numb, especially with people they were once close to.

Symptoms, according to the NIMH definition, are grouped into three main categories:

1. *Re-experiencing, such as flashbacks and bad dreams. "Words, objects, or situations that are reminders of the event can also trigger re-experiencing."*
2. *Avoidance, such as feeling strong guilt, depression, or worry and "losing interest in activities that were once enjoyable in the past."*
3. *Hyper-arousal, such as being easily startled, feeling tense or on edge, having difficulty sleeping, eating, and concentrating and/or having angry outbursts.*

In addition, the NIMH definition states: "It's natural to have some of these symptoms after a dangerous event. Sometimes people have very serious symptoms that go away after a few weeks. This is called acute stress disorder, or ASD. When the symptoms last more than a few weeks and become an ongoing problem, they might be PTSD. Some people with PTSD don't show any symptoms for weeks or months."

• • •

My personal journey into Post-Traumatic Stress began four decades ago, a process of research and learning that set the stage for *Surviving the Shadows*. In reading this book, you will find stories of men and women who have lived through—and are dealing with— deeply traumatic events in their lives. You will hear from doctors and counselors on the cutting edge of PTSD research and learn the physiological and psychological responses that take place within our bodies. I believe these pioneering perspectives of individuals in the medical community shed important light on treating the condition.

But I also am a firm proponent of a parallel and complementary method for helping people confront their PTSD—the peer-to-peer approach. People who have experienced traumatic events need to speak with others who have lived through similar situations.

I choose the word *similar* very carefully, because none of us can have exactly the same experience as anyone else. I have first-hand knowledge of the resistance that many cops and soldiers feel toward formal medical approaches for getting the help they need. Their objections usually arise from the unfortunate stigma attached to PTSD that still persists, as if seeing a professional were an admission of a weakness that might undermine their standing or reputation.

We need to change this perception of the disorder as some kind of mental deficiency. As with a concussion, it is an invisible condition and, left untreated, can lead to devastating consequences. For decades, pro football players did their best to ignore potentially serious head injuries, which have historically been written off as almost harmless and described by players as having their "bell rung," for fear of looking weak or possibly losing their jobs to other players should they take time off to recover. The National Football League has taken steps to deal positively with the concussion problem, just as society is gradually recognizing Post-Traumatic Stress as a real disorder with grave side effects if left unchecked.

That's where the peer-to-peer approach can be critically important. It is a first step sufferers can take toward self-awareness and acknowledgment that they have a problem, especially if they are not ready to seek more formal medical help—or if they are fearful of the consequences of making their problems known. Furthermore, it helps to verbalize the details of the trauma to oneself. We go from experiencing the event to holding it within, but avoidance and pushing the memory away is a dangerous path to take. Instead, we can use "self-talk" to address our feelings and bring them out into the open.

I learned this from having lived through PTSD. When I got to the point where I could hear my voice utter the words related to the traumatic experience, it was liberating. The simple act of talking about that painful situation—speaking out loud to myself—prepared me for the next step: discussing it with another person, a peer who had experienced something similar. That is truly where the road begins in feeling free from traumatic life experiences.

I share an image with folks when I make presentations. I ask people in the audience to picture me holding a balloon filled with air. How do we get that air out? If you let the balloon go, it flies around the room and you have no control over what it does or where it lands. If you take a pin and pop it, you can get the air out, but you don't have a balloon anymore. If you turn the balloon upside down, and you have enough patience to let the air out a little bit at a time, it will make that awful screeching noise that you might not want to hear, but when all the air is out, you have a full balloon in your hand that you can use again.

That's us—we need to get the air out of our own personal balloons. There is stuff inside of us that has to come out. The first step is talking about it—acknowledging it. But what I've come to find is that the first step doesn't have to involve psychologists and psychiatrists working with us to figure things out. Yes, their expertise and training can and does play a valuable part in the healing process. It certainly did for me, as I later describe. But sharing experiences with others who have endured something similar can have an enormous impact—and the stories you will read in the coming chapters vividly illustrate this point. In fact, each story mirrors in its own way the immense value of peer-to-peer sharing on the road to recovery. At the core, sharing with one's peers gives a deep and needed message: you are not alone. The connection to others can be a lifeline, the first sign of light.

The reality is this: If you don't talk about your pain and the anguish you've experienced, it's still going to come out somehow, some way. A cop who has lived too many nightmares might self-medicate by hitting the bar too often and then develop a drinking problem. Depression and anxiety might paralyze someone else. The bottom line is that living constantly in the midst of life-and-death crises takes a severe toll, not only on individual lives but also eventually on entire families. PTSD has a ripple effect, and it cannot be ignored.

• • •

I chose *Surviving the Shadows* as a title because that is what I hope will take place for those who are enduring the shadows of Post-Traumatic Stress Disorder. You can and *will* survive PTSD if you have a heightened attitude and awareness of the condition. You can help others suffering from PTSD as well. However, you must realize that there is no finish line. I wish I could tell you that if you just follow ten steps everything will be better. But surviving PTSD is a lifelong experience. In fact, the best thing you can do is change your thinking about what PTSD represents:

Process—Acknowledging, accepting, and becoming aware.

Time—Understanding that it's not going to be solved overnight.

Support—Relying on peers who have had similar experiences, and experts in the field.

Desire—Being dedicated to healing yourself.

My first insight into the condition—and how to help someone suffering from it—came in front of a television set many years ago. I was watching *M*A*S*H*—the classic CBS sitcom that ran from 1972 to 1983 about the 4077th Mobile Army Surgical Unit during the Korean War. Dr. Sidney Freedman often visited Captain Benjamin "Hawkeye" Pierce and his colleagues. The actor Allan Arbus played the Army psychiatrist who helped doctors and nurses on the front line deal with the invisible wounds that they were confronting. His steady, insightful manner brought attention and relief to those traumatic experiences.

That portrayal of the doctor always stuck with me. I realized, even in my early twenties, that we all need help dealing with *stuff*, even the professionals whose job it is to heal us. In the summer of 2009, I was at the Camp Diamondback base hospital in Mosul, Iraq, on a tour of the Army facility conducted by a medical staff member. When we entered the emergency room, I asked the attending doctor a question: "Who takes care of you?" He responded with a smile and walked with me to the rear of the hospital. There, behind a frontline medical unit in the middle of the desert, was a Zen garden, complete with grass and fountains. It was a place of solitude, a place where doctors and nurses could clear their heads and emotions, a place that made the ugly facts of war—the traumatic events they were facing every day—fade away. The garden gave the doctors and nurses an inner peace that rejuvenated them.

We all need that balance. And people dealing with PTSD need to find what brings them a similar inner peace—a crucial part of the process in dealing with the disorder.

As you read this book, I ask you to think about a traumatic event you have experienced, a situation that may have stemmed from service in the military, work in law enforcement, firefighting, or emergency services, or being the victim of a crime, a motor vehicle accident, or even a natural disaster.

The point is to use *your* experience for a better understanding of the chapters ahead. Think of how *you* would have felt living through those events, and put yourself in the shoes of those whose stories are told here. Storytelling is a valuable learning tool, and you are about to get to know many brave men and women who share their stories and experiences. They will provide you with greater insight into what it means to face PTSD—and the power of the human spirit that helps in the healing process.

This book does not attempt to provide a clinical step-by-step guide for dealing with the disorder. It is a collection of tales about real people and how they have coped with real tragedy and trauma. And as you will discover, the flow of the ensuing chapters mirrors the unpredictable paths of so many journeys. Just as you don't always know what lies around every corner, the stories you will read move from one to the next in a way that reflects the unexpected twists and turns on the road of life. They are united not by chronological order but by a common quest for knowledge, personal growth, and self-awareness.

Ultimately, I hope this book prompts discussion of and reflection on ways to work through PTSD and provides a heightened understanding of the emotional, psychological, and physiological facets of the disorder—all part of the path we are about to explore together in *Surviving the Shadows*.

(left to right) General Robert W. Cone, me, and General Ray Odierno at the Al-Faw Palace headquarters for the Victory Base Complex. Baghdad, Iraq, 2010.

CHAPTER TWO

A New Step in an Old Journey

"The greatest thing in this world is not so much where we are, but in which direction we are moving."

—Oliver Wendell Holmes

My name is Robert J. Delaney—D-E-L-A-N-E-Y."
The sound of the letters rolling from my lips was completely surreal. The mere act of speaking them aloud from the witness stand in a crowded New York City courtroom on that sweltering summer day in 2009 was like pushing the rewind button on some kind of personal time machine. Suddenly, I was hurtling three decades into my past—back to a world I thought I'd left behind on the murky docks of north Jersey, where for nearly three years I had lived an undercover life to infiltrate the Mafia.

The evidence I collected during that harrowing investigation led to many hours testifying in trial after trial throughout the

Northeast during the late 1970s. I'd hear my name called and make the long, solitary walk from the back of the courtroom to the witness stand. Each deliberate step was accompanied by a sense of my duty as a young New Jersey state trooper, a feeling that overshadowed the tension that inevitably pulsed through my body. No matter how difficult the circumstances were, my words always flowed from my complete commitment to the mission. I focused on whatever testimony I was about to give, with an overriding desire to follow it through to the end and put the bad guys away.

Now, on the witness stand more than thirty years later, I couldn't shake the cloud of agitation that had hovered over me for weeks. The experience was like tearing a scab off an old wound, exposing a painful and turbulent period in my life. Despite my success as an undercover agent and the landmark breakthroughs of our Project Alpha operation, those years living with a false identity had cast me into a world of darkness. Only after much personal struggle and help from others had I somehow found my way out of the shadows, ultimately discovering a new path.

Unlike those walks I had made to the witness stand as a young trooper, this day I entered from a small, well-guarded witness room outside the court of the Honorable U.S. District Judge John Gleeson. Looking straight ahead, I saw the attorneys for the federal government and the defense huddling at their tables, reviewing last-minute strategies as all of us waited for Judge Gleeson to emerge from his chamber and the jury to be seated in their box across from me.

The long wait further intensified my restlessness—a sensation I recognized from my twenty-four years as an NBA ref, that same adrenaline-tinged desire to get out of the locker room before a game and step onto the hardwood. Adding to my general discomfort were the icy looks on the faces of dozens of people in the gallery. I knew they had come to support the defendant in this case and regarded me with utter disdain.

Then, in a flurry of motion, heads turned and in walked defendant Michael Coppola, escorted by U.S. marshals. He wore tinted glasses, had grown gray and bald on top, and the years had put another twenty pounds on his stocky frame. But I could still recognize the face of the young, cocky mafioso I had come to know so well during my undercover duty from 1975 to 1977. I'd spent a good portion of those nearly three years doing business and socializing with Coppola and his friends, much of the time wearing a wire and recording his every word and those of his Mob brethren.

Coppola was one of more than thirty members of organized crime convicted and imprisoned following our investigation. The last time I had seen him was in a similar courtroom three decades earlier. Now, our paths were crossing once again in a celebrated trial covered daily by the New York tabloid media. The headlines and stories referred to him as "Mikey Cigars" Coppola, but I knew him by another code name, Andy, because of his onetime resemblance to the race-car driver Andy Granatelli. After more than a decade on the lam, he was now on trial for the unsolved 1977 murder of fellow mobster Johnny "Coca-Cola" Lardiere as well as a bevy of new extortion and racketeering charges extending back to my Project Alpha days.

After a few minutes, our eyes eventually locked and transported us to an earlier time: me, the Jersey trooper masquerading as a trucking company president doing business with the Mob; he, the swaggering wiseguy and right-hand man of the ruthless Genovese capo Tino Fiumara. Instinctively, we nodded and smiled despite ourselves, before casting our glances elsewhere in the room.

Finally, Judge Gleeson arrived. He took his seat and, in a heartbeat, I was plummeting back through the years. A member of the prosecution team for the U.S. Attorney's Office—a tough young lawyer I had met only weeks earlier, named Amy Busa—asked me to identify myself, then requested permission from the judge to proceed with her direct examination.

"Good afternoon, Mr. Delaney. Were you previously employed by the New Jersey State Police?" she asked.

"Yes," I said, relieved that the questioning had finally begun.

"When were you employed by the New Jersey State Police Department?"

I knew this mundane, building-block drill well and kept my answers short and simple as Busa established the foundation for my presence in the case.

"I graduated from the State Police Academy in 1973."

"And how long did you serve with the New Jersey State Police?"

"Fourteen years."

"Turning your attention to the period 1975 and 1977, September 1977, were you involved in a particular investigation?"

"Yes."

"What was your role in that investigation?"

"I was an undercover operative."

"And what was your undercover operative ID or name?"

"I took on the name of Robert Alan Covert, or Bobby Covert."

Bobby Covert. It was the name and double identity that would change the course of my life. As Bobby Covert, I lived and worked for three years in the constant, threatening presence of the Genovese and Bruno crime families. I was the president of Alamo Trucking, a fully functioning company created for our investigation. We carried out countless transactions with members of those crime families while gathering evidence against them—the distance between my survival and certain death was often as thin as the wire I wore beneath my shirt. I had put Bob Delaney's life on hold and created Bobby Covert's persona. After I surfaced from the investigation and tried to renew my previous life, I found myself on a road that wove perilously through psychological and emotional upheaval. Ultimately, the burden of being two people simultaneously, and the trauma that doing so engendered, caused me to develop a passion that has become central to my life: helping those suffering as I once did from the ravaging effects of Post-Traumatic Stress Disorder.

"And did Mr. Covert have employment?" Busa continued.

In my days as a seasoned trooper, I had learned the importance of speaking slowly for the sake of the jury. But for the previous two years, I had retrained myself to tell the complicated, nuanced story of my undercover life at a faster clip—a must for public appearances to promote the story about the experiences in my book, *Covert*. I *had* to tell the story quickly to hold people's attention in formats governed by time constraints and commercial breaks. So, without realizing it, I launched into my answer in my new, brisk cadence.

"When the investigation started, there were three FBI agents and two New Jersey state troopers as part of this New Jersey Joint Intelligence Operation, code name Project Alpha. We started a trucking company, Mid Atlantic Air-Sea Transportation in Elizabeth, New Jersey…"

I proceeded to explain that I was designated the owner of Alamo Trucking and detailed the other principal participants in our operation, answering Busa's questions as quickly as she could ask them. That's when I heard the abrupt, admonishing voice of Judge Gleeson.

"Excuse me. Sorry. But could you wait until she's done before you start your answer, and speak a little slower, OK?"

"Yes, sir," I replied, slowing my delivery down a notch.

There was still much about my trip into the past that I had to relive from the stand, and even though I wanted to speed through it, the judge was not allowing that option. But it wasn't the only significant trip weighing on my shoulders this day. A journey of nine thousand miles was scheduled to begin almost immediately after I completed my testimony. I would be flying into the war zone of Iraq—an opportunity to support soldiers fighting a ruthless enemy on the outside and to help them learn to subdue the demons that can arise within, as I had done following my work on Project Alpha. But for now, I had to push any thoughts of that trip out of my head and focus on the details from an old case that once again had me in its grip.

• • •

My presence on the witness stand, which stirred up long-buried anxieties in me, had its origins in a phone call I'd received a year earlier at my home in West Florida.

"R. J., how've you been?" asked the voice on the other end.

I go by a few names: I'm Robert to my mom and my aunts, Rob to my dad and my sister, Bob in my professional life, and Bobby to old friends. But when I hear "R. J." I know it's someone from my fourteen years with the New Jersey State Police.

The caller was Brian Lilley, a retired trooper who now worked for the New Jersey Criminal Justice Department. We spent a few minutes reminiscing about our trooper days, which was nice. But I couldn't help but wonder why he was calling. Finally, Brian got to the point: he asked if I would speak to FBI agent Kevin Brown. He was assigned to the Organized Crime Unit in New York City and was investigating some of the very same wiseguys I had helped convict in Project Alpha.

I was willing to answer whatever few questions the agent might have for me; I certainly knew the topic inside out. So several days later, Agent Brown and I had a phone conversation. He wanted to know more about the details of our investigation. In no time we were discussing the same names—in particular Michael Coppola—and code words that had been part of my everyday life as Bobby Covert.

Then Kevin told me he had first heard about my book *Covert* during a wiretapped conversation between two mobsters watching an NBA game I was working. "They said, 'That's the guy who wrote the book about workin' as a Jersey trooper undercover cop,'" Kevin explained. That's the moment he knew he needed to talk to me. We spoke for an hour and had several follow-up calls and then he visited my home. I was more than glad to provide background information about some of the key Mob players I knew and to interpret the language he was hearing through wiretaps in his current Mafia investigation.

I thought that would be the extent of my participation. But several months later, Kevin asked if I'd be willing to testify in court. "If you need me for your case, you don't have much of a case—I've been off the streets for thirty years," I told Kevin bluntly.

My response was similar to the one I gave during my rookie NBA season of 1987, when Grady O'Malley, a former NBA player who had become an assistant U.S. attorney, asked me to testify in the case against the mobster Jackie DiNorscio. Grady and I had different viewpoints about the value of my participation, and I did not share his enthusiasm for the case. My stance was eventually underscored by the jury verdict in what had become the longest trial in New Jersey federal court history, and it ended without a single conviction (the case was later portrayed on the big screen in *Find Me Guilty,* with Vin Diesel playing Jackie DiNorscio).

But Kevin didn't flinch. He arranged another visit to my house, this time accompanied by Assistant U.S. Attorney Busa and another FBI agent, Mike Lewis. They pressed harder for my testimony, and I pushed back with equal force. On the one hand, I assured them that I completely understood and supported their investigation; on the other hand, I wanted nothing to do with it as one of their prize witnesses. I promptly pointed out that I was no longer a trooper in pursuit of bad guys and that I'd done my time. I explained that the operational aspects of undercover work had long since ended for me. I had dealt with the emotional trauma of living two separate lives—one rooted in the Mob subculture and one in the law enforcement world. And I had endured more than enough abuse on the stand from defense attorneys using any tactic they could to get their Mob clients off the hook.

Still, they persisted and asked me not to shut the door on testifying. In the days that followed, I kept mulling over the idea. I was familiar enough with the legal system to know that if they wanted me there, all they had to do was serve me with a subpoena and I would be legally responsible to testify. I guess you could say I had one of those man-in-the-mirror talks with myself. I definitely did not want to be picking at that emotional scab, but maybe that wasn't the point. I had to admit that I had a unique connection to this case, so it was my obligation to testify. Besides, I was inspired by the way Kevin and Mike were so passionate about pursuing this case. I realized that they were now carrying the torch that I had once carried.

Reluctant or not, I was in, no matter how uncomfortable the ride would be. But that didn't change my feelings about Assistant U.S. Attorney Busa. When she visited my house, I'd tried to explain to her the complex, traumatic aspect of my undercover experience, and she seemed to brush it aside in her zeal to secure my participation in the trial.

"That was a long time ago—I'm sure you'll be fine," she'd said matter-of-factly.

It took all I had not to show her the door. She clearly had no idea of what I'd lived through, and this is often how Post-Traumatic Stress Disorder is dismissed in our society. The fact is, when I emerged from Project Alpha, I had no support system to help me sort through the storm of conflicting emotions. In the New Jersey State Police, there was no information about PTSD back then.

After my years as Bobby Covert ended and I tried to resume my regular life as a trooper, it was my friends and colleagues who reached out to help me when they saw my pattern of self-destructive behavior. A fellow detective named John Schroth was the first guy to help. After we'd been out on surveillances or after I testified in court, we'd stop off at a bar for a drink. And I'd find myself slipping back into my Bobby Covert personality, getting belligerent or acting like a wiseguy, buying rounds for everyone in the place as if I still had the endless cash that had been available to me during Project Alpha. John was the first one who called attention to my strange behavior. He had a background in psychology from Rutgers University, and that gave him insight into my problem. And he also had the courage to take me aside and say, "Something is wrong with you." I wanted to deny it, but I knew he was right.

And there were other signs of trouble. I felt an ongoing paranoia after learning that there was a Mob hit out on me—a conversation picked up on a state police wiretap that was supported by informant information. The mounting stress led to unpredictable outbursts at home; I'd punch holes in the wall, then cover them up with picture frames to hide the damage from visitors. I was exhibiting classic symptoms of Post-Traumatic Stress Disorder.

One incident captured all the raging emotions I was feeling at the time. One morning I opened up the door of my house to pick up the newspaper in my driveway. But the instant I stepped onto my porch, I heard a rapid-fire roar overhead and froze at the sight of a low-flying helicopter just above the trees. After everything I had lived through during the investigation, my brain interpreted virtually anything unusual as a potential threat to me and my family, as if somebody were out to get me at any given moment. Without time to analyze the situation, my fear took over and

"Protect yourself!" flashed through my mind. I quickly stepped back inside, slammed the door, and ducked for safety. What my mind and body had reacted to as imminent danger was only a helicopter for the Ocean County Mosquito Control Department. But that was my state of mind at the time—I was constantly agitated, unable to sleep because of the street noises I heard outside at night, and struggling to regain my equilibrium.

But I've always been lucky in life. And I got lucky again when I ran into my old psychology professor from Jersey City State College, Dr. Hank Campbell. I talked to Dr. Campbell about the episodes of fear, anger, and depression that had overtaken me after the investigation. At his suggestion, we began informal therapy sessions, and he eventually identified what I was experiencing. He said, "Bobby, you're going through Post-Traumatic Stress Disorder." At that time, the only reference to PTSD that I'd heard was in reports of guys coming home from Vietnam. I went into total denial.

But as I began to tell him about my emotional roller-coaster ride and listen to his comments, my eyes opened to reality. I did have a problem—and it was directly related to the deeply disturbing ordeal I had undergone while living two lives. I was having a normal reaction to a very abnormal situation.

Then, once again, a lucky break fell my way. Louie Freeh was an FBI case agent in New York City back in those days (before becoming the fifteenth director of the Federal Bureau of Investigation). We were working on cases that spilled over from Project Alpha, and he understood that I was going through a difficult time. So he encouraged me to talk with an FBI agent named Joe Pistone, someone many people know by his street name: Donnie Brasco. I first met Joe in October 1982 at a law enforcement-only dinner on Governor's Island in New York City, honoring him for his undercover work. Our relationship grew from that initial meeting, and he provided me with my first understanding of the power of peer-to-peer therapy. When I spoke to Joe, I knew that he knew what I was talking about. He had lived the same kind of life I had undercover; we'd gone through similar experiences. And Joe said it best to me one day: "Bobby, you know what your problem is? You've got one foot in the life of Bobby Covert and you've got one foot in Bob Delaney's life. You better get two feet in that Delaney life, because you don't like who Bobby Covert was, and that's a layer of your skin that you've got to shed…You've got to realize that what you did was the right thing. The people you worked against were the people who were wrong. You were doing your job. Nothing more, nothing less."

With the help of people like John Schroth, Hank Campbell, and Joe Pistone, I began to get my pain out into the open and to regain control of my life. I spent my spare time refereeing youth basketball. The purity of the games attracted me—they were a contrast to the evil and violence that had surrounded me. Before long, I realized not only that I enjoyed officiating but also that the game and my role in it gave me a sense of peace and balance. It was a kind of therapy in that it restored my confidence and hope for the future, and it opened the door to a second career in the NBA.

As I became more aware of the sources of my emotional turmoil, I saw my experience in perspective. We're all good at doing something in this world. And I was good at doing undercover work. I could be wired up, meet with the wiseguys, and go through my whole Bobby Covert routine—doing business with them, socializing over dinners, making plans for the next scheme. But after a meeting I'd get two miles down the road and I'd have to pull over and throw my guts up, or I'd have to find the first gas station I could because I had diarrhea. I didn't tell anybody about that back then because cops like to think of themselves as being able to leap tall buildings in a single bound. They tell themselves, "I can handle it." That's what I told myself, time and time again. But later I was able to recognize my behavior as a sign of traumatic stress.

In the years since my eyes opened to the impact of PTSD, I've frequently shared my story and insights with others. I've spent years talking with members of the law enforcement community and helping them cope with the emotional and psychological pitfalls of their work. I speak regularly at the Federal Law Enforcement Training Center in Glynco, Georgia, and for the Department of Homeland Security in Washington, D.C. and have addressed members of law enforcement from Europe, Canada, and Asia. The fact is that Post-Traumatic Stress Disorder can affect people in any walk of life, but those whose jobs place them in life-threatening situations and expose them to suffering, pain, and tragedy are in a higher-risk group. I can assure you that it's not normal to walk into a house and see multiple murder victims. It's not normal to go to a traffic accident and see multiple fatalities.

The images of the first such accident I worked as a young trooper are forever etched in my mind. It was my first assignment after graduating from the New Jersey State Police Academy. I was stationed at the Flemington State Police barracks. Early in my assignment, I was called to the scene of a motorcycle and truck accident where two cyclists had been killed. The phrase "traffic fatalities" doesn't convey the graphic, grisly images that I encountered at the scene. I'd never seen dead bodies before, mangled and torn apart. The sight was absolutely horrific, and it hit me like a sledgehammer.

The senior trooper I was with, Gary Rinker, appeared steady and cool. But I could feel my legs shaking. As we waited for emergency service workers to arrive, my immediate concern was that Gary would sense my deep discomfort and think that I wasn't up to the task. Gary, who'd done this many times before, puffed on a cigar, seemingly immune to the devastation. But I wasn't sure what to do with myself. Then I noticed that an emergency worker who'd arrived on the scene was smoking a cigarette, so I nonchalantly asked for one.

I'd never smoked a cigarette before in my life. I just wanted to project an image of being in control like my senior trooper, and I was oblivious that the cigarette the paramedic had handed me was a Camel, unfiltered.

I honestly thought I was going to pass out from the nausea and light-headedness that ensued; the cigarette's effects only compounded the nerves I was masking. All of this was the result of a charade—trying to hide normal human reactions because of the uniform I was wearing.

When we returned to the Flemington station, I quickly headed for the bathroom and cried my eyes out—I did my best to muffle the sounds, so no other trooper would overhear and think I was weak. Years later, when I recounted this story in talks before law enforcement groups, cops would often come up to me afterward and tell me that they'd experienced something similar.

We like to think we can handle anything, but it's imperative that we acknowledge that we have emotions, just like everybody else. We also have to move the bar for future generations so that they don't have to feel they're weak if they display normal emotions resulting from moments of crisis. Experiences like the one I had as a rookie trooper leave an imprint on even the toughest of cops, emergency service workers, and soldiers; such experiences cause reactions that they may not even be aware of as they steel themselves to carry out their responsibilities.

••••

All of my experiences contributed to my accepting an invitation to be part of a ten-day tour to support troops in Iraq and Germany, scheduled for July 2009. My personal story outlining my years infiltrating the Mob, followed by my transition to a new life as an NBA referee, had been told throughout the national media—HBO Real Sports, ESPN, and ABC Sports, plus a multitude of newspapers and magazines. All of this provided me with a platform to discuss PTSD. I was acutely aware of the disturbing reports—instances of PTSD rising to crisis levels in the military. Sadly, whispers and a stigma of shame still veil the condition, and I wanted the chance to help some of the brave young men and women dealing with those issues in the line of fire.

The trip—sponsored by San Francisco–based sports broadcaster Ron Barr—had been scheduled for months. We would take a flight from New York City to Kuwait, and then go on to Mosul, Iraq. But suddenly there was a new appointment on my calendar, a trip to federal court in Brooklyn to testify in a Mob case only two days before I was scheduled to leave for the Middle East. It was a stressful collision of emotions from my past and present, and I felt exposed and vulnerable.

It was hard to stay calm in the days leading up to my testimony, with all the painful memories and raw feelings that it was dredging up from my undercover assignment. I was anxious to get this job over with.

On Sunday, July 5, I flew to Newark. After a restless night's sleep, a security detail from the New Jersey State Troopers picked me up at 6:15 a.m. and drove me to the federal courthouse in Brooklyn. I met right away with Agent Brown and Assistant U.S. Attorney Busa—I was to be the lead witness and take the stand at 10 a.m. But as with so many best-laid legal plans, we hit one snag after another. A blizzard of defense motions produced a string of frustrating delays. I sat silently in a courthouse office, with my mind totally focused on the task at hand. By lunch, a jury had finally been selected and soon after I headed to a nearby luncheonette with my security detail. Then, like a sign of danger lurking from my past, I saw a man in a hooded sweatshirt standing on a street corner near the courthouse, hands hidden in his pockets. We were all on alert—hooded sweatshirts in July just don't make sense. The troopers approached him, shielding my path into the building. He turned out to be harmless, but his presence underlined the potential for danger—a reminder of old fears I could never fully lay to rest.

Finally, after what seemed like an eternity, the trial that I'd long dreaded—with all its gut-wrenching links to my past—was under way.

"I'm going to direct your attention to the recording on June 4, 1977—and you said this recording took place at an apartment: is that right?"

"That's correct."

"Is that an apartment where you resided?"

"On and off. It was an undercover apartment where I was purported to live…"

"Do you remember Michael Coppola bringing you sandwiches for lunch?"

"I don't recall."

The defense attorney Henry Mazurek, a short, nondescript lawyer, had been peppering me with endless questions about long-ago minutiae related to Alamo Trucking.

In response, I explained how all the Mafia factions wanted a piece of our business, but Tino and Michael wanted the whole show for themselves and eventually devised a plan by which I'd close Alamo and open up a new trucking line that they would completely control, thus shutting out all the other wiseguys who had their claws into us.

My purpose on behalf of the government was to connect Coppola to Fiumara and their criminal enterprises. I would be able to interpret Mob lingo and code names that I had learned in the 1970s and were still being used by Coppola and Fiumara. I would be able to establish their criminal activity over decades. The charges against Coppola were racketeering and the murder of Johnny "Coca-Cola" Lardiere. Mazurek's purpose in his cross-examination was to discredit me in any way he could, with the same kinds of lies and low blows that I had encountered on the stand thirty years before. He questioned my memory, insinuated that I had alcohol and substance abuse problems, and then held up a copy of *Covert* as he closed his long cross-examination.

"And after you left the New Jersey State Police you profited from your experience as being an undercover operative, correct?"

"I profited?" I asked.

"You financially profited from that period of time as a result of offering a book about your story?" Mazurek pressed on confidently.

"A book was authorized about the experience. The total experience, yes, and that would include Post-Traumatic Stress Disorder, which, to me, is the important layer of the book and the reason I wrote it."

Mazurek, clearly sensing that he was on the verge of a slam dunk, wasn't satisfied with my response. He wanted it on the record that I had earned money from the publication of the book, and indeed I had, in a manner of speaking. But as I tried to elaborate, he cut me off.

"It is very simple. Did you financially profit?"

"There is some money being gained from the book, yes."

"No further questions," Mazurek interjected brusquely, walking back to the defense table with the triumphant air of Perry Mason.

It became obvious to me that the prosecutor, Busa, had anticipated Mazurek's strategy of discrediting my role in the investigation, because she quickly opened a new line of questioning on redirect.

"Mr. Mazurek asked you about the proceeds from your book. Where did the proceeds go?"

I immediately explained that portions of the profits went to the

Blow the Whistle on Cancer campaign of the Jimmy V Foundation for Cancer Research, an organization for which I serve as national cochair, and to the Former Jersey Troopers Association for families of troopers killed in the line of duty.

I added, there was one more group: "Hope for the Warriors, an organization I work with to help Wounded Warriors deal with Post-Traumatic Stress Disorder."

I'm sure it wasn't a reply that Team Coppola had anticipated. I left the stand and walked out of the courtroom knowing I had done the right thing. My security detail promptly whisked me through the garage and into a state police car. I noticed another state police unit bringing in a Mob guy I knew who was in the Witness Protection Program. I realized then that Agent Kevin Brown had built a solid case—he was taking it one witness at a time to prove the criminal ways of Michael Coppola. I was just one piece of the puzzle, and Agent Brown was masterful in not revealing the full dimensions of his case to me so I wouldn't anticipate where he was heading in my testimony. The case eventually resulted in an extortion conviction against Coppola, but not a murder conviction.

• • •

That night, on the flight back home to Florida, I reclined in my seat and felt an enormous wave of relief wash over me. In less than a day, I would be flying back to New York for the start of a new experience amid the desert sands of Iraq, which were filled with many of their own uncertainties.

As the Tampa-bound jet reached cruising altitude, I thought

of the organization I had become involved with, Hope for the Warriors. Only three weeks earlier, members of the group had introduced me to a woman named Mary Gallagher. She had come to the official launch of the paperback edition of *Covert,* which was held at the National Basketball Hall of Fame in Springfield, Massachusetts. That night I gave a presentation on my experiences with PTSD, which was followed by a book signing.

Folks stood in line, and I greeted them one by one—and then Mary Gallagher was standing before me. I got up to shake her hand, and she pulled me close to give me a hug.

"I want to give you this pin," she said softly.

I looked down and noticed she was holding a silver insignia of the U.S. Marine Corps.

"I'd like you to wear this in honor of my husband, Gunnery Sergeant James Gallagher. He served in Iraq and committed suicide when he came home."

My heart sank as I absorbed her words.

"But I wish he could have heard you speak about PTSD," she continued.

Mary pinned her late husband's insignia on me. I hugged her again, and we both choked up. I quickly introduced her to my wife, Billie—partly to take a moment to collect myself. For the rest of the night, my thoughts kept returning to Mary. I kept hearing what she said about her husband and imagining everything she'd gone through after so devastating a tragedy. I decided I would wear her husband's pin proudly as a way of honoring him and others who have combated PTSD.

And I knew, as the jet began its descent to Tampa, that whatever uneasiness I'd felt on the witness stand that day paled in comparison to what the U.S. troops I would be meeting in Iraq were experiencing and what their families were living through.

I was ready to take new steps in an old journey and hopefully gain a deeper understanding of PTSD—and of surviving the shadows.

Mary Gallagher pinning the Marine insignia on me in honor of her late husband, Gunnery Sergeant James F. Gallagher.

CHAPTER THREE

Gunnery Sergeant James F. Gallagher

"Be kind. Remember everyone you meet is fighting a hard battle."
—T. H. Thompson

On a cool and gray November morning, I drove slowly along the quiet streets of Lynbrook, Long Island, noticing that each house I passed looked like a small but solid gem from my Paterson, New Jersey, youth in the 1950s and 1960s. Well-manicured lawns had faded to a patchy brown with the onset of winter, but a handful of pumpkins still rested on front porches, lingering images of another fun and festive Halloween gone by. Now, with Thanksgiving exactly one week away, I pictured families up and down the block preparing for a celebration with loved ones. I also imagined how different and difficult it must be in one particular home in this neighborhood, where the holiday would now carry memories of loss and heartache.

I knew the house without having to double-check the address. An American flag hung from the white-frame doorway on the stone facade. Resting on one corner of the redbrick front stoop was a rock emblazoned with the U.S. Marine Corps emblem and a pair of small American flags. To the right of the porch was a bright floral arrangement, highlighted by two miniature Marine Corps flags rising from the planter. As I pulled into the driveway, I looked at the arrangement of flags with purple, red, and yellow flowers, and saw hope, life, and pride amid the sorrow and pain that I knew resided here.

The front door swung open and there stood Mary Gallagher, smiling broadly, with her long, strawberry-blonde hair blowing in the breeze. "You found us," she said, waving me forward. The look on her face struck me. What I wouldn't know until I left some five hours later is that Mary's face is the *personal* look of Post-Traumatic Stress Disorder: it is a living reflection of the grim statistics and the nightly news stories; a mirror of many emotions—suffering, torment, and, thankfully, determination to triumph and come to grips with tragedy.

We hugged and exchanged hellos on the porch, and made easy small talk that helped create a bridge to the more difficult dialogue we both knew awaited.

Mary looked younger than her forty-four years despite all she'd been through. "I'm still unpacking," she told me. "I started with three hundred ninety-eight boxes and still have one hundred ninety-eight to go through. I did a hundred of them the first year. I would open up boxes and have to put them aside." Mary paused, falling momentarily into her thoughts: "You have no idea about the fear of simply opening a box and facing what might be in there."

Then she smiled, recalling how she opened one up filled with her late husband's old tube socks. She looked up at the heavens: "I said to him, 'Jim, do you know how much *stuff* you have?!'" I smiled, relieved to see Mary dealing with her grief and finding little things to chuckle over.

She gave me a quick tour of the home where she and her three children had moved two years earlier to make a new start. I was immediately aware of how the presence of Jim Gallagher filled every part of the house. In the front alcove, a small table held a framed photo of the Marine Corps flag raising at Iwo Jima and a ring of smaller flags depicting each branch of the military. A cluster of wooden four-leaf clovers on a wall bore the words "Luck, Love and Laughter"—a peek into the life Mary once shared with Jim. The sight filled me with admiration for her strength and commitment to carry on in the face of such unrelenting sadness. I knew that her feelings were especially strong in November, the month when the Gallaghers used to celebrate their wedding anniversary.

Just inside the living room, other pages of their story immediately came into view atop a wooden cabinet: a framed montage of Jim on the battlefields of Iraq; a snapshot of Mary and Jim in a happy time on a beach looking out at the ocean; and a portrait of Jim, a guy with all-American good looks and brown hair cut short in what Marines call a high-and-tight. He was sporting a chest full of medals and ribbons in his dress blues, with hash marks at the bottom of his sleeves denoting years of service. A motto accompanied the images: "Honor is the reward for what we give, not for what we get."

"That's what I buried him in," she said, as we moved into the kitchen and sat down at the dinner table. Within moments, the room bustled with activity. Mary's twenty-six-year-old son, James, came in with several friends—James's father had always preferred to call him "James II" instead of "Junior" because he believed it made him even more special. Not long after, Mary's daughter Jesse, then twenty-two, appeared, followed by Mary's sister Donna and two nephews. One of nine children in a working-class Irish family from Rockaway Beach, in Queens, Mary explained how good it felt to be surrounded by family. "I need to be with other people," she said. "I can't be by myself. It brings me to a very dark place. Being around people gives me strength."

For a while, we were immersed in stories and conversations that unfolded with bursts of laughter. But gradually, the crowd of young people and relatives filtered out. Mary and I began to shift our focus to the reason for my visit: a chance to reflect on the impact of Post-Traumatic Stress Disorder and the suicide of her husband only seven months after he returned from combat in Iraq.

She talked about the gratifying work she was doing with Hope for the Warriors, which reaches out to the wounded and families of fallen soldiers and works hard to enhance their quality of life. But she remarked how hard November had been on the job, even while surrounded by sympathetic co-workers. "My emotions got in the way and it caused a ripple effect at work," she said. "They were like, 'Mary, we understand.' But the truth is, they can't know. And I wouldn't want them to know."

But *I* wanted to understand what someone like Mary feels when she loses a loved one to PTSD. For starters, I wanted to learn about Mary and Jim, about their love story that began with two New York kids, a Brooklyn guy and a Long Island girl.

• • •

It was the summer of 1982—Mary was seventeen, five months older than Jim. She first saw him when he was on her mother's front porch at around 2 a.m. while peering out of her bedroom window to see what the commotion was all about. She went outside in her pajamas and saw a crowd of teens, friends of her cousin, who was living with Mary's family. They were all getting ready for a late-night run to the beach. "As I stepped out the door, I saw this boy who had the most amazing blue eyes I'd ever seen in my life," she said. "I was like, 'Oh, I'll be right back.' I ran upstairs, jumped into some shorts and a T-shirt, and we all went to the beach."

Jim and Mary talked until almost dawn. Jim was actually engaged to be married, even at such a young age, so he and Mary remained just friends. "I remember dying for him to kiss me, but thinking, 'Oh well, he's just not into me,'" she recalled. But one day, Jim, who worked two jobs—one at a Tastykakes bakery and the other a butcher shop—got off the bus and walked on to Mary's porch, sat down beside her, and gave her a kiss. He told her he had liked her from the day they met, but had wanted to end his relationship with his fiancée before starting one with Mary. "That just showed me right there the kind of person he was," she said.

They attended high school together and became parents during that time. Mary's father had died four years earlier, but her mother rallied to the eighteen-year-olds' sides, lending them money to get by and telling Mary, "It'll all be OK." Jim did his part, too. During Mary's pregnancy, he held plastic bags on the school bus in case Mary got sick. He worked any job he could get and paid Mary's mother back all the money she'd lent them. "He had a true sense of honor and was a great guy," Mary said. Her words reminded me of one of my favorite films, *Cinderella Man*, produced by one of my favorite people, Penny Marshall, in which Russell Crowe plays the boxer James Braddock, who repays a loan to the State of New Jersey Unemployment Office after winning a fight. As Mary talked, I realized that she'd had her own version of a Cinderella man.

After high school, Jim worked at a vet's office and a pharmacy, and he drove a cab. They married in 1986: the year the Mets beat the Red Sox in the World Series; the year the *Challenger* space-shuttle crash stunned the nation; and the sixth year of a war that raged in a distant land between desert nations that no one thought much about—Iran and Iraq. One day in 1987, Jim came home from work and told Mary of his dream. He wanted to join the U.S. Marines. "I said, 'Then go for it, Jim. I'll follow you wherever, and I'll be by your side.'" Two days after their first anniversary, he left for boot camp in Paris Island, South Carolina. Later, their new life as a military couple began in earnest when they moved to the Marine Corps base in Quantico, Virginia.

They lived in a townhouse, and for Mary, military ways took some getting used to. She described one such day, at a military base event, when she stood in a long line with her son, waiting with other military family members for a chance to shoot a real machine gun. An officer walked to the front of the line with his little boy and prepared to cut in.

"I said, 'Excuse me, the line starts back there—and he said, 'Well, I'm here with my son.' I told him, 'Yeah, and the line starts back there.' Then the officer said something like, 'Do you not see who I am?' And my response was, 'I don't care if you're God right now.' People in line were clapping. I come from a large family, and you just don't do that."

The exchange wound up getting Jim in hot water, but he wasn't harsh with Mary. He gave her a guidebook to read about military etiquette but added, "I wouldn't want you to be anybody but you, Mary—I can take care of myself.'"

Mary's story made me think even more highly of Jim. Her recollection reminded me of an anecdote in General H. Norman Schwarzkopf's book, *It Doesn't Take a Hero*, about his second tour in Vietnam. "By the time I got to the mess hall there was a long line—troops standing in the rain, NCOs [noncommissioned officers] bossing them around," the General wrote. "I took my place at the end of the line, which caused a mess sergeant to trot over. 'Sir, you don't have to stand in line; we've got a special section for officers.' 'Sergeant,' I said, 'if my troops have to stand in line out here in the rain, I'll stand here too.'"

At the time of that incident, Mary had her hands full with an infant daughter and a five-year-old son. Jim was a lance corporal and immersed in preparations for an eighteen-month unaccompanied tour—(named so because family members are left behind)—to Cuba for a year and a half. The preparation kept him too busy to help Mary as much as he would have liked to—even when she strained a ligament in her leg and had to move around on crutches while taking care of the kids. One day she called Jim to ask him if he could come home. He told her, "'Mary, it doesn't really work like that.' But I said, 'Well, can you at least try, because I'm in a lot of pain.'" When Jim put the phone down to ask permission, she could hear a senior Marine in the background loudly reprimanding her husband. When he got back on the line, he repeated the stern words from the superior: "Mary, you weren't issued to me. You need to place a pillow under your ass and get yourself around the house." Mary knew those weren't Jim's words: "I was in shock, and I never called again while he was on duty."

Gradually, she learned to become more self-sufficient and rely on the support network of Marines' wives. Once Jim was on Castro's shores, Mary spent a few months on the Quantico base with her young kids, then returned home to New York and moved in with her sister. This was long before the era of email and Skype, and the distance was vast. "We talked on the phone, we wrote, and I'd send pictures of the kids, but it was very difficult," she told me.

Finally, after Jim's tour was over, the Gallaghers were reunited. They promptly moved to Camp Pendleton in Southern California—and Mary and Jim had to restart their marriage. "What helped so much is that we only had each other in California, and we really, really fell in love in such a different way," she said. "It was wonderful."

They spent six years at Camp Pendleton between 1992 and 1998, followed by three years in Cape Cod, Massachusetts, at Camp Edwards—with Jim assigned to I & I, short for Instructor and Inspector. In that capacity, he handled color-guard duties for parades and funerals and recruited and trained reserves.

Jim and Mary enjoyed the assignment, although it was a difficult period. Mary's mother was dying from brain cancer in New York, which necessitated frequent trips there. And one of Jim's young Marines accidentally killed himself when he didn't lock his gun correctly—an incident that weighed on Jim terribly. After Mary's mom died in 2001, the Gallaghers relocated to New York, at the Garden City recruiting station. To make matters worse, Jim's father died soon after, in July, from pancreatic cancer. Two months later, when the 9/11 attacks occurred, Jim badly wanted to be in the fight, not on the recruiting front. But there was nothing he could do about it: his orders were to be a recruiter, so he put in three successful years before returning to his military occupational specialty as a gunnery sergeant in the infantry. The Gallaghers were reassigned to Camp Pendleton in August 2004, and Jim prepared for a tour of duty in Iraq. "He was transitioning well," Mary said. "I was happy for him, but at the same time I knew he would be going to war."

Jim never had his family see him off in person on his other, non-combat deployments, because he didn't want them to have to deal with the rush of sadness and emotion. "He always wanted to protect us from that kind of pain," Mary said. But this time, she and the kids went with him to Camp San Mateo to say good-bye before his company departed for Iraq. They returned to their home in tears, and Mary's phone rang. It was Jim. He wanted to see her again before he left. So a girlfriend quickly drove her back to the camp, and Mary and Jim shared time together, just the two of them.

"To have that moment with him," Mary said, then paused for several seconds and choked back tears. "It was so nice. But that's when it hit me that he might not come back."

• • •

Gunnery sergeants play a crucial role in a company; they're the core of the group, the ones who look out for the other Marines and make sure that all their needs are met. In Iraq, Jim was the one who got the water running so the soldiers could shower. He was the one who made certain that food supplies reached them, that vehicles were properly maintained. In short, he was the man who made everything work efficiently and effectively so the hundred or so Marines in his company could do their jobs in battle.

"Jim earned his title, and he was proud of it," Mary explained. "His responsibilities were very big. I remember Jim telling me once, 'Mary, I'm really not here to be their best friend. My job is to make sure they survive and know how to protect themselves.' He didn't coddle them—and he didn't coddle me, either. Once I had been in a very bad car accident and was afraid to get back behind the wheel. But he said, 'Mary, you have to do it.' If I wanted to go somewhere, he'd say, 'Fine, but I'm not taking you. You can be mad at me, but you'll have to drive.' He believed you had to push through things—he was always like that. He was a good Marine, and he was very well respected."

Jim's tour began in 2005, with his company—Bravo 1/5 (First Battalion, Fifth Marine)—stationed in Ramadji, Iraq. Communication with Mary was difficult from the war zone, but Jim stayed in touch frequently with postcards. "He'd send me a card, and sometimes it was just a picture of lips with a smile, and he'd say, 'I miss your smile,'" Mary said. "It was just as simple as that. It was Jim's style." Phone calls were harder to pull off, so they cherished the occasional times when they could hear each other's voices.

Early on in Jim's deployment, he was shaken by the death of the company captain, killed by a sniper's bullet. That haunted Jim, Mary said, because he hadn't been able to accompany the captain on the mission. Sand particles had entered Jim's eyes and affected his vision, so he was ordered to stay behind. "I remember so badly wanting to reach out—I wanted him to talk because he and the captain had a bond," she said. "I knew what he had was survivor's guilt. But he would say, 'Mary, I don't want to talk about it.' I want to know how the kids are doing and how you're doing. That's what I need. When I call you, I don't want you grilling me, Mary. I'm not going to tell you the horrors. I don't need you dealing with that image. What's that going to do, make you cry? You know I hate when you cry.' He always wanted to be our protector. So I tried to respect that, but it was hard."

It was hard because Mary continually heard stories about dangerous combat episodes from other wives on the base. But she decided not to bring them up to Jim; it made him angry. Mary also coped by trying not to watch or read the national news, so reports of battles and casualties wouldn't worry her, and she suggested to other wives that they do the same. She began to observe the different ways that deep-seated anxiety affected them. Some women would close themselves off, staying busy with their kids at home and not attending functions; others turned to alcohol to self-medicate and deaden the constant worry; some escaped through infidelity. Mary handled the uncertainty by trying to stay involved, by keeping lines of communication open with fellow wives, and by suggesting resources that would help them cope. "They didn't always want to hear what I had to tell them, but they were hurting, and just like Jim didn't coddle me, I didn't feel I was doing them a favor by coddling them," she said.

Mary's words instantly gave me a deeper understanding of the disorder. What she was describing was another layer of Post-Traumatic Stress. While their soldier spouses were dealing with traumatic events and the horrors of combat in Iraq that could lead to PTSD, their loved ones back in the States were experiencing another form of PTSD on a different level—something I describe as Active-Traumatic Stress Disorder. The circumstances that trigger the trauma in Active-Traumatic Stress Disorder are entirely different—one set results from battle experiences, and the other set unfolds with anxiety on the home front—but the impact on a person's body chemistry may be the same. Listening to Mary, I was struck by the multiple levels of PTSD and its ripple effect.

Jim, as Mary explained, dealt with increasing stress. Once on the way back from a mission, he saw a young American soldier who was engulfed in flames in a burning building. Without hesitating, he ran in and pulled the man out. Mary remembered the phone call with Jim after the incident and how he remained silent for an unusually long time while he was trying to compose himself. "I just don't get it," she remembers him finally saying. She asked what happened, and he described hearing the screams and seeing the soldier burning. Then, he told her about how he returned to his company and the first sergeant immediately berated him. "He yelled at Jim, telling him how irresponsible he was and shouting, 'What were you thinking?'" Mary tried to help Jim understand, suggesting that perhaps the first sergeant overreacted out of fear of losing his "Gunny." But she heard the anger rising in his voice as he responded, "Maybe I could see it that way if he didn't throw in, 'What was I looking for, some kind of medal?'"

I've seen that behavior from superiors before; it's usually because they fear that they couldn't have done the kind of thing Jim did. The first sergeant may have felt that kind of jealousy, but that jealousy also likely made him see a shadow of himself that he didn't like. The psychologist John O'Neil wrote in his book *The Paradox of Success*, "The shadow is our hidden self, the aspects of our personality that we don't like to acknowledge or we have been discouraged from showing." In the case of the first sergeant, his shadow might have been a disappointing or even humiliating realization that Jim did something the first sergeant could never do. In lashing out at Jim, he was also lashing out at his own shadow.

Mary told me it was no secret that the first sergeant and Jim did not get along particularly well. And she knew how much Jim needed to get that bad feeling off his chest—it was unusual for him to share anything like that with her from the war zone. About a month later, the subject came up again in a phone call. "What hurt Jim was that he'd kept asking about the soldier, and nobody knew anything," Mary said. "He never learned the young man's name, but finally he learned that he had died, and it really disturbed him, because he would have loved to talk with him."

• • •

When Jim returned from his tour in Iraq, he seemed fine to Mary. Like many of the spouses I've spoken to, Mary felt such an anticipation about the impending reunion—an excitement that built for months, like waiting for Christmas morning to arrive. But Mary had been told what to prepare for—that many returning soldiers needed space as they adjusted to their lives back home. Mary knew not to pry, and she did her best to give Jim time to complete his transition. She even prepared his own room in the house—a tranquility room, she called it—complete with television, computer, couch, and a wall filled with medals and symbols of his accomplishments. As she described it, I thought about the cave in my own home—most people would call it an office, but that need for a sanctuary is something I know very well, and my family understands my need for privacy. I even laughed to myself when Mary talked about his wall filled with medals and accomplishments, because I have my own scoreboard going, too.

If Jim needed time to be alone in his thoughts or away from the clatter of the household, that was his place to go and shut the door. "Honestly, he seemed like he was Jim when he came back, and I knew there were things he was struggling with, but he always could handle anything," she said. "He rarely cried. I think I only saw him cry four times in our marriage, and he always tried to hide it from me."

Jim had no downtime when he returned at the end of September. After only eight days, he had to report to a ten-week advance course program for gunnery sergeants. While he was attending the course, Jim learned that he would no longer be the company gunny for Bravo 1/5. Instead, he would be a weapons company platoon sergeant—a clear step backward in his career from senior company gunny. Jim was devastated by the move, which he believed his first sergeant had a hand in. But the first sergeant denied that he had anything to do with it and told Jim, "Don't worry, I've got your back."

Jim tried his best to keep his mind on the advance course, but it was tough. A Marine major noticed that something was bothering him; he listened to Jim's concerns and offered to help. That simple gesture brought some much-needed peace of mind to Jim, and he began to regain his focus, becoming excited about an upcoming new assignment in Japan.

Mary could tell that he was feeling better about things over the course of the following month. But one day, Jim arrived home with a six-pack of beer and a distracted demeanor. "I knew something was wrong right away," Mary said.

"You know who the new 'remain-behind' is?" he asked her.

Mary said, "No, Jim, who?"

He said, "You're looking at him."

The remain-behind, as Jim called it, referred to the position of family readiness officer. It was a traditionally low-rung job that was seen by peers as a distinct demotion, even though the U.S. Marines had come to view the position as increasingly important. It required a man with a steady hand and strong leadership skills to coordinate communications, programs, and events with the families of deployed troops.

"Jim looked at me and asked, 'Did you have a hand in this Mary?' and I told him, 'Jim, I'd never do that, never,'" Mary said. "Looking back, that was the moment we pretty much lost him, because he felt that everything he'd worked for was down the drain."

When Mary shared this story, Jim's words jumped out at me. He was displaying another symptom of PTSD: paranoia.

"He found it very insulting as a seasoned Marine, because normally when you were left behind, that meant you were the bottom of the barrel. I tried to explain to him that was no longer the case— the family readiness officer was the one who could multitask and didn't have issues. I said, 'Jim, this is a good thing, this could be a real career changer.' But he didn't want to hear it."

• • •

Seven months passed, and Jim gradually seemed to be adjusting to the idea of his new position. "We'll stay behind and have a good core of guys," he told his wife. Perhaps things were starting to turn around, Mary thought. She recalled how Jim had talked about counseling a young Marine who confided that he had suicidal thoughts after returning from Iraq. He told Mary how he couldn't believe the man would consider leaving his family in such torment. Jim felt he had helped the Marine, and Mary was glad he had opened up and shared the details with her. Slowly, life seemed to be falling into a normal routine.

I can relate to the frustration Jim had been feeling as he tried to adjust to his new role. It was similar to what I experienced when I surfaced from nearly three years of working undercover. I felt it was beneath me to have to drive a car to the motor pool like every other trooper had to do. When you're in positions of high energy and high adrenaline, when you're doing what's considered the "ultimate" job, you feel diminished when you are assigned to tasks that seem mundane or without the same level of importance. And in Jim's case, feelings of depression and lack of self-worth greatly intensify when coupled with Post-Traumatic Stress Disorder. It's as if you're sinking in quicksand, with no way out. At the same time, there's a level of personal pride involved: you don't go around telling everyone what you're feeling, because that simply exposes to others how bad things are. Even though the emotions are so strong within, you do everything you can to try to hide them.

Jim put up a good front for Mary, the same way I did for everyone around me as I tried to adjust to life after the investigation. Many soldiers even want to redeploy, because everyday life doesn't seem to matter after you've been on the front lines. There's a phrase I use with folks struggling to readjust to major changes: "If you are what you do, then when you don't, you aren't." That may well be what Jim Gallagher was feeling.

How was Mary going to know this, when her husband was so determined to put a mask over his turmoil? For Mary and for anyone else in this situation, you can't look back and take responsibility. It's unfair to expect anyone to connect the dots ahead of time. It's always easy in retrospect; things jump out that weren't so obvious earlier. I understand how Mary did not see the storm quietly raging inside her husband, beneath his facade that everything was fine. I'm sure he desperately was trying to convince himself of that as well.

On May 23, 2006—a Tuesday morning—Mary was busy with her daughters, getting Jesse ready for school and preparing to drop Erin off at the family of Jim's fellow Marine Jim Dinwoodie. She had a meeting to attend, and afterward she planned to pick up her girls and take them on a much-anticipated trip an hour away to Disneyland that afternoon and evening with the Dinwoodies. That morning, though, she noticed Jim was still lying in bed, uncharacteristically late for him. He apologized that he wouldn't be able to go along, but Mary knew how little he cared for amusement parks, and she didn't think anything else of it. Finally, Jim got out of bed and left for work, and Mary headed out with Jesse and Erin.

After her meeting, Mary's cell phone rang around 12:30 p.m. It was Jim. "I could tell he wasn't happy. And I said, 'Jim, do you not want us to go? I can call and cancel.'" But he urged her take the kids and have a good time. Then he added, "I just want to say that I love you Mary.' I said, 'I love you, too.' And he said, 'I'm just not having a good day. But I want you guys to have fun. I'll see you later on. I just want you to know that I really love you."

I watched Mary reliving her anguish as she recounted the details. Tears flowed down her cheeks as she paused to collect herself. There was nothing I could say to help her with the pain, so I just listened.

"Around two thirty, Jim called me again, just before I picked up Jesse. And I could tell he was upset—he was venting that his staff wasn't as good as what he'd been told. But then he said, 'You know I love you.' I had always given Jim a hard time for forgetting to say he loved me before we ended our phone calls, so I was really touched that he was saying it now. And I felt good that he was opening up to me about his feelings regarding the job, because he often kept his frustrations to himself. I told him I loved him, too, and would talk to him later on."

"So the day went on, and it was about five thirty," she continued, her voice cracking with emotion. "Jim called again. And he said, 'I just want to tell you I really, really love you.' And I said, 'I really, really love *you*, Jim. What's the matter?'"

"'I don't think I can do this,' he replied.

"Those were words I never, ever heard from Jim. I said, 'Yes, we can. We'll do this together—it's going to be OK.'"

They talked for a few more minutes, and Mary assured Jim that they would be home in an hour or so. He told her he was going to stop to get something to eat and would see her soon. And before he hung up, he repeated once more how much he loved her. "It was so repetitive, but I just didn't get it," Mary said.

She and the kids were delayed leaving the park by an hour or so and didn't get home until around 10 p.m. Erin, the youngest, tried to enter through the front door—they always kept it unlocked until everyone was home—but this time it was locked. She knocked several times, but there was no answer. Mary's heart raced as she called Jim's name but heard nothing. She instructed Erin and Jesse to go around to the garage.

They opened up the garage door, and Mary remembers only hearing them cry, over and over again: "Daddy, Daddy, Daddy." It seemed to her like forever.

"I was thinking, 'What's going on?' And then I saw the two of them standing there, so scared."

The moments that followed were horrifying. Mary described what came next, her voice halting as she sobbed.

Jim had hung himself.

"I just remember running in, and I tripped over something—and I was staring and looking—and then running into the kitchen, and trying to grab the phone and I couldn't get it to work," she said.

Her thoughts were colliding and nothing made sense. Suddenly she wondered whether an intruder had done this to Jim. In a combination of panic and trying to rationalize the irrational, she ran from room to room looking for any kind of answer. But the only answer was reality—and reality was in the garage. "And I just stopped in front of Jim," she said. "I tried to get him down. I tried so hard and I couldn't."

Mary's voice trailed off. Her sobs were coming full force, and she looked at me through her tears, as if she were trying to make sure that I understood how hard she tried to get him down. Silence filled the room, and I wasn't sure what to say or whether she'd be able to continue. But right then Jesse—who must have been in earshot a room away—walked calmly into the kitchen and stopped beside the chair in which Mary sat. She placed a hand gently on her mom's shoulder and said just above a whisper, "You can keep talking." That simple gesture was filled with so much love and support, and it seemed to give her mother the strength she needed to regain her composure.

Mary resumed speaking, slowly and quietly, in sharp contrast to the flood of words and emotion in her retelling of the unbearable events. "So I was just standing there, trying to hold him as long as I could. Until I realized that Jesse and Erin were standing there and staring at me. And I needed to let go and leave him. I told him, 'Jim, I need to go. Your two girls need me now.' It was very hard to walk away. I didn't want to. But I knew he was gone. I just thought if maybe I held on long enough he would come back."

They quickly got word to the family friends who'd accompanied them on the Disney trip, and within minutes Jimmy Dinwoodie arrived. Mary was sitting at the end of the driveway, with Erin crying and Jesse yelling for help. Soon after, an ambulance arrived along with military police, and Mary and her daughters were escorted into a neighbor's house. Then she faced the harrowing task of contacting her son to deliver the heartbreaking news.

All Mary could do then was hold her girls tight, feeling numb and wishing that the nightmare was just a dream from which she could somehow awake.

• • •

The funeral and memorial service took place three thousand miles away in Rockaway Beach. Then, on June 2, Mary and her children flew back to San Mateo for the military service. The large room where the tributes were paid was packed to capacity, and somber Marines and ranking officers shared many words of admiration.

The two months that followed were a blur. Mary returned to Camp Pendleton and only remembers signing the necessary paperwork related to Jim's death and crying, wondering if it all really happened. She went about the grim business of boxing up Jim's military gear and returning it to headquarters. She recalls how people inside the office didn't know what to say to her; many said nothing at all beyond the formalities, which hurt her deeply. At the same time, it was already July, and she knew that school would soon be starting again. She was no longer a Marine wife, and there was nothing to keep her in California. So Mary made plans to pack up and move with her kids to New York.

By early August, she and her children were back in Long Island. In just three months their world had changed completely. She remembers sitting on the front porch with her kids in the house they were renting when the moving trucks arrived with all their belongings from Camp Pendleton.

"That's when it just completely unraveled for me," she said. "I just couldn't function." Her children noticed and moved into action, making checklists of all the boxes and directing the movers to the right rooms.

"There must have been five different trucks that pulled up with our stuff," she said. "And then they showed up with my car, filthy and dirty from the move. Don't do that to a grieving family. I was ready to attack the whole moving crew. Then I noticed Jim's tool kit had been broken. The guy said, 'You know, you can replace it.' And I screamed at him—'You can't replace it when someone is *dead*! Get it?' I was inconsolable, and I was spiraling in so many different directions."

The spiral led to the night of September 5, 2006. Mary lay in bed with the lights out, holding a handful of sleeping pills in one hand and a bottle of red wine in the other.

"I didn't want to kill myself—I just wanted to go to sleep," she said. "I just wanted to reach Jim and understand. The pain was unbearable. I couldn't breathe. The pain was *crippling*. And I just thought everyone would understand, because I needed to meet Jim and I needed to find out what happened. And then I got a phone call out of the blue."

It was a friend and fellow Marine widow named Karen, whose husband, a major, had been killed several months earlier in Iraq by a blast from an improvised explosive device.

Karen asked, "What are you doing, Mary?"

"Nothing."

"Where are you?"

"I'm in bed."

"OK, what are you doing?"

"Nothing—Karen, I'm *just* in *bed*."

"What are you thinking?"

"I'm just thinking I don't want to hurt anymore, Karen."

"Well, can I ask you something, Mary? Did you look in the mirror yet?"

"Well, *yeah*."

"No, Mary. Have you really *looked* in the mirror and confronted yourself?"

"No, no, I guess not."

"Well, I need you to get up right now—you need to get up out of bed, go to the mirror, and look at Mary. You need to confront *yourself*, Mary. You need to look deep and hard and realize that this is *not* your fault. This is not Jim's fault. This is not anybody's fault. Mary, I don't ask why probably as many times as you ask why. My husband was blown up by an IED, but I still wonder why he was in that spot. And yes, Mary, I've also wanted to disappear. But that's not the answer. Because our children need us."

That moment—Karen's call and her blunt but loving words—changed everything for Mary. And I couldn't help but think what a wonderful friend Mary had in Karen—a woman grieving the loss of her own husband but whose miraculous intuition prevented another life from being lost in the tragic chain of PTSD. It was another great example of how peer-to-peer therapy can make such a difference in the process of dealing with Post-Traumatic Stress.

"It was an intervention in a very spiritual way for me," Mary said. "Until I got up and really looked in that mirror, I wasn't looking at myself. I was ashamed of looking at myself. Because I felt like such a failure—as a friend, a wife, a lover. And every morning for months after that, I went to the mirror and talked to myself—*every* morning—to remind me who Jim was and that it wasn't anyone's fault. The therapy sessions in front of the mirror got me through it. The sleeping pills went down the toilet. And I also stopped drinking wine for a while."

Mary continued: "I was like, 'You know what? I need to find Mary.' And I'm still trying to find Mary. I see some of me coming back. But I'll never be the same Mary."

• • •

In listening to Mary talk about how someone reached out to her in a time of profound need, I recalled how friends of mine had helped pull me out of the destructive darkness that left me spinning out of control thirty years earlier. John Schroth and Joe Pistone did for me what Karen did for Mary. I asked her if she'd gone on to get more formal therapy, and she had—just as I had done with Dr. Hank Campbell, who diagnosed me with PTSD. Mary's path out of the shadows underscored what I had come to learn: when people who have similar experiences talk with each other, it can be a crucial first step in overcoming PTSD. That first step is the foundation of healing.

Today Mary is a project coordinator for Hope for the Warriors and a peer mentor for the Tragedy Assistance Program for Survivors, or TAPS, an organization based in Washington, D.C., that gives emotional support and guidance to spouses of fallen soldiers. Her work is a way of dealing with her own pain, which she does every day. Mary has learned that talking about what happened is healing in its own way, although not everyone knows how to react.

"It's just nice for people to be there and listen, and if you're uncomfortable, tell me, 'I'm not good with it,'" she said. "That's OK. I don't ever want to make anyone uncomfortable. I can sense if someone is, and then I pull back. I remember people asking me, 'Oh, your husband died in Iraq?' And I'll say, 'No, he killed himself.' They don't know what to say—and sometimes there are no words for it. But if a person might reach out and touch me when I say that, I know through their body language that it's safe to continue."

Mary realizes that she will never be able to fully understand what happened, and she still plays out in her mind all the events leading up to Jim's death.

"If Jim could die like this, then it could happen to anybody— that's really all I can think," she said. "You become a detective, and boy, do you beat yourself up repeatedly. I really just couldn't function anymore. I didn't see it coming. And people say, 'Well, didn't you notice?' And you respond, 'Oh, God, how didn't I?' But I know the answer now is that he didn't let me in. It was because of who he was—my protector. He always protected us all. He would say, 'I'm the Gunny. I'm fine. It's OK. I've got it right here.'"

Mary pointed to her heart.

"But, you know," she added, "you can only put so much in your heart until it absolutely fails you. It just bursts."

She shared that she has felt anger toward Jim as well, sometimes kicking and screaming at the sixteen-by-twenty-inch color photo of him that was used at his memorial service at Camp Pendleton. "I felt so bad being angry because I felt guilty at the same time, but when I allowed myself to truly feel anger—that was another healing process. I said some very mean things and would yell, 'Come back at me! Come on! Do you see what you caused?' But did he do this intentionally? No. It wasn't him."

At the same time, Mary acknowledged that in the wake of Jim's death, she felt an intense desire for vengeance toward the first sergeant because of his treatment of her husband. I told her that one of the main symptoms of PTSD is a thirst for revenge— and I shared with her a story from my undercover past. I had planned, but not carried out, the murder of the ruthless Genovese family capo Tino Fiumara, who was the source of so much of the torment I felt during my undercover days. After nearly three years, I had begun to feel trapped by the lengthy investigation and wanted badly to return to my old life. I thought how easy it would be to kill Fiumara—doing so would end the investigation instantly, and I rationalized that the world would be a better place without such an evil man. What I was experiencing was unresolved frustration, which can lead to aggression. But I realized that taking such an action would make me no better than the bad guys.

Mary epitomizes the phrase I use so often: "normal reactions to abnormal situations." She feels frustration and anger, and those feelings have to come out into the open—I know that firsthand. I told Mary that her honesty with herself is precisely what has gotten her to where she is now and a powerful lesson for all of us in how to take care of ourselves in the face of trauma and tragedy.

She faced her pain and fear in the most amazing way. She returned to their empty house at Camp Pendleton in 2007, standing outside for nearly two hours, reflecting on all that had happened, thinking about Jim in the good times and the bad. Neighbors saw her from their windows but, out of respect, gave her time alone in her continuing journey to come to terms with her husband's suicide.

"We don't know how to grieve as a society," Mary said. "And we don't know how to allow somebody *else* to do it."

She stopped and looked down at the table, collecting her thoughts, then quietly reiterated what she had told me that night we met—that she wished Jim could have had the chance to talk to me.

The truth is, I thought to myself, I wished that I could have had the chance to talk to Jim, to help him understand where the internal pain and suffering were coming from and that he wasn't alone.

A few more moments of silence at the table followed. Finally, Mary spoke.

"I don't want Jim's death to be in vain. I don't want people to define him by suicide. I want them to remember that he was this incredible guy who served our country—willing to die for us. But I do want people to know *how* he died. That has to be brought out into the open. It's all part of the healing process—and that's something I do every day."

*The Gallagher family, posing for a photo
on October 1, 2005, a few days after Jim
returned home from Iraq.*

CHAPTER FOUR

The Physiology of Post-Traumatic Stress

"Live to learn, and you will learn to live."

—Portuguese proverb

In the summer of 2007, I had been feeling unusually tired and drained following another long NBA season. At first, I attributed it to the months of running up and down basketball courts in arenas across the country and the generally hectic pace of the job—I was always rushing to catch a flight to the next city, checking in and out of hotels, and nursing aches and pains as I went. But no matter how hard I hit the weights in the gym, I could tell that something wasn't right. My energy level was teetering on empty.

So I sought out Dr. Guy DaSilva, a specialist in my home area of West Central Florida—an expert in the fields of pathology, internal medicine, and anti-aging.

Dr. DaSilva knew of my profession as an NBA referee, but he didn't have a clue about the dangerous work I had done more than thirty years earlier, work that plunged me into the shadows of prolonged anxiety with a double life infiltrating the Mob.

In a way, you could say I was the perfect test case for the man in charge of the Sarasota, Florida-based DaSilva Institute. It was hard not to worry about what might be conspiring to undermine my health. But like a good detective—and I've been around plenty of them in my life—Dr. DaSilva carefully collected and analyzed the evidence. In this case, he drew that evidence from vial after vial of my blood. When I saw the number of little tubes awaiting me on my first visit—no fewer than fourteen—I literally thought that the nurse was preparing not only for me but also for everyone else in the waiting room. But the extensive blood work would become the key to unlocking a mystery, determining what specific physiological factors were causing my problems.

When Dr. DaSilva completed his diagnosis, I was not only relieved but also truly amazed by his ability to connect the dots and give me a vital, new awareness of the biochemical connection to Post-Traumatic Stress Disorder.

Today when I speak to members of law enforcement, the military, and other groups, I talk about more than the emotional and psychological pitfalls that result from experiencing a trauma. I convey how essential it is to have an understanding of the physiological roots of PTSD, an approach that sets Dr. DaSilva apart as a pioneer and an important voice in treating the condition.

He is a groundbreaker, yet breaking through the walls of traditional medical approaches remains a formidable challenge. Without question, Dr. DaSilva helped me understand why I felt the way I did, and he opened my eyes to a whole new world of potential help for PTSD sufferers.

Our relationship has grown from patient and doctor to one of collaborators in a search for a better understanding of Post-Traumatic Stress.

I asked Dr. DaSilva to share in his own words the core of an approach that hopefully will one day be used widely in treating PTSD. These are words that may help you or somebody you know gain a better understanding of how the body reacts to traumatic stress, and provide another layer in the healing process.

My medical practice is very different from most due to my particular background and training in pathology. I immersed myself in that branch of medicine throughout the 1980s—studying why people die, looking at organs taken directly from the body of a deceased individual who had suffered a prolonged period of stress, such as an extended stay in intensive care. My goal was to present findings to the medical staff, saying, "This is what we don't want to do again, and this is what we have to understand." After my years in pathology, I moved to internal medicine to broaden my background beyond the medical school and clinical training I'd received at New York University.

Growing up, I was always someone who liked to take things apart. The computer I use today would have been in pieces on my desk when I was thirteen, and the challenge to put it back together was what drove me. I needed to know how things worked. And it's the same for me with the human body. I've strived to gain a deep understanding of how the body functions and how it is designed, guided by the premise that you could easily surpass the century mark by living right.

Of course, the trouble begins when you live wrong.

With that in mind, I started my medical practice to get away from all of the knee-jerk responses from many in the medical community. Here is what traditional medicine is based on: you provide your chief complaint to a doctor, then that doctor treats the symptom with a drug prescription and sends you on your way. Essentially, you have five minutes to talk and don't really get to say much, since doctors might need to see one hundred patients in a day.

A patient might go to a traditional doctor and explain that his antidepressant is making him even more tired than he was before. That would create a cycle: the patient comes back and gives the doctor another layer of a complaint, and the doctor prescribes another drug. It's a pill for an ill. And in reality, it's not really the ill we're treating, but just the *symptom* of an ill.

When I first saw Bob Delaney, he told me he was feeling sluggish. But I had no clue of what was going on in his life to make him feel that way; it could have been anything. Hence the reason for my approach: to start by performing a biochemical analysis. I looked at hundreds of different biochemical markers that I call the Bio-Age Analysis. In short, the process equates to looking at fourteen different medical specialties and how those chemicals will translate into a certain symptoms or signs—even years before they manifest as a disease.

With Bob, what really stood out was that he looked like a completely healthy and physically fit man in his fifties. He was a respected official in the NBA, running up and down the basketball court with LeBron James and Kobe Bryant. As a result, I didn't expect to find much wrong with this man from a fitness perspective. In my mind, he was just coming in for a health evaluation. My guess was that I'd give him a shot of B_{12} and he'd go away feeling better.

That's what the situation *looked* like. But it couldn't have been further from reality.

After I performed my analysis, one thing jumped off the charts: his testosterone levels were low. I thought perhaps that was from all the exertion caused by running up and down the hardwood. Maybe it was that, or maybe not. All I knew was that something was disrupting his hormone production. That's never a good thing.

Next, I started to see from my tests a tiny little marker called cortisol. We hear about cortisol in TV commercials, and it's most often because the levels are excessively high in some people—individuals who are stress junkies. In basic terms, cortisol is a hormone produced in the adrenal gland. Think of it as your speed, the way you get your energy in life. Bob's complaint was sluggishness, which means his cortisol was way too low. When cortisol is low and you continue to be under stress, the adrenal gland will "steal" from the other hormones—typically testosterone in males and progesterone in females. That's because the adrenal gland's job is to save your life, and it will do anything to achieve that.

Now, as a pathologist, I'm used to dealing with the extremes of life. Either you're sick on the too-high side of life or you're sick on the too-low side of life for biochemical reasons. If you're in between that range, you're called "normal" in the eyes of traditional medicine. But as a laboratory doctor, I have never looked at that in-between range as normal. It's not. At one time, for instance, Bob could have had testosterone levels at 1,100—a level at which he's going to be feeling good. When he came to me, his level was at 241. Yet, medically, he would still be viewed as normal by our accepted standards.

How can that be normal when you compare 241 to 1,100? It's absolutely not normal for Bob, who was telling me, "Doc, I feel terrible."

It's important to bear in mind that many diseases are not diagnosed until your levels get so low that you need a big-gun drug or hospitalization. With Bob, all I knew was that his levels, while not critically low, were unusually low for a man his age—or *anybody's* age. What happens in that case? Well, you can become hypoglycemic, when suddenly your blood sugar drops very low, and the next thing you know you're feeling as if you're going to black out. And it all ties back to a deficiency of cortisol. That's what caused Bob to lack energy.

Why does this cause a lack of energy? Because cortisol's job is to deliver sugar to the brain and keep you alert. To frame it in the most basic of terms, you're ready to run from the tiger. In a primeval context, the cortisol-producing adrenal gland was made for fight or flight. You see a tiger. You get supercharged. And you're ready to run. You don't have time to think of grabbing a Snicker's bar. Your body instantly starts breaking down the stored tissue so it can immediately get that energy to the muscle and then to the brain. That way, you can figure out how to get away from the tiger and not end up as its next meal.

How does this relate to Bob—or anybody who has faced traumatic stress in life? First, remember this: the fight-or-flight mechanism was meant only to work for three to five minutes at a time, not for prolonged periods—days, months, or even years. Think of a sponge filled with water. If we constantly take that sponge and squeeze it, sooner or later we're not producing any more water. That's the adrenal gland. It's a vital organ, actually two small triangular glands that sit on your kidneys. You wouldn't survive twenty-four hours if you lost it, unless somebody rushed to your assistance to provide a replacement for the crucial hormone produced by the gland, cortisol.

The bottom line is that Bob, and everyone with Post-Traumatic Stress Disorder, has what is known as adrenal fatigue. They are constantly working their adrenal gland. And the sponge doesn't produce any more water.

From a pathology perspective, that's a real disease we're seeing today, and it has a name: Addisonian Syndrome, the common link among PTSD sufferers. At one point in time those individuals felt good. But they were put into some kind of stressful situation and—in that unrelieved period of stress—the sponge kept squeezing and squeezing. Finally, it was as if that gland said, "I can't do this anymore."

This takes place when the brain comes under stress or simply under a perceived stress. With Bob, even after he finished his undercover mission, he actually lived several additional years of it because there were triggers, like testifying in court cases, that reminded him of his dangerous duty. Even though he wasn't physically there with the mafiosos any longer, he really *was* there from a physiological perspective—in every way. What happened was that Bob's adrenal gland never got a rest. It wasn't as if his superiors could send him on his way and say, "Bob, it's over. You're going to be well protected. We'll make sure nobody's going to harm your family." He was still tied to that traumatic experience. As part of the healing process, you have to have a period of nurturing and caring to shut off the adrenal mechanism that's communicating with the brain.

Anybody who has watched the movie *Jaws* probably has thought back to the scene in the movie in which the young woman swimming in the ocean is suddenly and violently shaken like a rag doll as she is attacked by the great white. You can relive that scene physiologically just by visualizing the scene. You know it's a movie, but your adrenal glands don't know. The perceived stress that you experience can be just as bad as being there. When our palms get sweaty watching a scary scene in a movie, that's the adrenal gland kicking in. Moreover, what we embed in our brain stays there for a long period of time. Does thinking about a traumatic experience make you feel a little agitated and scared? Yes, it does. Do you find yourself shallow-breathing? Yes, you do. That is the perceived stress you continue to live with post-traumatically. The word "post" is there for a reason. Your adrenal gland does not shut off after the event. So we need to help you with that.

You might wonder why these glands are so small when they do so much.

Again, it reaches back to our ancient ancestry, to when we were hunters and gatherers and only needed adrenaline in a short burst. The glands didn't need to adapt into larger organs; we'd hunt our game, kill it, digest our food, and rest. We weren't meant to have prolonged stress.

When you do experience a trauma—or lengthy periods of extreme stress—there are certainly ways you can be helped psychologically. But that medical approach still doesn't do everything for you. It doesn't address or help heal all the physiological aspects related to that stress. Here's where I come in.

Our job is to replace what is missing. The reason: I need to restore the physiological gland so it will be able to handle the next stress, whatever it may be. Remember, in the final analysis, PTSD victims are suffering from adrenal fatigue. They are unable to benefit from a gland that is supposed to make them happy, bright, energetic, and wanting to be around people. Think of the adrenal gland as a survival kit that helps fend off disease. When the gland stops functioning properly, so does your immune system. In fact, people with unchecked PTSD are at a higher risk for cancer and illnesses involving other organs. Bear in mind that cortisol works in every organ in the body, so a disease can strike where the weakest link happens to be in a particular person.

The symptom of isolation is actually a telltale sign of PTSD. Being around other people agitates sufferers. They get to a point where they can't put up with it and lose their interest to be around others. Not surprisingly, they tend to be susceptible to depression. That condition is really just a state in which a person's entire mental attentiveness is suppressed, because if you're not delivering cortisol, oxygen and glucose to the brain, why would the brain go to work? Things that normally would have brought you pleasure in the past no longer do. Consequently, I don't treat depression as a mental or psychiatric issue but as a physiological issue. Why else would individuals suffering from PTSD all exhibit the same symptoms? Shouldn't there be some kind of organ or physiological reason for that?

Let's return to Bob's story. I knew virtually nothing about him other than his NBA credentials. I saw that his cortisol was very low. I didn't care what he said to me or how energetic he looked on TV. I could tell he had a big problem, but I didn't know why. Then I asked him if he'd ever experienced any prolonged periods of stress in his life—something that would sap his cortisol levels and adrenal gland.

"Doc, you have *no* idea," I remember Bob telling me as he sat there across the table. "You may want to think about canceling your next few patients, because we're going to be here a while." Then he told me the story of Bobby Covert and the nearly three years he spent infiltrating the Mob as a young New Jersey state trooper.

There was my answer.

My methodology with Bob—and all of my patients—is to take fourteen vials of blood to begin extensive testing. I measure not ten or twenty but two hundred different biochemical markers. It's a process akin to the proverbial peeling back of the onion's skin, trying to locate what's really going on with a person.

Now I should point out that NASA knows all about the importance of the adrenal gland. They test astronauts before they go into space to make sure the gland is functioning properly. If you chart out a properly functioning adrenal gland for the astronauts, the line resembles a ski slope. It starts high at the upper left of the graph and gradually curves down to the lower right. Ideally, you want to start out at the top of the ski slope in the morning and at night end up toward the bottom when it's time to unwind and go to sleep.

But in Bob's case—and in the charts of individuals suffering from PTSD—the lines of the adrenal gland are flat. In fact, some cases display an *upward* incline toward the right side of the graph. Bob's sheer willpower and mental capacities had gotten him through the day, but it took a tremendous toll on the rest of his body. He knew something wasn't right—a disconnect between what he *wanted* to do and what he *couldn't* do. The couldn't-do part of the equation for Bob was the physiological response he was living with all those years: the condition we call Post-Traumatic Stress Disorder, otherwise known as adrenal fatigue.

When I examined Bob's charts, I had the proof that his PTSD translated into the physiological need for cortisol. According to his markers on the graph, I could see that the only time he felt good was when he fell asleep. The rest of the day he was struggling. That's why if a doctor does not help you and replace what is missing, your problem can intensify. The question then becomes, What replaces cortisol?

Many doctors will tell you the answer is prednisone. That is the traditional treatment that evolved in the 1980s, when drug manufacturers followed the lead of a University of Virginia researcher who stressed the need for cortisol replacement in cases of depression. The companies, however, thought it made sense to create a drug that was essentially one hundred times more powerful than the original cortisol molecule in your body. Their goal was to make a drug that appeared similar to cortisol, but it wouldn't *be* cortisol—and of course could make them a nice profit. Suddenly, big business was pushing the drug prednisone as a method of replacing cortisol. Yet the irony is that cortisol remains readily available and highly affordable in pharmacies. There's just no financial incentive to market it because it has no attachment to the drug companies.

Prednisone, meanwhile, has become problematic as we've gained greater awareness of its side effects. If you've ever seen anybody who has taken prednisone for a long time, they gain tremendous amounts of weight and develop a moon face. Why? Because prednisone breaks you down. It was made to *act* like cortisol—that natural spark to help you run fast and escape the tiger without thinking. But when we make something one hundred times more powerful than that, it creates the cortisol-fueled adrenal response *all day long*.

Through my extensive testing of Bob's blood, I discovered that his adrenal functioning was deficient because of a lack of norepinephrine, which creates the actual adrenaline response. So my first task was to put him on a regimen that raised his norepinephrine levels to where they needed to be. At the same time, his serotonin—which is supposed to be there to relax and calm a person—was too high. The reason: since his body didn't have enough cortisol, his body automatically compensated by overproducing serotonin to get him through the day and help protect him. This is why it is absolutely essential to examine the physiological aspect of PTSD. You can actually balance and fix the levels and help a person deal more effectively with what they have endured.

No, doctors like me can't take away the fact that Bob was undercover in life-threatening situations for three years. We can't take away the experiences of war or other tragic events. But we can make sure your body thinks it can handle the next phone call that might deliver bad news or serve as a potential trigger to the original trauma.

My goal is to help PTSD sufferers' adrenal glands catch up with their emotions, to get the adrenal gland to a point where they feel OK and can handle a terrifying memory. They can still experience a trigger that makes them feel as if they're reexperiencing the trauma, but they don't crave the dopamine affect that comes from drinking alcohol or taking drugs. Indeed, some people with PTSD typically experience a sharp drop in dopamine levels, which can lead to gambling, sex addiction, or substance abuse because of a constant need for pleasure. Others coping with PTSD see a *rise* in dopamine levels. These are the people who exhibit symptoms of hypervigilance, always looking around and hearing multiple conversations in a room all at once—something Bob has experienced.

You or your loved one might be going to a psychiatrist to help you with this issue, but you still can't stop the cravings—or curtail the hypervigilance—because your dopamine is either too low or too high. It's almost like having an inflammation of the brain, not with mercury or lead or an infection, but with thoughts. So that's when we have to raise or lower the levels accordingly to truly help you feel better.

An increasing amount of science tells us that our thought processes—the negative ones such as anger and fear—produce what's called apoptotic chemicals. Apoptosis is cell death. It starts stabbing away at your neurons. After a period of time, people with apoptosis suffer what we know as dementia, where they are no longer able to remember anything in their life because their neurons have been destroyed for so long.

This is why I also study neurotransmitters in urine, because I want to know exactly what neurotransmitters—which govern the flow of chemicals to the brain—are off balance. There are eleven essential amino acids involved in the process, but we don't create them in our body. We have to get them through our food.

If you're eating a proper diet, you can manufacture all necessary neurotransmitters because you're eating these essential amino acids that make them. But let's say you encounter a traumatic experience, perhaps seeing your spouse killed in a car accident. Your regular diet took care of the neurotransmitters you needed to live a normal, happy life. Now, because of the shock of the trauma, you not only use up the neurotransmitters you already have, but you may stop eating properly. The result is that your neurotransmitters quickly become depleted.

Meanwhile, your state of hypervigilance can elevate sharply.

This is your body's way of compensating for the suddenly lowered mood, tied to the lack of neurotransmitters. As always, your body will naturally try to equalize what's happening internally. But the result is an unhealthy state of hypervigilance and an individual in a perilous spiral.

For example, a person who has lost his or her spouse in such a tragic way may try to move forward in life, but now has a hard time being around other people. The person in turmoil knows something isn't right, and that's why it is so crucial to study their neurotransmitters. That's one of the first things I did with Bob, followed by a program of rebalancing them. As in a basketball game, rebalancing allows both the offense and defense to operate at an effective level for a person suffering from PTSD.

I wish I could tell you that the medical establishment is moving in a direction that accepts my school of thought. Unfortunately, it's not. But some are beginning to see the value in this approach. I'm getting an increasing number of referrals from psychiatrists who have heard about and seen my work. Now they're starting to send patients my way when the tools they have are no longer working. I truly believe that the physiological method of treatment represents a breakthrough in helping people suffering from PTSD.

Sadly, its value is still not being widely recognized right now. More than anything, I attribute that to an inherent flaw in our medical system. Here's the problem. If you're being driven by insurance companies and see hundreds of patients a week, and give them an average of 5.2 minutes each, there's simply no way this medicine can be practiced on a wide scale.

Think of what Bob and countless others have experienced in a traditional framework. After his brief checkup, he leaves the office while a doctor dictates notes into a tape recorder and moves on to the next patient. But when Bob and I confer, the session might last forty-five minutes while we examine the results of the extensive blood tests, and the work is ongoing as we continue to adjust his uneven levels. It takes more time than most doctors have to spend with their patients in the current system.

My operation isn't big enough to bring it to the masses. It will take funding for alternative forms of treatment that complement and go beyond what traditional medicine offers. Meanwhile, I will continue to be a voice pushing for new and effective ways of dealing with the tragic epidemic of PTSD. The approach is rooted in science that is readily available and works wonders. Bob Delaney is certainly living proof of that.

In fact, so much proof exists about ways we can help PTSD victims biochemically. Even timeworn human rituals underscore that. Think about the ageless tradition of bringing plates of food to the home of someone grieving the loss of a loved one. We think of it only as a custom of providing solace and support. But in a very tangible way, it helps encourage a person suffering a trauma to eat—and, in doing so, maintain the vital neurotransmitters we need to remain in balance so we can function well and avoid a potential physiological decline.

We help grieving individuals with laughter, something that shouldn't be underestimated biochemically. If you're sitting there by yourself within your sorrows, we know the physiological damage that can occur. Sorrows cause a certain kind of chemical to be released in your brain that causes neuron cell death (the condition called apoptosis). And laughter does the opposite. It creates chemicals that excite the stem cell and can promote neuron growth in the brain. Laughter and happiness promotes their growth; sadness, anger, and fear destroy those neurons.

I was able to share with Bob the physiological causes of PTSD. But because of its complex nature, I wanted to make him aware of landmark work being done in alternative psychological and emotional treatments for PTSD by Dr. James Gordon in Washington, D.C. I knew Dr. Gordon was someone who could shed further light on the topic. So I suggested that Bob visit Dr. Gordon as another worthwhile step in his unfolding journey.

I would make that trip to Washington, D.C., three summers after my first meeting with Dr. DaSilva. Arranging a meeting with Dr. Gordon was no easy task. He is a man who travels around the world to places of extreme trauma and is in great demand. In an upcoming chapter, you will meet Dr. Gordon.

The knowledge that important new ways exist to help people have a better understanding of ways to deal with PTSD fuels the parallel efforts of Doctors DaSilva and Gordon. My hope is that society—and the mainstream medical establishment—will one day embrace those methods as we continue to learn more about this debilitating condition.

Dr. Guy DaSilva

CHAPTER FIVE

Collisions

"Out of every crisis comes the chance to be reborn."

—Nena O'Neill

The email instantly got my attention. It was from a federal agent who had attended undercover law enforcement training schools where I'd taught. From the tone of the message, I could sense at once that she was at a crossroads.

I knew Sabrina Martin as someone who looked more like the girl next door than a tough undercover operative who had helped foil a major bank-fraud scheme in New York City. With her diminutive athletic frame and attractive appearance, Sabrina hardly conveyed the standard image of a hard-core, relentless investigator. She could always rivet a roomful of cops with her story, telling it with a gentle, youthful voice that contrasted sharply with the pressure of her high-stakes assignment. As a teenager, she had been a contestant in a national pageant competition, and she was an accomplished singer. But she was just as comfortable handling an M16 as a microphone, and she could stand her ground with anybody. So her message took me by surprise, although the sentiment she expressed was by now familiar to me:

Bob—I have just received a request to sing the National Anthem before about 25,000 spectators at a sporting event next month. They want me to perform; otherwise they will need to make arrangements for someone else. Of course, my first instinct is yes, but then I thought of Angela. She'll be released from prison soon. This would be the first time I performed since the case went down.

The case that Sabrina spoke of had changed her life. It was an intensive investigation that put Sabrina in harm's way. Undercover work is always dangerous—you live with criminals and experience constant fear that they might find you wearing a wire and think you're an informant. And in that world, informants die. Sabrina methodically built a case against an East Coast woman who had made millions defrauding bank customers. Sabrina helped convict Angela and send her to prison, but the prospect of her impending release was clearly preying on Sabrina's mind:

I immediately thought to send you a quick email for advice. Should I take the plunge, go out and sing, or should I just stand down and not be in the public eye?

I thought of the time in my life when I surfaced from the undercover investigation, knowing that there had been a threat on my life from the bad guys. And I thought of the decision I'd made to follow my passion into officiating on the floors of the NBA, not to live in fear of what might happen or give the Mob guys any say over my decisions or dreams. I wrote Sabrina back urging her to follow her heart, to take that step out into the spotlight, if that's what she wanted. I reminded her what my old friend Joe Pistone, a.k.a. Donnie Brasco, had once underscored to me—that I'd done nothing wrong. And I told her to do what I did: to hide in plain sight and not allow those who broke the law to have any power over her choices in life.

I knew that Sabrina had grappled with Post-Traumatic Stress Disorder following her investigation and dealt with it more than a decade later following a terrible car accident. In a very tangible way, she was a PTSD sufferer in two distinct sets of circumstances, yet the clouds from each still entwined in her life. I wanted to talk with Sabrina more about what she had experienced and how she was coping, knowing that her strength and insights could be an enormous help to others lost or trying to find their way.

Soon after, we met in her hometown over coffee. Sabrina told me in detail about her younger days as a hardworking young Catholic-school student who had a knack for math and numbers.

We talked about how she wound up, quite by accident, on the front lines of law enforcement, experiencing the aftershocks that would follow.

She told me about something else as well: how the waves of fear and paranoia from her undercover days—sometimes just a desire to be alone and away from family and friends—still shadowed her daily life. I knew that what she was experiencing was a reaction shared by many who have dealt with the effects of PTSD—isolation and avoidance. They were symptoms I'd lived through. Over the past thirty years, I've presented at countless undercover training programs and before thousands of undercover agents. I've been called in by organizations to work with undercover operatives who are struggling after their missions are complete. I understand that their lives have depended on being completely secretive about their identities. Couple that need for secrecy with the fear that lingers from the people they dealt with, and you have a collision that impedes honest and open expression of feelings. It took many years before I could reveal my innermost emotions. So I understand the reluctance a person only a few years removed from an operation would feel. And that's the case in Sabrina's story. The names I've used in this chapter are fictitious to allow a story of personal courage in the face of trauma to be told.

• • •

"My plans were to become a forensic accountant," Sabrina said. "I'd been reading a magazine one day when I was in high school and it stated that of the up-and-coming careers for women, that was one of them. When I read the prerequisites, I saw law enforcement and I saw military. And I thought, how can I stand out among the rest of the candidates for the job?"

Sabrina told me that she made a decision then to enroll in the Reserve Officers' Training Corps (ROTC) program when she got to college, planning to get military science training. She reasoned that the structured military environment would be no problem given her Catholic education. I had to chuckle. I was a product of the same schooling as a youth and knew the rigors firsthand.

"It was when I was in ROTC that I learned I could possibly become a federal law enforcement agent," she said.

And Sabrina still had a knack for numbers. She was so good, in fact, that by the age of nineteen she had landed a full-time junior accounting job off campus during the day and found a way to take her entire college course load at night. On top of that, she maintained her full commitment to ROTC, in formation by 5 a.m. each day, followed by other duties and meetings, then leaving for work at 7 a.m. and getting home past 11 p.m. This is something I see in many members of law enforcement: total dedication to whatever task they take on. Nobody's ever watching the clock; it's about putting in whatever hours are necessary to get the job done.

Sabrina could easily have stayed on the accounting track after college, but instead she decided to pursue the federal law enforcement route. She attended the academy, excelled in her class, and was hired after spending only four months on the waiting list, compared to others who had been waiting for two years. Her fast rise actually wound up causing Sabrina some problems once she began working. At her first office, many of her colleagues wouldn't talk to her because they suspected she was secretly working for Internal

Affairs, simply because she'd leapfrogged so many on the list. But after several months, Sabrina's coworkers warmed up to her—not hard to do given her friendly, cheerful disposition and excellent work ethic.

Then, one day, her supervisor asked the staff a question that would ultimately change the course of Sabrina's life.

"He wanted to know if anybody would be willing to translate documents used in investigations from Spanish to English," she recalls. "Because I came from a Castilian family and spoke Spanish fluently, I thought it sounded interesting. We were also told that it would have be to done on our own time and that we'd get no extra pay."

She would find time to translate documents and tapes whenever she could. One agent was assigned to drop off and pick up the evidence. They became better acquainted, and he asked Sabrina about her career ambitions and what she had done before joining the agency. She wasn't sure about her long-term goals, but she told him how she had managed to hold down a full-time junior accounting day job off-campus while in college.

Sabrina definitely made a good impression; several weeks later the agent had a new question for her. He asked if she would consider working undercover.

"As it happened, they had put out an announcement agency-wide looking for a female who spoke Spanish and had some type of financial background," she said.

It was as if the job description had been made for Sabrina. She was excited by what felt like a once-in-a-lifetime opportunity and was told the assignment would last only thirty days.

As Sabrina spoke, I mentally leaped to the moment I was offered my undercover life with the New Jersey State Police—a job that was supposed to last six months, only to drag on and on with no end in sight. I could understand the thrill Sabrina felt in taking on an important, new challenge—to help with the investigation and track financial irregularities of a corrupt banker in Manhattan.

Sabrina's supervisor laid down two ground rules: She wasn't allowed to tell her fellow agents anything about the undercover assignment. They would just assume she had received more translating work and wouldn't be around much for a month. In addition, Sabrina wouldn't receive any extra compensation during the assignment. For many of her colleagues, that would have been a deal breaker, because they would have wanted to be paid. "I thought, 'Oh, I can pull this off for thirty days and see what it's like,'" she recalled.

But thirty days soon turned into sixty days, then into ninety days, and then into a request to stay indefinitely. In the meantime, her colleagues continually asked about her and grew resentful that she wasn't being drafted to work holidays when they were. "That started a whole 'where's Waldo?' hunt for Sabrina," she said. "Everybody was upset that I got away with getting July Fourth off. Labor Day, Christmas, New Year's Eve, you name it. And they all had to work."

One day, her group supervisor called and demanded that she start coming into the office each day to fill out a time sheet—a virtual impossibility since her undercover job required that she take the train each day to New York City. She alerted the agent who controlled her undercover job, and he intervened on Sabrina's behalf. But what she didn't know at the time was that a different undercover investigation was going on within the agency. The more she was absent from her office, the more her coworkers began to assume that she, in fact, really was with Internal Affairs and had been investigating *them*.

When Sabrina finally finished her undercover job and returned to her federal agency office, she was shunned. People she had developed friendships with would no longer talk to her. Her closest friend on the job called one day and said, "How can you do this? I thought you were my friend." Sabrina was heartsick: "I couldn't even say anything. All I wanted to do was tell her, but I knew I couldn't."

I was struck by the similarity to the experience when I went undercover, when my superiors sent out official paperwork showing I had resigned from the state police, and speculation began swirling that I had criminal charges pending as a result of a fight in Miami before disappearing. I shared with Sabrina how my trooper partner and mentor, Bob Scott, had planned to donate the life savings he and his wife had put away to help with the legal defense he thought I needed. When he called me one day to offer his assistance, I couldn't tell him the truth, either. And I'll never forget the sense of hurt he expressed toward me or the tears that welled in my eyes on the other end of the telephone. Lying is an essential tool of an undercover agent. You have to lie to both the bad guys and the good guys—you feel terrible having to mislead your own, but for security reasons you cannot share even the smallest details. As a result, blocking honest feelings is another emotional pitfall that can lead to PTSD.

"There's such a feeling of isolation," I told Sabrina. "It's an isolation from who you are, and what you're a part of—an organizational isolation. Then there's a personal isolation from your inner circle. That's not normal for our psyche."

Undercover operatives take on multiple personalities, and that was a stress Sabrina endured that wasn't normal, either. As she delved into the details, I could tell the toll it took on her.

Her assignment was to work as the assistant to the vice president of a booming business within one particular Manhattan financial institution. The woman Sabrina would work for had created various shell companies within the bank, and informants had alerted the government of the fraud. When investigators approached the institution in question, its top officer promised to fully cooperate. All signs of wrongdoing pointed to the executive in charge of the banking operation, Angela.

Angela was making a fortune through her phony companies and discreetly wanted to expand her illicit business practices. So she had simply asked her superiors at the bank if she could hire an assistant to help with the banking workload. The official immediately notified the investigators, and it was decided that it was the perfect opportunity for an undercover agent. That opened the door for Sabrina to be Angela's new assistant.

Sabrina's responsibilities for Angela were to file endless documents, check the status of foreign currencies, and work with the one that offered the best deal. "The one common denominator when I first started looking at the paperwork Angela told me to file was a signature; it was the same on the incorporation papers for more than a hundred different companies," Sabrina said. "That's when I knew there was a problem."

Sabrina experienced instant problems with Angela, who had

wanted a friend to get the job—someone who would no doubt assist in perpetrating more scams. So Angela did her best to trip Sabrina up, constantly changing numbers after the fact and accusing her of picking the wrong currency and falling short on the job.

"At first, I thought, 'Wow, I must be under a lot of stress because I keep messing up, but then I realized that I couldn't have messed up *that* much," Sabrina said. "I'd done this kind of financial work forever and knew what I was doing. But when I spoke to my controlling agent, he advised me to start marking the papers I was filing."

Sabrina devised a system and marked her work in ways only she would recognize. And, sure enough, she quickly learned that Angela was changing it or having two of her accomplices alter the work in an attempt to make Sabrina look bad, even if it meant damaging the bank in the process. All the while, Angela berated Sabrina for her "poor" work and blamed her for creating costly problems. Her mindset was that the more quickly she could get Sabrina fired, the more quickly she could bring in her own assistant.

"I knew that Angela was notorious for hiring private investigators to check up on the people who worked for her," Sabrina said. "She wanted to make sure nobody would interfere with her operation. I didn't learn until later that she had been keeping a whole file on me, and not for banking purposes."

But Sabrina was also keeping meticulous notes on Angela, studying documents she had obtained at the bank and turning over potential evidence to the agents on the case. Through the course of nine months, she sneaked out countless documents in her oversized tote bag, analyzing them late into the night to help build a case and lay the foundation for a search warrant and arrest warrant.

As the time neared for Sabrina to be pulled out of the investigation, a story had to be concocted for her departure to prevent Angela's suspicions from being raised. Sabrina came up with the plausible tale that she was moving to California to be with her boyfriend, who had gotten a new job. "She was so excited I was leaving. She pretended she was happy for me, but I could tell she could hardly contain herself now that she'd have her way," Sabrina said.

Sabrina's unpleasant experience back at her law enforcement office—getting the cold shoulder from all her colleagues and lost in a wave of isolation—fortunately didn't last long. One of the investigators she worked with let her know of a new job opening. She jumped at the opportunity to get away from the difficult environment she found herself in.

Not long after, when the affidavit for Angela's arrest arrived, her case agents in the investigation were elated and assumed that Sabrina felt the same way. "I remember thinking, 'Yeah, she was really cruel and nasty to me,' but at the same time I had a lump in my throat that they were about to arrest her—and I couldn't figure out why I felt so bad." On the day of the arrest, Sabrina chose not to go along, instead staying in what the agents called the war room—a location that is also known as the command post during a raid. The door was open a crack, and she saw Angela coming down the hallway. "I felt sick to my stomach and didn't come out of the room all day," she said. "I'd never had a problem arresting people for committing crimes. But I kept thinking of Angela's husband, whom I had gotten to know, and her kids. I thought about them, and I felt horrible."

Sabrina also felt terrible about having deceived another woman at the bank, an honest employee who frequently asked for her advice in personal matters. Understandably, Sabrina worried about the woman's reaction once the arrest of Angela was made and Sabrina's identity as an undercover agent came to light. "I knew she'd think that I didn't take her seriously, that everything she'd confided in me was being recorded," Sabrina recalled. "That made me feel awful. So I asked my controlling agent if I could buy her a book—the kind of thing I would do for any friend of mine. And I wrote a little message in it that wouldn't make sense at the time, but when she knew who I really was, when I surfaced from the undercover job, it would make a world of sense to her. She was one of the good people, and I cared what she thought."

I understood from my undercover experience why Sabrina felt the way she did. Her true nature was to be loyal to friends. And then her undercover work had forced her to betray those friendships. It's very much like what I went through, feeling that I had betrayed some of the mobsters I'd become friendly with and then had to arrest. The betrayal created a complicated psychological layer that prevented me from feeling good about the work I'd done, when in fact I should have been proud.

It comes down to this: When trust is part of your core values, and you're asked to sacrifice that trust as part of your work, you may pay a price emotionally. Then, when you realize that your broken trust is the reason for a person's undoing—even if that person is a criminal—it can create a lingering turmoil that plants the seeds for Post-Traumatic Stress, just as it did for me and many other undercover agents.

Sabrina never had to face Angela in court; the evidence was overwhelming, and Angela pled guilty. Sabrina never saw Angela again. Yet in the weeks and months that followed, she was overcome by a sense of paranoia—a feeling that persists in some ways to this day. "Ever since the operation, I know I'm different," she said. "I'll go into a room and scout out everybody there. If I'm in the tristate area, I'm always looking to see who I recognize and who might know me. If I'm in New York, anywhere around the bank, I still wonder if someone there will recognize me. I'm always looking over my shoulder. I'm afraid to engage in certain things that might link me to Sabrina from the bank."

I experienced a similar feeling of paranoia after I surfaced from my undercover assignment, thinking everybody was out to get me and every car that went down the street was suspicious. I hear similar reactions from soldiers who return from the Middle East and look for IEDs as they walk down the street back home in the United States. It's all part of the baggage that comes with PTSD.

Sabrina, however, didn't know much about the condition and did her best to push aside her paranoia and hypervigilance, forging ahead with a successful career as an agent in the years that followed.

But then came another life-changing event, a completely different kind of trauma that by all rights should have cost Sabrina her life.

• • •

"I'm sorry—I get so emotional when I talk about it," she said, her voice quiet and quivering. She paused, and I assured her that it was completely understandable, that the retelling of a trauma serves as a trigger for reliving the nightmare. But I also know that the more we talk about that emotional roller-coaster ride, the less scary it becomes. She eventually gathered herself and described an incident that took place a few years after her undercover experience.

It happened on a Monday. She was driving north on I-95 thinking about her plans for the week. What happened next seemed like a slow-motion movie scene she was observing rather than living. A truck plowed into the back of her car, completely flattening the trunk and backseat with a force that would instantly have crushed to death anyone seated there. The crumpling metal narrowly missed Sabrina, who had the fleeting sensation that one of her arms had been severed. She remembers the truck passing her on the left side and pushing her car to the right across two lanes and directly toward a stalled van on the shoulder. Her only thought was to keep from hitting the van head-on—not for her own sake but because she feared that she might injure any passengers who might be inside. Her quick reactions, rooted in the driving skills she learned early in her extensive law enforcement training, made all the difference in the millisecond she had to consider her options.

"I turned the wheel away from the van, but as I did that, the car rose up—and I think that's what saved me," she said. "Because as the car flipped, the entire passenger side got completely smashed down. Had I gone into the van head-on, I would have gotten crushed inward. I remember the loud roars and noise—like thousands of soda cans being crunched. I didn't know what it was then, but I learned later that it was the crunching of my car. I'll never forget that sound. To this day if someone crunches a soda can near me, I jump."

Seconds later, an eerie, peaceful silence settled over the shredded car. Sabrina looked up and recalls seeing what she thought was a light, creamy fog surrounding her. It turned out to be the particles of powder from the air bags that had deployed floating inside the car, another strange and surrealistic sight from her waking nightmare. She felt a momentary wave of relief in knowing she was alive and conscious.

"Thank you, God," she thought.

But suddenly Sabrina looked up and saw vehicles barreling toward her on the interstate and was frozen by another thought: "Oh my God, they're going to hit me." The traffic slowed as it neared her mangled car. As she related the details to me, Sabrina's voice trailed off, and I could see how difficult it was for her to relive the memory.

As an undercover agent, I knew Sabrina had experienced Post-Traumatic Stress from a set of circumstances most people will never encounter in life—living a double life as I had. But as she spoke, I realized that she had experienced it again through one of the most common causes of PTSD: an automobile accident. Several doctors approached Sabrina before her release and told her that they didn't know how she had survived, the same thing the troopers had told her at the scene of the crash.

"There were some good Samaritans who had pulled me from my car—they wouldn't let me look at it," Sabrina recalled. "One of them was a nurse who saw the accident coming from the other direction. She pulled over and jumped the divider, and put an oxygen mask over me and told me I'd be OK. She took care of me and asked me what hurt. But being a law enforcement agent, I didn't want to appear weak and told her I was fine. I did tell her my head hurt, and when I touched it, I couldn't figure out why my hair was wet. Then I looked at my hand. It was covered with blood. I remember she held my cheeks and told me to just keep looking at her, and kept repeating I'd be OK. Thank God she was there. Because of her, I think I made it through."

Sabrina had the presence of mind to tell everyone helping her that she was a police officer and had a gun, worried that the troopers might mistake her for a criminal with a concealed weapon. When they arrived, she turned over her gun and reminded them to be careful; there was a bullet in the chamber. They assured her not to worry and marveled at her presence of mind—to even think about their safety under such duress.

When Sabrina saw photos of the accident, she finally understood why people kept telling her how lucky she was to have survived. There was no right side of the car remaining, and on the left was a big hole exposing the gas tank, surrounded by mangled metal.

Fortunately, Sabrina was in top physical condition. That helped her withstand the physical trauma she had endured in the horrible crash. When the paramedics took her blood pressure on the scene, she knew instantly that the readings were extremely high but nothing her finely tuned system couldn't handle.

"I honestly believe, with all my might, that had I not been physically fit, I would have died of a heart attack," she said. "A lot of people suffer heart attacks from these traumatic accidents and die from that—not from the physical impact."

In the days and months after the accident, Sabrina would awaken from strange, unsettling dreams that combined both of her Post-Traumatic Stress experiences—often dealing with giving her gun away or not being able to find it. Her waking thoughts frequently focused on the van and how she might have died if it hadn't been stalled in front of her, forcing her car to flip on its passenger side while protecting her on the driver's side.

In spite of the suffering she'd undergone from her undercover bank investigation, Sabrina looked at herself as a happy-go-lucky person, a self-described social butterfly who made friends easily. But for two weeks after the accident, she didn't want to get out of bed. And as is common with PTSD victims, many of the things she held in high regard simply meant nothing.

"I didn't really care about anything anymore, and that's not me," she said.

Meanwhile, the lingering physical pain from a fractured collarbone and internal bruises throughout her body only made matters worse. She had glowed in the pageant world as a teen and cringed when she looked at herself now.

By the third week, she went to see her primary physician, who recommended that she see an orthopedic doctor. A close friend steered her to two top physicians, one specializing in orthopedics and the other in internal medicine. Six months of physical therapy followed, three days a week, from four to six hours daily. Progress was slow at first, and she found herself worrying about gaining weight, then feeling guilty for being selfish and simply not being grateful she had lived.

"I looked around and saw people with major illnesses—I had

just been in a car accident; that was nothing," she said. "But in time, I realized it's OK to be hurt, and I started doing research online or in the bookstore to buy medical books. But the whole time I was so upset with the truck driver. How could he have done that? The report said he didn't see me, but I thought, 'How did he not see me?' So I Googled 'car and truck accidents,' and that was the first time I read about PTSD."

She pored through all the information she could find on the topic and how it related to her situation, reading articles from the Mayo Clinic and the *New England Journal of Medicine*. The more she read, the more Sabrina realized that she probably would benefit from receiving psychological counseling. But the age-old stigma that surrounds any mental or emotional condition held her back. Her feelings underscored an ongoing problem for people in uniform who experience a trauma—the fear of how others will perceive them and the feeling that they need to be able to leap tall buildings in a single bound. For Sabrina, going it alone seemed like the safer route under the circumstances.

"I thought to myself, 'You're a strong person—if anyone knows how to get somebody back on track, it's you,'" she said. "You need to treat yourself like you're a patient. So that's what I did. I read books on wellness and PTSD. I put the two together, and I knew I still had a problem. I had two choices: I could continue on my downward spiral, or I could change, remind myself every day that I didn't want to become a statistic. I didn't want to lose the person I was."

It wasn't easy for her. She remembers putting on a happy face whenever her colleagues came to visit—not so different from my false front of hanging picture frames over the holes in the walls I punched, which stemmed from the storm of anger and frustration I felt after surfacing from my undercover mission.

Noises startled her and triggered memories of the accident, so she didn't watch television. "All I did was read and write," she said, her voice weak and tears streaming from her eyes. "I think that helped me get myself out of that dark place. But I still start crying when I think of the accident."

Sabrina has never gone for formal therapy, but she has continued to work on empowering herself through her own research and self-awareness efforts. When she felt ready, she began sharing her experiences at law enforcement training conferences. That's where I heard her speak. I was so impressed by how she used her story as a teaching tool and asked her to recount her message to me.

"I remind the students that trust and safety are intertwined," she said. "And if they don't trust the people who are with them, they won't feel safe. A lot of people say that undercover work is dangerous, but if you trust the people covering you then you'll feel safe. And I show them the picture of my car and say simply driving home from work may not be safe. I'll remind them to pay attention to their training on the driving course—training that helped me turn the wheel away from that van. And I remind them to be present in every moment, because you never know what the next one will bring."

One such moment in Sabrina's life occurred with that unexpected invitation to sing the national anthem at a major sporting event. She had deep-seated fears that Angela or the others whom the undercover investigation had affected would see her, knowing that the event took place in the same general area as the undercover investigation. I understand this feeling. The fear is twofold: it's a concern for physical danger, as well as the possibility that coming face-to-face with people from her undercover past would trigger the flood of emotions tied to that traumatic experience.

"Go for it! You've done nothing wrong," I emailed her back after she had first contacted me for advice.

A few weeks went by and I didn't hear anything from Sabrina. I occasionally wondered what her decision had been but didn't want to put any pressure on her by asking. Then, out of the blue one day, she emailed me to let me know she'd done it. She had sung the national anthem before a packed crowd, and the spectators cheered enthusiastically.

I was proud of Sabrina, even though I knew she would have a long way to go in her own journey, one that continues to have its challenges. Fears from her undercover past continue to linger and cause her to remain guarded about her identity. The trauma from her accident, both mental and physical, still weighs on her.

"The reality is I have many more steps to take," she said as we walked out of the coffee shop.

I knew from my own experience that Sabrina had taken an important one. It was a step toward pursuing a passion in her life, a step away from letting fear control her actions. For all of us dealing with a traumatic situation, that's a step in the right direction—away from the shadows.

"This is my hideaway, a place where dreams are born and heartaches erased," Sabrina told me. It reminded me of the oasis that the doctor showed me at the frontline base hospital in Iraq. We all need a place to go for inner peace as we travel the healing journey. Be sure to take time and find yours.

CHAPTER SIX

Healing from Within

"What do we live for, if it is not to make life less difficult for each other?"

—George Eliot

When I made my appointment to see Dr. James Gordon, founder and director of the Center for Mind-Body Medicine, I had envisioned a bustling Washington, D.C., cityscape packed with pedestrians, Metro buses, and marble office buildings.

Instead, the cab driver dropped me off in a quiet, tree-lined section of Northwest Washington just off Connecticut Avenue—a neighborhood of two-story residential houses that looked as if they dated back to the 1940s and 1950s.

It definitely wasn't the downtown office complex I had pictured, but I would soon learn that traditional expectations and preconceptions simply don't apply to this doctor.

I began walking along a sidewalk looking for the address to the renowned psychiatrist and expert in the field of Post-Traumatic Stress, prolific author of a dozen books on mental health, and former chair of the White House Commission on Complementary and Alternative Medicine Policy under President Bill Clinton.

In moments, I located the house and knocked on the front door. No answer. I waited and knocked again. Still nothing. As I stood on the porch, pondering my next move, I noticed three women walking up the sidewalk. One of them asked, "Can we help you?"

I told her I was hoping I'd found the office of Dr. James Gordon but might be lost. "You've found it," said the woman, explaining they were members of his staff returning from a break. We walked inside, where I took a seat in the front foyer, waiting for Dr. Gordon to arrive. Five minutes passed, maybe ten, and then I heard the sound of footsteps—steady and unhurried—coming down the stairs.

A man dressed casually in an open-collar shirt and slacks, and looking right at home in his bare feet, came into view. Once again, my mental image couldn't have been further off the mark. I stood up, extended my hand and asked, "How are you, Dr. Gordon?" He replied, "I'm doing fine—and so is Jim."

His warm smile, informal manner, and quick wit—cleverly giving me permission to call him Jim—set the tone for our meeting.

I'd sought Jim out in hopes of learning more about his groundbreaking work with PTSD sufferers in the line of duty at home and war zones abroad. I was eager to listen to his words. But Jim did all the listening at first—the mark of a master communicator. He immediately put me at ease, the way he undoubtedly does with so many others. He is a unique individual who has dedicated his life to helping people throughout the world with a different approach to psychological and emotional healing; he is a person who moves to his own beat in breaking down personal and cultural barriers.

The son of a surgeon and grandson of a pediatrician, Jim earned his undergraduate degree in English from Harvard University and trained as a doctor at Harvard Medical School. He attended Woodstock in 1969 as a volunteer physician, then went on to become a research psychiatrist in the early 1970s at the National Institute of Mental Health in Bethesda, Maryland. As a member of President Jimmy Carter's Commission on Mental Health, Jim directed the Special Study on Alternative Services. In 1980, he joined Georgetown Medical

School, where he serves to this day as a clinical professor in the departments of psychiatry and family medicine.

His work in the alternative medicine field led him in 1991 to found the Center for Mind-Body Medicine, a training organization that integrates breathing and relaxation techniques, meditation, guided imagery, and physical movement to help people look within and share feelings, thus creating a healing environment for those suffering from disease, chronic illness, and PTSD.

Jim has traveled the world, putting his methods to use in trauma-ridden hot spots such as Bosnia, Kosovo, Gaza, Israel, and Haiti. He has turned bitter enemies from Israel and Palestine into friends through his small-group therapy sessions. And he has faced stubborn New York City firefighters who sat with arms folded, refusing to take part in his unorthodox methods, and won them over. Along the way, he's trained some 3,500 professionals to conduct the intimate group therapy sessions that yield the amazing results I had read about.

In addition, Jim has won research grant money to work with U.S. troops returning from Iraq and Afghanistan and their families.

We sat in a cozy back room, with a picture window overlooking lush greenery. Sipping our cups of freshly brewed tea, I listened intently as the barefoot doctor reclined in his chair and began painting a picture of how trauma can be treated and overcome. And if you were with me that day, this is what you would have heard.

The truth is, the approach we developed wasn't initially geared to helping people deal with Post-Traumatic Stress Disorder. But it has made a significant difference in the lives of men, women, and children suffering from the condition. Simply put, our program is designed to help people understand and express themselves, to become aware of what is going on with their lives and learn how to take care of themselves and one another. We teach our methods to mental health professionals and peer counselors, as well as military personnel, firefighters, police, and others—at home and around the world.

When we started collaborating twenty-five years ago, there were three major groups with whom we worked to apply the methods and techniques we had created: People suffering from chronic physical illness, inner-city school kids, and medical students.

Why medical students? Because they are always under stress, and 90 percent of the time they don't know why. You say, "How are you doing?" They say, "I'm stressed out." You say, "Why?" They say, "Because I'm a medical student." But that doesn't really explain anything. You ask, "What is it about *being* in medical school that makes you stressed out?" Every answer was somewhat different. One student wanted to be in the top 10 percent of the class. Another wanted to be more attractive. Another wanted to be smarter than her roommate. Another was worried about his father two thousand miles away.

After our first five years of working together, we saw that the approach worked extremely well, that people in our target groups were feeling more relaxed and more in control. So we expanded, extending our work to medical school faculty and with kids in some of the most difficult schools in Washington, D.C.—children who were so troubled and unruly they couldn't be in the normal school system. And we began working with people suffering from cancer, HIV, and other life-threatening illnesses, as well as PTSD.

What became apparent was that our method was effective with all the populations we were dealing with. The reasons are clear. First of all, it takes people as they are. You come to us without a need to define yourself. You don't have to have a diagnosis. You just have to come and be interested in looking at what's going on inside of you and in learning about things that may be helpful to you. In that sense, it's highly respectful. Second, it's practical. We teach simple, easy-to-learn techniques such as breathing deeply and relaxing—creating an environment in which people feel they can make a change in their own lives.

One of the problems with most traditional medical approaches— and you'll see the analogies to PTSD—is that people tend to see a doctor as someone in authority who will do the work for them. But with most chronic problems of any kind—physical or psychological— what the doctor can do is limited. And if major change is going to happen, it's going to come from within. So it's important to give people a sense that there is something *they* can do. For instance, if you breathe deeply, in through your nose and out through your mouth for five or ten minutes, your body begins to relax. We've done this with soldiers in combat situations. I've done this myself in a combat zone when people were shooting outside my hotel. I had to remind myself to relax. I couldn't do anything about the shooting, but I could do something about my reaction to the shooting.

With our approach, people get the feeling, right from the beginning, that there's something they can do to help themselves. We give them an opportunity to put their hopes and fears into words. We ask, "Who are you? Why are you here? What would you like to get out of this experience?" At first, people are wary, reluctant to reveal private worries. One might hold back talking about her cancer; another might be a kid who has just come to the United States from El Salvador; another a police officer, a firefighter, or a member of the military. The last three groups are definitely hesitant to talk. But little by little, they become comfortable saying who they are and what's going on in their lives, and sharing their experiences. And then people do the exercises that we teach them. We actually call those exercises "experiments," because we found out that people like to do experiments, especially kids.

One of the things we do in the groups is work with drawings. Somebody might say, "Here's my drawing. My biggest problem is I can't sleep at night because I'm so anxious and I want to punch the wall." Somebody else says, "You know, what he showed in his drawing is the same thing for me." We create a safe place for doing the experiments—a safe place to share inner thoughts.

Ultimately, participants have the chance to see similarities between themselves and others. And in the context of a small group—a group in which we don't let people argue, interrupt, or analyze one another—there is an opportunity not only to learn about one's self but also for *others* in the group to learn at the same time. And *I* may learn something that, as group leader, I can share with everyone. When I do that, it's not moralistic, not talking down to anyone. I, too, am a member of the group. I do the drawings, the mental imagery exercises, and the deep breathing. When we get up and dance and shake our bodies, I do it, too. The basic idea is that we're all human, and we all have certain kinds of experiences in common—*similar* experiences, not necessarily the *same*.

When we work with military personnel, for example, we usually train civilians in the same sessions. Groups might include people on active duty or working full-time with the military, a doctor who's an anesthesiologist in Kansas, a social worker from New York City public schools, and somebody working with a local police department. They're all there together—and they're seeing similarities in one another.

They're discovering that some guy they thought was an idiot on the first day turns out to be pretty smart on the third day. They're learning how their own prejudices, preconceptions, and fears shape the way they look at the world. They realize, "Hey, if I could be that wrong about him, then there really are a lot of things I have to look at in my life—a lot of ideas about myself and other people."

Even in group meetings held in the Middle East, conflicting participants begin to change their views about people from the other side, realizing, "Maybe they're not all as evil as I thought they were." After the war in Kosovo, our training sessions included both Serbs and Albanians. We work with Israelis and Palestinians, helping people from Gaza and the West Bank, as well as Israeli Arabs and Israeli Jews. The basic idea is that everybody has the capacity—no matter how troubled they may be or how distressing the circumstances—to gain power over their lives, to feel more in charge of themselves, to feel more whole as human beings.

That is our goal: to empower people in those particular ways. Part of being empowered is being stronger, but it's also being able to accept one's vulnerability. Working with members of the military suffering from PTSD, I have learned how difficult a step that is for them. But if you can't accept that you're vulnerable, it's very hard to feel truly strong. You're simply putting on a show for the outside world. When we work together in these therapeutic sessions, people begin to acknowledge their true feelings—and still be tough.

My staff and I work with people from all walks of life in serious states of PTSD. In fact, what our studies show is that the more serious the PTSD, the more effective our approach is. We're just finishing research in what's called an open trial including the first five hundred adults we worked with in Gaza in a small-group model and the first five hundred children treated in our program. We had people who were very severely traumatized, as well as those with fewer PTSD symptoms. And we found that those who had the most severe symptoms made the greatest improvement. The groups continued to hold two-hour sessions once a week over the course of ten weeks. Improvements continued to be seen in a six-month follow-up period, in spite of the fact that living in Gaza often feels like a prison, and a difficult one at that.

Why would those most severely traumatized make the greatest strides? Partly, I think, because there's so much motivation. The easiest people to work with before we started helping those suffering from PTSD were individuals afflicted with cancer and HIV, because their lives were in jeopardy. It's just human nature that when your back is up against the wall, you work harder. Of the major symptom clusters for PTSD, the most ominous one is withdrawal from other people and life. Sufferers are trying to retreat from anything that might remind them of their trauma or make them feel vulnerable. In our groups, those people have the opportunity to feel safe for the first time.

One teen from Kosovo sticks in my memory. He was a very nice kid, and his teachers wanted me to work with him. He was an A student before the war, but after the war he was failing and couldn't concentrate. We learned that *during* the war, he felt that he was too old to flee with his family to Albania, and he remained home to fight for his country. But the Kosovo Liberation Army decided he was too young to fight and instead gave him a job— burying the bodies of the dead at night. By day, he hid out to avoid capture by the Serbians, who would have killed him.

After the war ended, he had constant nightmares, imagining hands reaching out of the grave. He felt very strange and disconnected, saying, "I'm so different from all the other kids." He talked with me for an hour, and he agreed to attend a group session I was conducting with students. We had about twenty children sitting in a circle, and each one talked about his or her situation—"I saw them burn my house," "The Serbian troops killed my father," "I saw my sister get molested," "I was molested." Finally, it was the boy's turn, and he said, "Please forgive me. I'm smiling not because what I think you're saying is funny, but for the first time since the war began, I do not feel like I'm so weird. I feel like I'm somebody just like all of you who's been through something terrible."

There are times people will come to the group emotionally out of control. If you can teach them breathing techniques, which enable them to feel an inner change, it creates a sense of hope.

Another young boy from Gaza was throwing rocks at Israeli tanks. We found out that he did it because his best friend was killed while throwing rocks at the tanks. He felt terribly guilty and thought the only way he could honor his friend was by getting killed.

He didn't tell any of us that at the start. But at one of the group meetings, he discovered that he could relax in the safe setting, and that was a turning point. In a later session, he did a guided imagery exercise, in which ultimately he imagined his dead friend appearing before him. He asked what he should do, and the friend told him not to keep throwing rocks. That was a life-changing moment. But the first step was simply being able to feel comfortable, and that little change helped get him past his state of despair.

Our goal with this boy, as with others in pain, is to create a situation in which people can come back from PTSD and feel connected to themselves and to others.

We also work with caregivers, such as police psychologists, military clinicians, and squad leaders. All too frequently, these givers are so concerned with taking care of others that they don't take time to care for themselves. They can be effective leaders for the type of therapy I've described, once they are able to take that time and once they understand that it's OK to be vulnerable and to acknowledge that they have similar problems as others. Until they reach that level of awareness, they remain too afraid of confronting their own feelings to accept them and move forward. In our sessions, we stress the importance of caring for themselves, not just for others in the field. That's the starting place.

The techniques we teach always focus on the balance between *being* and *doing*. It's a cycle of relaxing, becoming aware, and expressing. The relaxation techniques—which I explain in my book *Unstuck*—derive from basic meditation. The idea is that meditation is simply relaxing and being present in the moment. There are thousands of meditation techniques. The slow, deep breathing—saying to yourself "soft belly" as you inhale through your nose and exhale through your mouth—is technically known as concentrative meditation. Repetitive prayers—a prayer to Jesus, a Hail Mary—are also concentrative meditations. Another type of meditation is mindfulness, or becoming aware of thoughts, feelings, and sensations as they arise. There's also expressive meditation, such as fast breathing or shaking and dancing.

All of these meditation styles are useful, and we use and teach each one of them. If you're extremely stressed out, you need to move your body. That's healthy. It's a way to rid yourself of some of the stress. In other situations, slow, deep breathing is perfect.

We've now trained more than 3,500 people in the basic course of mind-body medicine. Taking that course is the beginning of a rigorous process. Certification for our program takes eighteen months, and it includes two trainings and sixteen weeks of individual supervision as people use our work with others. We choose our faculty from among groups that have received the certification. We have some seventy-five English-speaking faculty members and another forty who speak only Hebrew, Arabic, or Albanian.

First, they learn about all the science underlying the program. Then, they experience the techniques we use in our small-group settings. We work with up to three hundred people at a time, in small groups of ten, in our initial five-day training. In the smaller groups, participants begin to look at their own inner struggles, to put conflicts in perspective, and to use their imagination to resolve problems that previously seemed insoluble.

In the second phase, the advanced training, we teach our students how to lead the same kind of small groups that they've participated in.

Supervision is essential, not only during training but also throughout the whole process. For instance, a military psychiatrist who we have trained—whether in Afghanistan, Walter Reed Hospital, or Bethesda Naval—will receive support and supervision from our leaders as the doctor begins to use our methods with troops and their families. It's irresponsible to simply train people and send them out in the world, especially when they will be working with severely traumatized individuals. The stress can sometimes be overwhelming and stir up feelings of frustration or failure. We've created a system of psychological support for trainers and caregivers that ensures that no one is cut off from the help they themselves need as they help others. Wherever we are—in the United States, Gaza, Israel, or anywhere in the world—we always allow time for group leaders to share with one another.

We've begun to do work in Haiti, following the devastating earthquake in 2010 that killed more than 250,000 people. Our goal is to create a national program of self-help and mutual care, and we are cooperating with the Ministry of Health, the Haitian Red Cross, the hospitals, the medical and nursing schools, the police, and the Catholic Church. They all understand that they need our type of program to deal with what will become their leading public health problem: Post-Traumatic Stress. After the visible wounds are attended to, the invisible wounds will linger on for generations.

Most people at the highest levels of government in the United States and abroad, including the military, are very supportive of our work. But we also encounter resistance in our attempts to help—not only overseas but also in the United States. That resistance stems from the traditional medical model, which says, "I'm the doctor. I'm in charge. I'm going to tell you what to do. I'm going to give you pills. I have the answer." Traditional medicine can be a very good thing, but medicine is also conservative in a way that's not always helpful. I liked the conservative training I had at Harvard Medical School; it taught me to be discriminating and to ask hard questions. But there is a lot of medical dogma out there, and when you say to some people in authority, "Listen, I can teach the people you're treating to help themselves," it makes them nervous and uncomfortable with us. It exposes an area of vulnerability for them.

What I've found in working with various medical centers is resistance and difficulty dealing with the stress that caregivers and their institutions feel. People in authority sometimes don't want to open themselves up to the possibility that they themselves are troubled or that the way they work together is inefficient and unsupportive. Consequently, hospitals are often difficult, stressful places to work.

It can also be difficult to bring our work into schools, where people in charge can be equally resistant, insisting that traumatized students are already in academic trouble and that there isn't enough time to include our program in the school day. But we explain that if the students can learn to relax, to alleviate their stress, and to be a little more creative and active, they will have a better opportunity to learn in school. Unfortunately, systems become so entrenched in their traditional ways of working that the notion of taking care of oneself sometimes feels almost un-American. It's not part of our ethos.

If someone goes through a traumatic experience, sharing with others—just as Bob Delaney is doing—can open a door to healing. That's why it is incumbent on us to create an atmosphere where people can openly speak about their innermost feelings—so that these feelings do not get bottled up and cause havoc. There are three major symptom clusters of PTSD:

1. *agitation and hyperarousal*
2. *flashbacks and nightmares*
3. *withdrawal or emotional numbing*

The approach we use, even though we didn't develop it to treat Post-Traumatic Stress, in fact addresses all three of them. We help people relax at a physical and psychological level. We give them tools to gain perspective on overwhelming thoughts and emotions, and we teach them techniques that give them the experience of having control over their bodies and minds. By creating an environment in which people can share with one another, we can help them overcome the sense of isolation. Little by little, in sharing with others, they can overcome the numbness. They learn something vital to their recovery and that they are far more like others than they were imagining.

And they are learning to heal from within.

I left Jim Gordon's office reflecting about the connections of his research and work to every person I have met dealing with Post-Traumatic Stress Disorder and to my personal experience with the condition. What struck me was the relationship of his approach to the heart of my own, peer-to-peer therapy: the participants in his groups begin to relax because they feel safe and reassured speaking to others who have undergone similar traumatic experiences.

I thought about the young boy from Kosovo who had felt so disconnected from life until he realized that there were others who had dealt with their own horrors and suddenly felt relief and a surge of renewal. This is the power of bringing your pain out of the darkness and into the open, with others who are traveling the same road and can ultimately help change the direction you are going.

Dr. Jim Gordon and Linda Metayer, Center for Mind-Body Medicine, interviewing and counseling survivors of Haiti's earthquake at the Champ de Mars tent camp in December 2011 on one of his many visits to the country following the devastating 2010 earthquake.

CHAPTER SEVEN

Behind the Badge

"Nothing liberates our greatness like the desire to help, the desire to serve."

—Marianne Williamson

I understand the significance that a badge carries for all police officers. The day my father, Captain Robert D. Delaney, presented me with my badge ranks as one of the proudest in my life. His number was 978, mine 2853. In the New Jersey State Police, badge numbers are consecutive—meaning that my Dad was the 978th person to become a Jersey Trooper and I was the 2,852nd. (Badge 1921 was never issued, since that was the year Colonel H. Norman Schwarzkopf, father of Gulf War General H. Norman Schwarzkopf, founded the New Jersey State Police.)

Each department has its own badge system, and that badge becomes a cop's identity.

I have been around the law enforcement community my entire life. I have worked with officers from all over the United States at the federal, state, county, and local levels. I have been with police from Canada, Europe, and Asia. And I find them all to be very much alike in one fundamental way: they are givers. They become cops because they want to make a difference—and they believe they can make a difference.

I have spoken at police training programs around the world and have lived through many changes in the law enforcement community. When I became a trooper in 1973, we didn't even wear bullet-proof vests. We carried revolvers—six-shooters. Moving into the 1980s, we learned that we needed to protect ourselves with body armor and more sophisticated weaponry. Today police officers know that they can be physically hurt, and they constantly have to remind themselves that they can be psychologically hurt as well.

Cops face traumatic events as part of their job—and a monumental challenge befell one of the greatest cities in the world on September 11, 2001. So many stories of courage in the face of death took place on that tragic day, from the collapse of the twin towers in New York City to the inferno at the Pentagon in Washington, D.C., and the crash site of Flight 93 in Shanksville, Pennsylvania.

I choose to share the story of NYPD Officer Carol Paukner as a symbol of the entire law enforcement community: a tale of heroism, compassion, dedication, and service. These are traits I have witnessed firsthand from so many men and women behind the badge.

As with Carol, their sacrifice often comes at a high price.

• • •

There's something in Carol Paukner's experience then and now—something in her earnest brown eyes that still fill with tears in retelling those events—that conveys the essence of going above and beyond the line of duty. There's something that defines what it means to be a survivor of the immense physical pain Carol endures to this day—and the emotional turmoil of the PTSD she has managed to face and rise above. Something that gets to the heart of being among New York City's finest, even when her own heart was broken by the treatment she endured immediately after 9/11.

I met Carol at a conference of the National Association of Women Law Enforcement Executives in New Jersey, where we both had been invited to address the annual gathering. Her account of rushing to the scene of the World Trade Center as an NYPD officer, on a morning that had begun routinely patrolling the subways in lower Manhattan, had everyone in the large meeting room completely captivated.

I wanted to know more about Carol and the traumatic aftershocks in her life. We spoke for months by phone and email after the conference, and finally arranged to meet at the Lindencrest Diner one Saturday afternoon, near her hometown of Long Island.

The place was packed when I arrived. She and her longtime domestic partner Geralyn Garcia were waiting for me at a table. Carol beamed, showing no hint of the darkness she had lived through. That is, besides a small pin on her black leather jacket depicting an American flag against the digits 9-11-01.

We hugged and made small talk amid the din of nearby conversations and the clattering of tableware. I knew Carol was suffering from a mysterious infection in her sinus cavities—a malady her doctors attributed to the toxic blend of jet fuel, smoke, and chemicals she inhaled for hours at the Ground Zero site. Antibiotics had proved useless, and she faced the likelihood of surgery—one more in a series of operations over the past decade that included repairing a damaged shoulder and torn ligaments in both knees.

She wore her short brown hair pulled back and pointed out the thinning that had resulted from the biological upheaval in her system. As she talked of her ongoing ailments—headaches, gastrointestinal problems, and asthma—I noticed her frequent smile and feisty humor coated in a classic New York accent. "I have to fight," she told me. "If I don't get up, what's the alternative? The pain—I'll deal with it. As long as I feel pain, hey, I know I'm alive."

We placed our orders, and I asked Carol to retell a story she now relates to law enforcement audiences several times a year all over the country—therapeutic work that has helped her heal the invisible wounds she has carried all this time, well past her retirement from the force in 2004 because of the *physical* wounds.

She grew up in Long Island as the youngest of three siblings, dreaming of becoming a police officer from the time she was a child. Her father earned a living digging for clams along the coastline, but Carol was drawn to the idea of fighting bad guys and helping others. She was always an outgoing, caring child, and her people skills and natural athletic ability would serve her well as she worked toward her goal. "I could always talk the hair off a peach," she said.

After earning an associate's degree in criminal justice and studying psychology, Carol got her first taste of law enforcement as a

Veterans Administration police officer in the early 1980s, a job that brought her in frequent contact with PTSD patients and emotionally disturbed individuals. From there, she made the grade as a member of the NYPD Transit Division and soon found herself doing lonely, dangerous duty: patrolling New York City subway stations and cars in the dead of night.

I could imagine how tough the job was for a newcomer. But Carol, who packed plenty of power in her stocky five-foot-four frame, was up to the task. She worked out with weights rigorously and had a passion for softball—playing doubleheaders after twelve-hour days on the job, batting cleanup, and competing in the Police Olympics. There was no question she could take care of herself physically.

"I rode the trains from eight at night until four in the morning by myself a lot—and it's survival," she said. "You can't confront somebody on a moving train by yourself. You have to have tactics and think safety. How am I going to take on a three-hundred-pound man who's making trouble? I was involved in quite a few scary incidents—rolling down a flight of stairs with a couple of perps.

"I also did buy-bust narcotics undercover work on the street for a short time. In one case a guy came at me in Harlem with a baseball bat." The day she was attacked, Carol wasn't carrying a weapon. Undercover cops often don't—I never did during my work infiltrating the Mob. She wasn't sure where her backup, or "ghost," partner was, so she instinctively used her verbal skills to calm down the menacing, would-be attacker and escape unscathed.

Despite the hazards, Carol loved the job and was a true professional. She looked forward to work each day. Just as she did on that cool, sunny morning of September 11, 2001.

In the locker room at 6:30 a.m., her biggest decision was whether to wear long sleeves with her police hat or short sleeves without it—an option in the NYPD dress code. She decided on the latter, not wanting to wear a hat on a beautiful day that she expected would warm up.

At 7:05 roll call, Carol was assigned to the Broadway-Nassau station a block away from the World Trade Center. She was paired with a rookie partner. They were underground in the station, keeping an eye on rush-hour commuters. Shortly before 9 a.m., a call came over their radios—something about an unknown condition at the World Trade Center.

"With that, we ran up the nearest flight of stairs, got outside to the street, and saw a bunch of debris and a lot of people running at us," Carol recalled. "As we ran toward the World Trade Center, I got on the radio because I could see a plane hanging half in and half out near the top of Tower One. I actually saw the plane when it was outside—most people didn't, because when it exploded it went further inside the building. I immediately put it out over the radio: "Confirmed—plane hit the Trade Center. Officer needs help.""

Carol's confirmation was one of the first filed in the wake of the attack. With so much debris flying at her, she couldn't reach Tower One, so she and her partner raced to Tower Two, where panicked throngs of people were rushing out after seeing the plane hit the adjacent building. Carol radioed in that they were helping to control the crowd, and they were told to continue. They had no idea of the magnitude of what had just happened, as the aircraft appeared to be a small plane from ground level. But the degree of urgency changed minutes later when an FBI agent approached them with words that shook Carol to the core.

"He looked at us and said, 'This is terrorism. You're not a coward if you want to leave, but if you stay, you're going to die.'"

Amid the nonstop clatter of the diner, I asked her how a person processes words like that. Tears filled her eyes at the memory of that moment. Soldiers, she explained, go into combat with an expectation that they might die in battle. Police officers come in contact with death on the job, but they don't go to work expecting to die themselves. It's a different mind-set.

But in that moment she decided that this was what she had signed on for—to serve and protect. "I wasn't going anywhere" she said. "I couldn't leave all those people, even if it meant I was going to die trying to help them."

• • •

Carol and her rookie partner evacuated frantic and confused office workers, trying to maintain a sense of calm while hurrying them a safe distance from the falling objects. Then Carol dashed inside the building to help those who had been injured, becoming separated from her partner in the process. She came across a woman who appeared to have multiple sclerosis and was unable to walk. Without a second thought, she picked the woman up, climbed an escalator that had stopped working, and brought her out onto Broadway.

"I had this weird sort of adrenaline—you *do* have extra strength," she said. "Under normal circumstances, I couldn't have carried that woman up those steps. When I got her up to the street, I saw this big guy with Army fatigues and said to him, 'Take her downtown to the hospital. Get her away from this building!' I told everybody I brought out of the building, 'You need to leave! Don't look up.' I didn't want them panicking more than they already were. I just tried to keep people together and get them moving away as quickly as possible."

"I saw a guy walk out of the building and his arm was totally dislocated," she added. "He was in shock, and I said, 'Hey listen, do you need me to take you anywhere?' He said, 'What do I need to do?' And I said, 'You need to get far away from this building— just walk downtown to the hospital, straight down that road!'"

As Carol related the story, I could still hear the forceful, authoritative voice she must have used that day.

"A woman behind him said, 'I'll walk with him.' And I said, 'That's wonderful, Miss.' Anybody who walked out of that building by themselves, I made sure they had somebody to walk with: 'You go with her! You go with him! You two stay together!'"

Carol was back inside the building when jet fuel cascaded down the elevator shaft and rocked the ground level with a sudden explosion. People screamed and pushed their ways toward the doors. What she didn't know was that a second plane had just crashed into Tower Two. Instead, she found herself dealing with a surreal sight of her own—a chunk of metal the size of a car hood slammed into the ground only several feet away. "It just missed me, but when it hit the ground, the rush of air knocked me off my feet and threw me against the outside of a Borders bookstore."

A handful of fellow cops saw Carol slam into the wall and yelled for her to get up and run. She did—heading back *inside* the building to continue searching for people in need of assistance and carrying out anyone she could. She recalls holding the door open for a battalion of firefighters who had arrived to help fight the blaze and pull anyone they could to safety. "Those poor firemen—they were all in their gear with hoses and pickaxes," she said. "I'm yelling at the people running out, 'Clear the way! Let these fellas in!' I swear to God, I held the door open to their death. Because those men never came out. That thought stays with me."

In the midst of the chaos, unbeknownst to her, Tower Two began to implode in a horrible roar—with floors pancaking into themselves in a cloud of debris, dust, and death. At that instant, Carol was on the mezzanine level, and the impact of the collapse blew her through the air. But as the force hurled her toward an open door and certain death below, she thrust her left hand out at the last second, grabbed hold of the frame and held tight, despite the enormous strain on her shoulder. Her quick wits and strength prevented her from being blown through the opening and crushed beneath falling concrete and twisted steel. "Being in shape saved my life," she said. "People were blowing past me and under me, and they died."

Carol continued to grip the door frame with all her might, surrounded by the deafening noise—and with no idea what was going on.

"Suddenly, my free hand hit this leg; I pulled it and then I realized it belonged to a man right beside me," she said. "He was yelling, 'Grab my hand.' I reached—but first looked close to make sure the hand was attached. It was, so I grabbed it and pulled myself to that person."

They clung to each other in the darkness, lying amid dead

bodies while overwhelming noise and blasts of concrete and metal continued to swirl around them. She heard the man yelling, "Do you have a flashlight?" She pulled one off her belt, and it barely illuminated their path. She held tight to his hand—unsure if he was a civilian, cop, or firefighter. And then the roar around them suddenly gave way to silence. Carol thought there had been a nuclear attack. They began to crawl, still gripping each other's hands, toward anything that felt like an opening.

"It was the silence of death," she said. "It was very, very eerie. We just kept crawling along together through the debris. Everywhere we looked, there were body parts. It was terrible. As we inched forward, I kept hearing this voice repeating, 'Holy Mary, Mother of God'—over and over. I couldn't see where it was coming from." Carol paused, tears welling in her eyes. Then she continued, her voice breaking with emotion, "But you know, my father had died of cancer not long before that. I truly believe that was my father, protecting us from dying as we worked our way through the rubble."

Finally, in front of their path, was a welcome sight—a row of trees. They had somehow found their way outside. At that moment, Carol learned that the man she had escaped with was Richie Vitale, a fellow NYPD cop. They hugged and thanked each other for "saving my life."

But outside there were new grisly images to confront. Police trucks and ambulances were burning, and bodies were lying dead everywhere they looked. Carol and Richie had trouble seeing because their eyes burned so badly, and both were vomiting from the noxious gases they had inhaled. Carol remembers thinking, "It's not *if* we're going to die—it's just a matter of when."

Somewhere in the horrifying blur of events, Carol saw people jumping to their deaths from upper windows of both towers—a memory that haunts her to this day. She also heard a woman nearby screaming, "Where's my pocketbook? I lost my pocketbook!" The woman's simple concern was such a bizarre image in the midst of the carnage all around them. She and Richie ran over to her and walked her away from the scene of devastation arm in arm.

After finding someone to care for the woman, Carol and Richie—bonded by the mayhem—grabbed bottles of water from a deli to soak their eyes and wash the soot from their faces. They moved to another building, but the fumes Richie had inhaled overcame him, causing him to collapse in what looked like a heart attack. Fortunately, a paramedic on the scene quickly administered oxygen and got Richie back on his feet—just as the rest of Tower One fell, sending smoke billowing everywhere. Carol and Richie took brief refuge inside a garage with a group of firefighters to escape the smoke and ash, then began walking toward the West Side Highway.

"I was numb, but I wasn't scared," Carol said. "You didn't have time to be afraid."

By chance, the route they decided to take led them to Richie's lieutenant. She asked him to notify her superiors at Transit District 2 that she was OK but had become separated from her partner. The lieutenant obliged and informed Carol that she was now under his command. They continued to assist dazed and injured passersby and handed out bottled water to anyone on the scene providing care.

Eventually, Carol received her own care—first at a triage center, transported by a police barricade truck, along with other injured cops and firefighters, and then at St. Clare's Hospital, where she and other first responders had to share oxygen bottles because of the dwindling supply.

Treated and released after several hours, Carol found her way to Richie's precinct house, where they learned good news amid the bad: Carol's partner was fine and so were Richie's two partners. Later, Carol returned home to Long Island, with both knees aching and a searing pain in her left shoulder—the same shoulder that had saved her life.

She had survived and helped countless others to safety as well.

But nothing could have prepared her for the next round of devastation.

• • •

On September 12th, Carol awoke from the little sleep she could manage—coughing up fluid stained by black smoke, her eyes stinging from scratches on her cornea, and the left shoulder throbbing. Then a call came in from her precinct sergeant.

"She was ordered—absolutely ordered—to come in to work and show her face," Geralyn said. "I got on the phone and said, 'Her shoulder's dislocated. She can't move.' And I was told that I had twenty-four hours to present her. It was *nonnegotiable*."

Carol got dressed with Geralyn's help. They made their way into the city, surrounded by buildings and cars that were still on fire and soldiers and cops patrolling with machine guns.

"We walked into her precinct house—the place she worked and had been the morning before—and I expected people to come running over and say, 'Carol, my God, are you OK?'" said Geralyn, her voice beginning to quaver with emotion. "You know what they did? Carol went up to her sergeant to turn in her radio and tell him she wouldn't be able to work that day. He took her radio and threw it across the room. Then he verbally attacked Carol for abandoning her partner. *Everybody* there was told that she left her partner." Carol stood there speechless. Then she was ordered to immediately leave and report to the medical division to receive a psychological evaluation.

She felt sick to her stomach. Twenty-four hours earlier, she had been trapped in the rubble of a fallen tower. Now she was accused of being a coward. She protested, trying to explain what she had gone through during the attack, but it did no good.

There is a name for what Carol was going through that moment at the hands of her sergeant—Second Injury. The condition today is being studied and taken very seriously in the law enforcement community. It occurs when police officers feel that they have been trained to do a job and follow the prescribed procedures only to be second-guessed or blamed at the supervisory level—and made to feel as if *they* did something wrong. Carol did her job, yet she was criticized harshly for abandoning her partner and responsibilities as a law enforcement officer. That's a clear-cut example of Second Injury, and it can be just as devastating as the first. In many cases, it may be more hurtful, because it comes from your peers.

Carol felt completely abandoned as Geralyn drove her to the evaluation, where she was brought into a room for a session with an NYPD psychiatrist.

"I said to him, 'You know what? I am so done here, it's not even funny,' and I took my gun out, put it on the table, and told him I didn't want it, that I was lucky to be alive," Carol recalled. "I told him, 'You're gonna have a lot of people to treat, but you don't need to treat me, because I'm not crazy and I know what I did and what happened. You want my gun? Take it. I will not have the police department do this to me.'"

She says the psychiatrist put her at ease, telling her he had no reason to doubt her. He told her to take her gun and go back home. "The sergeant sent me to that doctor just to cover himself, to say that I needed psychological help, and here I had a psychiatrist telling me, 'You're fine, Carol. What you're experiencing is totally normal.' Other than Geralyn, that doctor was the first person who validated me after what happened."

It made little difference, though, to counter the rumors that swirled around the department. In the days that followed, she found herself ostracized from colleagues, told she should be in a Nike commercial because all she had done was run. Several of her friends in the department stood by her and spoke in her defense, but the situation didn't change until word of the injustice reached Richie Vitale.

"He came in and spoke to the captain," Carol said. "He was fuming, and said, 'I don't know where you get your information, but that woman saved my life. And if you don't stop this nonsense, you're going to push her over the edge.' He told them all the rumors were outright lies."

That made an impact. But the real turning point occurred when Richie happened to look at a collection of Ground Zero photos, hanging on a wall in a downtown gallery. His eyes focused in on one particular shot and his heart jumped. It showed three people, blackened from smoke and ash, walking arm in arm amid the chaos. The picture was of Carol, Richie, and the woman who had been screaming that she'd lost her pocketbook.

The photo changed everything. Richie called Carol to tell her about it, and she couldn't believe it. When he brought her a copy, she could instantly smell the overpowering, deathly mix of ashes and chemicals that filled the air that day. Looking at the photo was a trigger that plunged her into a sensory reaction to the events of that day.

She handed the photo to her superiors. "It was proof of what had happened," she said. "When everyone saw it, they backed off."

The dramatic photo that showed her on the scene doing her job—not *running* from it—was a transformative moment for Carol. There was actual verification, in addition to Richie's corroboration, that she had acted heroically. But there was still lingering bad blood with the sergeant, and her injuries made it difficult to do her job.

Carol was soon transferred out of the Transit Division into an administrative position in the medical department, and she was glad to be in a new environment. She underwent surgeries on her shoulder and knees and began to make friends in her new unit, advising injured police officers about the best doctors to treat their injuries. She also did for one distraught police officer what Richie Vitale had done for her.

"This undercover detective came in one day—his superiors were having a lot of trouble with him," she recalled. "He would just break down and cry. He had long, straggly hair, and it was obvious that he was really hurting emotionally. I felt so bad for him. I knew him even though I didn't work with him. So I went up to him and I said, 'Dude, what's the matter?' He said, 'Nobody believes me that I was there on 9/11.' I said, 'What do you *mean*? I saw you there.'"

The man's eyes lit up, and his entire demeanor changed. He wanted to be sure he'd heard her right—did Carol really see him? She assured him that she had. "You were right by the bookstore and you had your shield around your neck and you were evacuating people," she told him. "He yelled, 'Yes!' Everyone thinks I'm just lying to get money from the job and retire. I looked at him and said, 'I will validate this—even if it has to be in court, I will testify for you.' I went over to the sergeant and said, 'I saw this man at the towers. He was there that day.' The man was crying, and then I was crying. And after that, he seemed to be OK. We stayed in touch, and his wife even stopped in to thank me. He'd come by the clinic and bring in doughnuts. It was wonderful to see—and I was glad I could help him."

All the while, Carol was still struggling. The doctors she worked with would remind her of everything she had experienced, telling her she had miraculously survived a building collapsing on her. She didn't want to think about that; instead, she felt a lingering sense of regret that she could not have done more, could not save more people. She was still having trouble processing the enormity of everything she'd been through, a common trait of PTSD.

In January 2002, the department held a Medal of Valor event, and Carol was among those to be honored. But she didn't want to attend.

"I was ordered to go," she said. "I didn't want to go, because I didn't feel I deserved a medal—too many people died, and I felt that I had failed. What could I have done differently to save more lives? I was in my full dress blues and I looked up and saw all these snipers on the roof of a building for the ceremony. They were there to protect us. That's when it finally hit me. My physically being at that ceremony allowed my body and mind to begin to come to terms emotionally with what happened."

Still, lingering anger and resentment brewed inside her. The police force brought in mental health counselors to provide therapeutic support—called 9/11 training—to help officers reeling from the trauma they had experienced at Ground Zero. It had been a year since the attacks, and Carol's new supervisor in the medical division informed her that she needed to report to training.

"When my boss told me I had to attend, I said, 'Absolutely not. I was a first responder—I was there three minutes after the first plane hit. And you're just coming to me now to offer help and see if I'm all right?' I was not happy and said I wasn't going, that I'd call in sick if they tried to make me go."

Carol soon relented and attended the group counseling session, but she sat there with arms folded. When her turn came she refused to talk. "They said, you have to tell us what happened, and I said, 'No, I don't. The only thing I can tell you is three minutes after the first plane hit, I was there. I was severely injured. I'm having another operation and this is the first time you're getting to me? That's enough.'" Carol made it clear she would have nothing more to do with them.

Meanwhile, she continued to experience triggers that sent her mind rushing back to the World Trade Center nightmare. The first came the day after the attacks. Carol heard a military plane flying over her house and raced out the front door, ducking for cover. That reminded me of how the sound of a chopper after I surfaced from undercover made me fear a Mob hit was under way, when the chopper was just flying low to spray for bugs. It's a classic PTSD reaction—paranoia.

Then in 2002, she was attending an outdoor Melissa Etheridge concert in New Hampshire with Geralyn, talking with band members after the show, when a loud sound overhead caused her to panic. "All I could think of was the towers exploding and I start freaking out, grabbing people and yelling, 'Take cover!' Well, it turned out to be a helicopter coming in to pick up Melissa. People are staring at me like I'm crazy and calling me a druggie."

A year later, in August 2003, Carol was riding a crowded subway car late in the afternoon en route to meet Geralyn inside the Penn Station at 34th Street when a real crisis occurred. Carol was using a cane following one of her knee surgeries, and she stood near the subway door as it rumbled beneath the city. "Then I got this eerie, eerie feeling," she said. "Something didn't seem right." Carol, who knew subway sounds intimately from her decade on the job, sensed an uncharacteristic silence—perhaps the sign of mechanical trouble as the train glided to a halt at 51st Street and the doors opened. Instinctively, she thrust her foot to keep them from closing—knowing there would be no way to get out of the train if the electrical system went dead. Poking her head outside, she could hear the sound of power fading and see lights flickering. Carol was terrified—could it be another terrorist attack? But she maintained her composure and immediately went into cop mode.

"People are screaming and kids are crying," she said. "And I tell them, 'Everybody relax! We're going to evacuate—walk straight, feel the wall with your hands, the stairway is straight ahead.' So I get everybody off the train and walking up the stairs. Meanwhile, I'm sweating profusely, wondering what is happening. And when we get up stairs, everybody is looking up at the sky, thinking we might be under attack again.'"

Carol, doing her best to mask her fear, spotted a police car across the street and approached, identifying herself as a cop and asking what was going on. The two rookies inside told her they didn't know. "All I cared about now was finding Geralyn, so I said, 'I need a ride.' They refused, and I jumped in the backseat and said, 'I'm a senior officer and you give me a frickin' ride and take me to 34th Street now! Put the lights on and *go*!'"

They didn't argue and dropped Carol at her destination. She hobbled down a flight of steps into Penn Station, fighting the rush-hour crowd of people being evacuated up the stairs—all the while unsure if Geralyn was trapped on a train somewhere. But she found her in the darkness, all alone, just where they had planned to meet. They embraced tearfully. They learned soon after there was no terror attack. It was a massive power outage that would be dubbed the Northeast Blackout of 2003.

Anybody would have been terrified under the circumstances, but I could understand how the horrors of 9/11 had magnified Carol's fear. She was experiencing a PTSD trigger. But I was impressed by how she displayed such strong leadership—fueled by her innate toughness, willpower, and years of NYPD training—even while fighting through the flashbacks to that morning in Tower Two.

Carol continued to excel in her desk assignment, immersed in paperwork, at the medical division. She enjoyed the camaraderie but missed being out on the street. Then, in 2004, she received word that the police department was going to retire her—the consequence of the physical injuries suffered at the World Trade Center. Her boss at the medical department offered to let her stay on in a new, ambassadorial position—going around the city to give inspirational talks about her experience. But she wanted to stay only if she could serve in a more active law enforcement role. She declined, and her retirement became a reality.

• • •

But in her own way, Carol has wound up doing what her boss had suggested. She has become a compelling voice in the tapestry of stories tied to the deadliest attack ever perpetrated on American soil. The 2002 book *Women at Ground Zero* told her first-person account from the morning of September 11. And she is today an in-demand speaker at law enforcement functions around the country, although the constant ailments she has dealt with since that day often make travel difficult.

Carol has benefited from ample peer-to-peer counseling in recent years through the National Association of Women Law Enforcement Executives and friends from the job, such as Roe Manghisi, a retired New Jersey State Police captain. She's also had some more formal counseling offered to 9/11 survivors through the World Trade Medical Monitoring Program—embracing the process and self-awareness she has gained, in stark contrast to the resentment and distrust she felt toward the department's efforts a year after the attacks. Sharing her experiences with fellow law enforcement officers has helped bring her harsh memories under control. She also remains close to some of her former colleagues, and she keeps in touch to this day with the cop who became forever bonded with her in the rubble, Richie Vitale.

But Carol still feels the sting when talking about the sergeant who wrongfully accused her of abandoning her partner and the cruel treatment she received from others in the wake of the attacks. There is still the concern she feels from mysterious infections in her lungs and sinuses, and she wonders whether a medical cure even exists for them. She refuses to take many of the medications her doctor prescribes for her, fearful of the potential side effects and preferring to deal with the pain. But that pain is a constant reminder of the job she can no longer do on the street and in the subways—and of the softball games she can no longer play.

On top of that, there are constant reminders of the severe trauma she endured, triggers that can still cause her pulse and mind to race. On the sixth anniversary of 9/11 in 2007, she and Geralyn were getting set to watch the coverage on television at home when a massive water leak began. Carol ran down to the basement to check on it. When she looked up to see tiles peeling and falling from the ceiling, it instantly thrust her back inside Tower Two with debris tumbling all around her. It was another example of how a PTSD sufferer remains forever vulnerable to triggers.

She has never had an easy time when 9/11 rolls around on the calendar. But each time the date arrives, her phone rings nonstop with calls from friends, offering words of support.

Through it all, Carol perseveres with that friendly smile, good heart, and quintessential toughness of a New York cop—a cop who held tight to an extended hand in the midst of a living hell and extends a steadying hand to others by sharing her story.

"I make the best of things," she said. "Every day is a good day I wake up. People say, 'Oh, I'm so sorry you were involved in 9/11.' But I say, 'Yeah, but I'm here to bitch about it.' I'm a survivor."

• • •

Carol is, indeed, like so many of the cops I have come to know over the years. Her amazing efforts—unfolding on one of the most traumatic days in our nation's history—typify the dedication and selflessness I've seen from law enforcement officers for decades. It may be a cop in Houston involved in a shooting or a police officer in Chicago pulling somebody out of a car wreck. It could be a constable across the pond thwarting a robbery in downtown London. They put themselves in harm's way without hesitation. Their goal is no different from anyone else's—to go home to their families and friends at the end of the day and retire knowing the work they did made a difference. Along the way, they see things the rest of the world doesn't, things that can cause scars that may not be visible. But the injuries are just as real as a broken leg or gunshot wound. Carol Paukner can tell you that. And so can countless other cops who have sacrificed to make us a safer, better society—dealing with injuries seen and unseen as they work behind the badge.

*Police officers Carol Paukner and Richie Vitale help the woman
who had been screaming that she'd lost her purse at Ground Zero
on September 11, 2001.*

CHAPTER EIGHT

Trauma Resilience

"There is a growing appreciation of understanding one's emotions, how they operate and how to manage them."

—The Dalai Lama

When Dr. Bengt Arnetz was a medical school student in his native Sweden, he spent the summer of 1977 as an intern at Walter Reed Army Institute of Research. His academic focus was in the field of stress, and his work was underscored by many cases of depression and stress-related disorders he observed in patients at the renowned Washington, D.C., military hospital. That internship would ultimately spawn a career as one of the world's most respected research stress physicians studying the impact of trauma on first responders and on ways to prevent those experiences from developing into Post-Traumatic Stress Disorder.

Dr. Arnetz is now a professor at Wayne State University in Detroit, Michigan, and director of the school's Division of Occupational and Environmental Health. His pioneering work continues to put him on the front line of PTSD research, targeting a wide range of groups that include law enforcement, the military, and emergency services workers—and today Iraqi citizens who have fled their country.

In fact, his ongoing study of Iraqi war refugees, which deals with stress resiliency and social programs aimed to reduce PTSD, is among the largest of its kind ever undertaken, funded by a $2.6 million grant from the National Institutes of Health.

Dr. Arnetz's resume reflects years of expertise in the field. He earned his medical degree, followed by a PhD in psychophysiology, from the Karolinska Institute in Sweden, and he added a pair of master's degrees from Harvard University's School of Public Health. He's certified in occupational and environmental health in both the United States and Sweden. And his specialty lies in identifying individual, social, and environmental factors that can create trauma and stress disorders, as well as ways to combat them by enhancing training methods and coping skills.

In speaking with Dr. Arnetz, I learned that distinct parallels exist between his extensive PTSD research and the conclusions I've reached over the years about the condition, especially as it relates to the power of peer-to-peer therapy. I admire his advocacy for positive action and believe that his studies can provide new pathways for people facing trauma in their lives.

"Most of my work has been stress-related research," he told me. "But the more I worked with Swedish police in the 1990s, the more I saw PTSD, and I grew increasingly involved in studying the science of it. But I've also been very critical of how people with PTSD have been treated. It's almost like we lock them up in a negative spiral, instead of helping them deal with it and move forward."

His first major foray into the study of stress and how it leads to PTSD took place in Stockholm in the early 1990s, centering on members of local law enforcement.

"A physician colleague of mine who worked with the Swedish police and the police training academy came to me to discuss stress training for officers," he recounted.

As Dr. Arnetz spoke, I was excited to hear his thoughts. Law enforcement's existing training emphasizes skills in technical areas—becoming proficient at shooting, driving, and tactical response—but omits any awareness of an emotional connection to critical events.

"We wanted to combine tactical skills with emotional regulation, which means how do you recognize your feelings—not just during, but *after* a critical event—and how do you deal with it?"

He based his research on seventy-five Swedish police cadets with emphasis on both technical and mental training. To test his hypothesis about the need for an emotional aspect to training, he and his staff created a series of mock scenarios for the cadets to handle, all related to building the imagery-based skills that he considers a key element of training.

In developing their work on image skills—drawn from concepts used in sports psychology—Dr. Arnetz and his team reviewed the literature and conducted multiple interviews with first responders about the situations they regarded as the most stressful. They surveyed some one hundred police officers and asked them to rate the degree of stressfulness of more than thirty-five scenarios that had been identified.

From those, they chose a set of ten experiences, including being called to a domestic violence scene, a car chase, a bank robbery, and a situation involving a dead child. Members of Sweden's Special Forces were brought in to work with the cadets, training them to handle those scenarios mentally—using techniques for reaching optimal relaxation and mindfulness, imagining the different stressful scenarios, and learning how to cope with such situations. This imagery-skills training involves creating a checklist of three or four main courses of action to keep in mind when confronting each challenge.

"We found that better-trained people fared much better over time and had less stress, better mental well-being, and fewer behavior issues after a stressful event," he said. "We took nontrained people and ran them through a reenactment of a bank robbery. In the real bank robbery, one police officer had been shot to death. And we reenacted that."

Dr. Arnetz continued: "The comparison in responses between trained and nontrained groups revealed clear differences. What we found was that the people who had been trained were better able to follow procedure. And when the situations were extremely critical, they were much, much less stressed. They had more control. Furthermore, they had a more accurate memory of what happened— indicating that the kind of training you get seems to affect how you perceive a critical incident. This ties in with one theory about PTSD—that you don't really have a clear mental picture of what took place. The brain tries to re-create a picture of the situation, but when you re-create that picture, you create one that the brain doesn't really understand—and that contributes to PTSD."

Dr. Arnetz has noted that more than two-thirds of the general population will experience a traumatic event during their lifetime. But because police, military, and other first responders face potentially traumatic experiences much more often, they are at a greatly elevated risk of mental health problems—including adjustment disorder, depression, acute stress disorder, and PTSD.

Specifically, he notes, the number of police officers dealing with PTSD-related disorders caused from experiences on the job stands as high as 19 percent, compared to 4 percent for the general population. In addition, he has written that police officers who deal persistently with critical incidents are at a heightened risk for suicide, substance abuse, spousal abuse, and divorce. They suffer work-related problems more frequently, which undercuts their ability to serve the public effectively. And for many, their quality of life is severely undermined.

Now at Wayne State, Dr. Arnetz has worked on comparative studies between U.S. and Swedish first responders that explore the effectiveness of imagery-based techniques and better training in helping first responders deal with a crisis. I wholeheartedly embrace one of the central themes in his approach: the goal of keeping Post-Traumatic Stress from turning into the *disorder*—using methods designed to keep cops, firefighters, soldiers, and emergency service workers from getting PTSD.

"If you know that you're going to experience violence and threats and very difficult situations, you would think you'd be trained for it," he said. "The only proven treatment today is *after* you've been exposed, *after* you've developed PTSD. It's important that we move toward prevention. Psychologists in general tend to overstress studying some of the symptoms of PTSD. But I think you can turn it back—you can prevent people from *developing* the condition."

Dr. Arnetz has done in-depth research with the City of Detroit Police Department in hopes of furthering that goal. In 2009, he conducted a study at Wayne State that revealed sobering data. He explained a statistical formula that found that the Detroit police force leads the nation in suicides—with twenty-eight per one hundred thousand Detroit police officers killing themselves each year, well ahead of Los Angeles (twenty), Chicago (eighteen), and New York (fifteen). He attributes the suicide trend in Detroit—as with that in every city—to working in an atmosphere of sustained stress, coupled with factors such as depression, individual personality traits, and exposure to trauma.

In tailoring his work with rookie Detroit cops, Dr. Arnetz has replicated the special cadet-training program he conducted in Sweden with an emphasis on imagery skills. "We developed a variety of critical scenarios, and we'll train police officers in similar fashion—together with experienced police officers, who'll discuss how each situation should be handled," he said.

But Dr. Arnetz has also added a new wrinkle to the training. He's created a system designed to improve the communication skills of police officers, on the premise that better communication can diffuse stress and potential cases of PTSD. "The new component we've added is this: 'How do you talk to one another?' What we've found is that when you talk to police officers, they might say something like, 'I had a lousy day.' But they don't really talk with one another about anything that has psychological relevance to their work experiences. We want to help them recognize their feelings, because sometimes police officers are so confused about their emotions that they can't really express them."

Dr. Arnetz continued: "We're attempting to train officers to express their feelings in a way that's acceptable within a police department. But we want them to be able to say a little bit more than, 'I'm pissed off at my supervisor.' Or 'I'm stressed.' We want to teach them how to express emotions more clearly, so they can get better support from one another."

Dr. Arnetz and his team have developed a communication process for police officers that creates a vocabulary for talking to one another about extreme stress. His theory is that with training of this kind, performance will improve. "Hopefully," he stated, "we'll see fewer incidents of aggression at home and other domestic problems. And ultimately we hope to see fewer cases of depression and PTSD."

That perspective on communication is right on the money: it relates directly to the effectiveness of peer-to-peer support and interaction. Just going to a bar and talking about the football game doesn't help release emotions—doesn't let the air out of the balloon. The result of not communicating is avoidance and a continued pattern of not facing pressing personal issues. I know how it goes: you're sitting next to a person who went through a similar experience, but you actually avoid speaking about the very thing you need to be talking about.

We need to know how to get the talk started, what words to use.

I'd like to see the kind of approach Dr. Arnetz describes applied in not only police departments but also in every walk of life. Effective levels of communication can only help efforts to keep PTSD from taking hold.

In thinking about this, I was reminded of my trip to Oakland, where I spoke to the police department following the shooting deaths of four officers in one day. During presentation breaks, cops approached me in the back of the room or hallways. They were angry and needed to vent. As stated earlier, another symptom of Post-Traumatic Stress is a thirst for revenge—and cops need to acknowledge that they have that level of anger, because the potential for undisciplined reactions to everyday situations can result. It's also important to acknowledge other feelings, whether caused by a traumatic event, pressure at home, or other personal difficulties. Speaking about problems is essential, because doing so can prevent isolation, the feeling that you're alone. Without venting, you'll feel as if you're the only person dealing with the simmering rage.

Dr. Arnetz further emphasizes, "It's very important that the PTSD focus be expanded to the family—that's been underestimated in the past. Fortunately, we've received great support from the Detroit police force, and there's very good leadership in place. We collaborate with the police at the training academy—they do the technical training. And we combine that with the knowledge from our team of psychologists and stress physicians. The whole program is designed with the police. It's theoretically driven, but they are the ones who actually oversee the training of rookie cops. At the end of the day, you need to have police providing training to police. That's critically important."

Another significant finding by Dr. Arnetz is that PTSD can develop even without experiencing a highly traumatic event.

"The thinking has been that to get a PTSD diagnosis, you have to have gone through a specific traumatic event. What we see increasingly is that a continued stress—not necessarily an extreme stress—can create an equally strong risk factor for PTSD. The research is moving much more toward not just the big event but the aggregated, chronic exposure to stress."

That makes sense. We can easily see the effects of a major traumatic event that plays out over and over on CNN. But what about the twenty years that firefighters have been battling blazes three times a week or police officers have been handling years of fatal accidents—and the accumulated stress they face? What about the abused spouse who has suffered from years of ongoing domestic violence? That adds up to layers upon layers of stress. Dr. Arnetz's view is that this kind of continual exposure creates a higher baseline level for trauma, thus making an individual more susceptible to developing PTSD when a major event does take place.

Dr. Arnetz has more recently turned his energies to studying a group of people who have lived in an environment marked by chronic stress and exposure to major trauma. His groundbreaking research into Iraqi refugees tracks their experiences assimilating to life in the United States, specifically examining trends among the high population of Iraqi immigrants in Detroit.

"There have been a huge number of studies on refugees, but very few that have been based on random selection and studying them after they arrive in a new country," he said. "We track them very early and truly know their mental health when they get here. We want to follow them from the beginning—when they arrive, and then again after two years—gauging them in the areas of PTSD, depression, prior experiences, and resiliency. And then we're going to compare that data with data from immigrants from other Arab countries who have not been exposed to war."

Dr. Arnetz explained that the National Institutes of Health funded his project because of their basic goal to look at the importance of institutional stresses and resources in adjustment to the immense pressure of migration. "My theory is that the better the postmigration training, language training, occupational training and health care there is, the less likely they are to develop PTSD when they come to this country. Those factors will increase their immunity after what they experienced in Iraq. So we're basically taking a systematic approach in attempting to attenuate the risk for PTSD—instead of just proposing going to a psychiatrist. We're looking at the entire public health aspect of the situation."

He continued: "We also know that the trauma exposure in Iraq is huge. We looked at refugees who came here before and after the 1991 Gulf War, and the number of cases we found among the people immigrating here now is vastly higher—roughly one hundred individuals compared to one back then. And we know they will face additional substantial stressors in this country, separate from what they experienced in the war. We're studying this issue just as we would a police officer who experienced a major trauma."

"In looking at Iraqi refugees, we're trying to determine how much the stress exposure here adds to the risk," he said. "The problem is that they leave Iraq and think that family members or friends already in this country will take care of them. But Iraqi families over here say, 'We don't have time. We're working like Americans. We can't drive you all over the place.' So the refugees become very disenchanted. They have this expectation, and then they don't find it in the Iraqi culture here. There are a lot of issues going on."

That kind of creative, comprehensive work by Dr. Arnetz—with an emphasis on resiliency training as a defense against PTSD—reminded me of what I saw in Fort Hood at its Combat Reset and Resiliency Campus.

Meanwhile, Dr. Arnetz told me about the important efforts undertaken by Dr. Amy Adler, a clinical research psychologist and chief of science for Walter Reed Army Institute for Research who works at the U.S. Army Medical Research Unit in Germany. Adler helped developed the "battlemind" approach.

"The premise is telling soldiers returning from Iraq that it's completely OK not to be able to sleep or to be hypervigilant," Dr. Arnetz said. "You need to be that way in Iraq or Afghanistan. But now we're going to change your brain so you can adjust back to life at home. They have changed their whole approach—to switch the entire mind-set before one might get a diagnosis of PTSD."

Dr. Adler's work represents another piece of the PTSD puzzle. It is a puzzle Dr. Arnetz continues to help solve with his cutting-edge research and training—at home and abroad—and substantial contributions to creating a resilient response to the many faces of trauma.

His work underlines the need for preparation—we all need a level of trauma preparedness. It's no different than when we get on a plane and the flight attendants provide the information about what to do in the event of an emergency. We become mentally prepared by visualizing the actions we might take if needed. Being prepared emotionally for traumatic experiences will help us deal better with them as they occur, and hopefully—as Dr. Arnetz's research has demonstrated—diminish their long-term impact on our lives.

Dr. Bengt Arnetz at Wayne State University.

CHAPTER NINE

Defining Moment

"Photography deals exquisitely with appearances, but nothing is what it appears to be."

—Duane Michals

remember when I first saw the photo—a riveting battlefield image of a U.S. Army private in full combat gear cradling a wounded Iraqi boy. It was the morning of March 26, 2003, and I'd just opened the door to my hotel room in Salt Lake City, where I was in town to officiate a game between the Utah Jazz and the Portland Trailblazers. I looked down at the copy of *USA Today* by my feet and saw the picture splashed across the front page. Then I took a closer look: the soldier—a young medic, Private First Class Joe Dwyer of the 7th Cavalry Regiment—had carried the child to safety following a brutal firefight one day earlier near the Euphrates River in the opening phase of the Iraq War.

I felt a surge of gratitude for his selfless act. While I was flying from Sarasota to Salt Lake to run up and down an NBA basketball court, he was running across a battlefield to save a life. Joe had rushed toward the four-year-old's frightened uncle, who held his nephew and a white flag, and bolted back with the little boy to receive medical care. His courage spoke volumes about our troops as they pushed toward Baghdad and into the perils of frontline combat. No matter what political beliefs we hold, that kind of military sacrifice is worthy of our admiration and keeps our country strong.

In no time, the iconic scene captured by *Army Times* photographer Warren Zinn made the rounds in newspapers and other publications throughout the nation. The previously unknown enlistee was hailed as a hero—embraced as an uplifting symbol of the new war. The Army awarded him the Combat Medical Badge for his efforts during active ground fighting, although he downplayed the accolades and insisted he was just doing his job.

Back in the States, the close-knit Dwyer clan—parents Patrick and Maureen, a daughter, and four sons—had thought Joe was stationed out of harm's way in Kuwait until they saw the photo in the paper, and they were shocked to learn that he was actually on the front lines. But they couldn't have been prouder of the second youngest in the family—Joe had joined the Army on September 13, 2001, just two days after the attacks on the World Trade Center, eager to do his part in the mission to strike back against the terrorists. Even so, they were feeling a little overwhelmed by the sudden media attention. In an era of instantaneous, 24/7 news, for a while, everyone wanted to know more about him.

But as the fighting intensified and America lost track of the brave medic, Joe soon slipped from the national radar. That is, until another headline surfaced on June 29, 2008. Somehow, in barely five years, the tale of his inspiring battlefield rescue would shift into a tragic narrative about the ravages of PTSD.

This is the story of Joe Dwyer—how he died a shell of his former lively, irrepressible self; how he fought imaginary Iraqi enemy forces that haunted his waking thoughts long after returning from war; and how he ultimately succumbed to a chemical aerosol spray called Dust-Off, an electronic equipment cleaner, after regularly inhaling it to dull the relentless and gruesome memories of war.

It's also the story of what has happened since—how a Dwyer family friend has made it his mission to keep Joe's memory alive by raising awareness about PTSD.

That friend—Iraq War veteran Chris Delaney, no relation to me—has worked closely with the Dwyer family and their oldest son Brian, a veteran police officer in Suffolk County, New York, to achieve two important objectives. First and foremost is to lobby military powers to have Joe's death officially listed as the result of side effects from Post-Traumatic Stress Disorder, signaling a real change in the way the condition is regarded. Second is to create a groundswell of support to turn the famous image of Joe saving the Iraqi boy into a U.S. postage stamp, to memorialize his heroism and underscore the PTSD crisis among returning veterans.

Chris is constantly on the run to further his quest. In fact, running is one of the many things he's done to honor Joe's memory and underscore the importance of fighting PTSD. As a way of drawing attention to the cause, Chris donned his full, fifty-pound combat uniform—military boots and all—to compete in the Long Island Marathon on May 2010. And beneath the gear, he wore Joe's Army uniform shirt.

"I did the training run the week before and I didn't have any problems," he said. "The weather was beautiful, with the temperature in the sixties. But the day of the race, the temperature jumped by twenty degrees and the humidity was through the roof. And at mile marker four, my feet were bleeding from blisters. I thought for a minute about taking my boots off and showing everybody all the blood on my feet, and that I might not be able to continue."

"But I knew if I took the boots off, I'd never get them back on," he said. "So I just kept on going. It's only nine more miles to the halfway mark—what's the longest it could take me? Three or four hours? I decided to just keep trudging along."

Chris pushed himself along for some 13.1 miles to complete a half marathon—more than enough to thrust Joe Dwyer and his battle with PTSD back into the national news. Brian Dwyer also competed that day, serving as the family's point person to help Chris stand up for the memory of a good man overcome by an unseen but brutal enemy.

I had a chance to catch up with Chris and Brian at the Hope for the Warriors annual five-kilometer race fund-raising dinner in New York. I had to marvel at their commitment and at what they had achieved in such a short time in focusing attention on Joe Dwyer's life and the issue of PTSD.

"I'm not doing this to put *my* name on any of this; I just want to rekindle the memory of Joe's life and don't want him to become a statistic," Chris told me. "We're doing this because there's an issue out there that needs to be looked into, and there is some progress on that front. But we still have a long way to go."

Chris has dedicated himself to changing that, in hopes that mental health care will improve for returning veterans. And there's something else remarkable about that: he's doing it in the name of a fallen soldier he never even met.

• • •

Chris didn't know any of the Dwyers until he became friends with the third oldest son, Danny, when they attended the Suffolk County police academy together in 2000. They formed a close friendship and later became coworkers in their current occupation as corrections officers.

The Delaneys shared a lot in common with the Dwyers and their working-class roots. The father in both families had been NYPD cops. And though he didn't know it at the time, Chris had something in common with Joe—an anger that welled inside and crystallized into a desire to stand up for his wounded country.

The day after the attack at the World Trade Center, Chris went to Ground Zero and stared in stunned disbelief. He called his wife of two years and told her he was going to enlist in the Army, to go after the terrorists that had perpetrated such a horrendous crime against America. But she implored him to think through his decision before acting.

"She asked me not to do anything rash and told me she'd support anything I wanted to do," he recalled. "She just wanted me to look at all the branches of the military to make the best choice.

And because I had her in my life, I wound up going to recruiters from every branch to see what they had to offer."

Ultimately, he enlisted with the U.S. Coast Guard. And because of his law enforcement background, Chris was assigned to a special, post-9/11 unit that patrolled New York City Harbor and conducted stop-and-search missions on incoming freighters and tankers. "That's where they thought the next terrorist threat would come from—something coming in through the channels," he said.

After completing his Coast Guard duty, he returned to his corrections job alongside Danny, where he learned that Danny's younger brother, Joe, had signed up right after the attacks. "I often asked Danny how Joe was doing and then, all of a sudden, that amazing photo of him hit the press," Chris said. "I'll never forget the headline on the front page of our local paper, *Newsday*—'Making Mom Proud.' They plastered the article all over work. But you have to understand—the Dwyers are very low-key people. You could tell Danny was very proud of his brother, and he was very gracious with everyone wanting to talk about it, but he didn't want to make a big deal out of it. It wasn't his style."

Chris knew Joe had returned from combat after his three-month tour of duty ended, but he had no idea of his troubles until reading a 2005 *Newsday* story that detailed Joe's incident with police in El Paso, Texas, and his struggles with PTSD. Danny was reluctant to talk about it, but Chris reached out to his good friend and expressed his concern. They occasionally talked about Joe, and Chris learned that the situation was deteriorating. It angered him that someone who had volunteered to serve his country could be suffering so much from the courageous service he'd given.

One day in June 2008, he noticed Danny wasn't at work. He didn't know why until he saw the paper that evening. The valiant medic, who had made international headlines only five years earlier, had died the day before in North Carolina at age thirty-one, following a prolonged downward spiral and accidental overdose of a toxic household inhalant.

"It really hit me hard, because I'd wanted to join the Army right after September 11 just like he did," Chris said. "And I thought, 'This is a disgrace—this guy did all he did for his country, and then he came home and in *our* backyard, something like this takes place. This is what happens? It's just not fair. I read in the story that he had a wife and a little girl—and I kept thinking, 'This isn't right.' Then I wondered, 'What if this happened to me? Would I want someone to step up for me and do something?'"

When Danny returned to work, Chris expressed his condolences and his feelings that they needed to do something for Joe. "I said, 'Listen, we just can't let this go. I know your family likes to keep to themselves, but at least we should try to raise some money and make sure Joe's wife, Matina, and daughter, Meagan, are taken care of.'"

In the early stages of his involvement, dreaming up different ways to help, Chris would broach ideas with Danny, who would relay them to older brother Brian. Then Chris received a phone call—it was Brian, and his tone was hardly upbeat.

"It was like I was being interrogated," Chris said. "He wanted to find out why I wanted to do all this and what my motives were."

"Basically, I said, 'Why are you messing with my family?'" Brian interjected.

But they sat down and talked, and it became clear that Chris had only pure intentions—and that he felt a kinship with Joe from their similar reaction to the terrorist attacks. From that point on, everything Chris has done in Joe's name has been with the permission of the Dwyer family and Joe's widow, Matina.

One of his first ideas came to fruition six months after Joe's death, in December 2008. A crowd of family, friends, combat vets, and city officials gathered in nearby Mount Sinai, Long Island, for a special dedication. A section of Pipe Stave Hollow Road, where Joe Dwyer had lived as a child, was renamed "PFC Joseph P. Dwyer Road."

"I challenge anybody to find a street in this country that was named after a soldier who wasn't killed on the battlefield but who actually died here due to the side effects of PTSD resulting *from* the war," Chris said proudly.

Chris eventually did his own six-month tour of duty in Iraq during late 2009 and early 2010 as part of Operation Iraqi Freedom. His time in the war zone made him even more committed to his personal mission to speak up—and effect change—on behalf of Joe.

"When I came back from my deployment in February, understanding the conditions we lived in over there and how everything was, I found myself in a transitional period," he said. "I was walking around thinking, 'Nobody *cares*.' You read the paper, and there's nothing in it. We're fighting in two wars, but Lindsay Lohan is getting all the front-page coverage. And I get back and I'm just baffled. Then I came across this quote that had received a lot of attention in the media—a 2007 photo of a message written by a Marine on an erasable board at a base in Iraq: 'America is not at war…America is at the mall.'

"That kind of struck a chord with me. Because Americans are doing everything pre-9/11—as if 9/11 never happened. And yeah, the men and women who went overseas to defend the country are getting homecoming parties and pats on the back. But you know what? Those 'Support the Troops' bumper stickers are starting to fade. After that month or two of welcome-home parties, people forget. And if you don't have the visible wounds—you're not missing a limb or don't have a scar—people don't know about the wounds you may carry inside."

Chris decided to take matters into his own hands—and feet. He had left for Iraq weighing 240 pounds and returned in top physical condition at 205. After getting clearance from the Dwyers and Matina, he decided it was the perfect time to implement his new plan of action—he would run the Long Island Marathon wearing his battle gear.

And Chris didn't stop there. He has since competed in an array of other distance runs in combat attire, always with Joe's shirt beneath the layers, to keep PTSD awareness on the front burner. When he had to return his own military equipment, Chris found a creative solution: he located a fifty-pound firefighter's training dummy, strapped it to his back, and competed in a five-kilometer race to keep Joe's PTSD story alive.

On another front, he worked with Brian and Matina to commission a large oil painting based on the original Zinn photo—a powerful and vivid portrait by a local artist, Angelo Marino, depicting Joe running with the Iraqi child against the backdrop of a rippling American flag and a smoldering sky signifying PTSD—with the silhouette of a soldier saluting him. The artwork, titled *Defining Moment*, was displayed all over Joe's hometown area—first at the Suffolk County legislative building, where a replica of the painting now hangs—then at the Babylon, New York Town Hall, and later in the community of Brookhaven. Moving the framed memorial from town to town has become something of a symbolic ritual, carried out at a series of motorcycle rallies that Chris and Brian have orchestrated to spread Joe's message geographically.

"Our goal is for people to see this image and remember," Chris said.

Their ultimate goal is for the original oil painting to be displayed prominently in a place of national honor: the Pentagon.

"We want to make this story come full circle. There's the heroic tale of someone who enlisted right after September 11 and did something very special while serving his country. Then there's the tragic side of the story of everything he and his family went through. And now, we want to bring it back to the story of true heroism—as a way of honoring Joe and helping others."

• • •

Chris's enthusiasm motivated me to learn more about the man with whom he feels such a bond and has devoted so much time and energy fighting for. I wanted to know Joe's story better so I could gain a deeper understanding of how PTSD can derail and then take such a promising life. I turned to his big brother Brian, who helped paint the picture for me—one of a fun-loving practical jokester who was devoted to his new wife and little daughter, only to lose his grip on reality and everything he held dear.

The Dwyer family lived in a small, three-bedroom home in Mount Sinai—with Christine the oldest of the children, followed by five boys: Brian; Patrick, who became a New York City transit cop; Dan; Joe; and Matthew, who joined the Air Force.

"Growing up, we had everything we needed," Brian said. "Everyone was so close. We didn't really have a choice—there was no fifth or sixth bedroom where we could just close the door and be by ourselves. Joe was a kid with a great sense of humor. He loved fishing and golf, peaceful things in life."

"But God forbid our parents would go out to dinner and the movies and be gone for four or five hours. Joe was like, 'Great, we have time for all my friends to come over and go nuts.'" Brian continued: "I was older and was working by then, and I'd come home and there were kids all over the place. I'd go, 'Joe, what are you *doing*?!' But he was doing what we all did growing up—when our parents went out, it was our time to have fun."

Brian will never forget one prank Joe had at the expense of brother Dan. He took a plastic office mat designed to let desk chairs glide smoothly and flipped it upside down, exposing the spiky plastic tips meant to grip rugs. Then he placed it outside the door of the bathroom, waiting for his brother to come out of the shower. "That was the Dwyer household—watching one of your brothers jumping around and cursing," Brian said, laughing at the memory. "It was hysterical. That's the way Joe was and we all were."

When Joe enlisted, he calmed his nervous parents and newlywed wife Matina, telling them that his medical unit would be located in Kuwait far from the front lines. In reality, his unit would be assigned to the 7th Cavalry Regiment, which would lead the initial charge into Baghdad as part of the "Shock and Awe" phase of the war.

The next thing the Dwyer family knew, a world-famous photo had certified Joe as a hero—and they hadn't even known he was in Iraq. The picture didn't diminish their daily concern for Joe's safety, but it gave them a sense that he was OK and excelling at a tough job under intensely difficult circumstances. They weren't aware, though, of the other sights, sounds, and smells that were part of his life in Iraq: tending to the horrible wounds from gunshots and shrapnel, the excruciating cries for help from the injured, the soldiers who died as he tried to save them. Those were the parts of the job Joe kept to himself.

His family and friends couldn't wait to welcome him home in June 2003. On the Fourth of July, Dan hosted a party for him at his house in New York, complete with a bagpipe band in the back yard that greeted him when he arrived. Joe looked gaunt, having dropped some forty pounds from his normal weight of 220, but he told everyone the loss was due to the steady diet of prepackaged military meals in the desert. And he put on a good front, laughing and making easy conversation with well-wishers. "It was a very proud moment, and everything seemed to be all right," Brian said. "Knowing Joe, he was just so humble, and he was saying, 'This is unnecessary—enough, enough. But he didn't show any signs of turmoil inside of him. The first five or six months were actually a nice period. It was like, 'OK, he's back. We've got him.' He was quieter, but we felt he'd come around, and it wasn't like anything was bad."

By Christmas, though, Joe began to show outward signs that

something wasn't right. He dwelled constantly on his experiences in Iraq and, according to Brian, seemed to be reliving events in his mind and wanting to avoid contact with other people as much as possible. He had trouble sleeping, sometimes staying awake for two days straight, feeling agitated and increasingly paranoid. "We talked to Matina on the phone and realized, 'OK, now we have a problem—where do we go as a family to figure this one out?" Brian recalled. "I went down to talk to him and he was like, 'No, nothing's wrong.' If you tried to pull anything out of him, you would never get anything. I guess he really wanted to talk to somebody who had been through the same thing. He wasn't going to open up to anyone in the family. Joe turned down offers to go out to eat or see movies—being around people bothered him." These are two signs I know all too well with PTSD—avoidance and isolation.

Joe was finally diagnosed with the condition a year after being back in the States, stationed at Fort Bliss in El Paso, Texas. A doctor prescribed antidepressants, but Joe's emotional decline and display of erratic behavior continued while living off base in an apartment with Matina.

There was an incident when he was driving and thought he saw a roadside IED and swerved, hitting a store sign. Another time he told Matina and friends that he was sure he saw hostile Iraqi combatants lurking nearby, and he began answering the door to his house armed with one of his guns. The situation worsened in the summer of 2005, when he turned his apartment upside down, claiming that he was searching for the enemy.

That incident resulted in his being admitted for three days to the base medical center, where he received treatment for an addiction to Dust-Off—an inhalant that has become a problem in the military, with some soldiers "huffing" the dangerous and potentially deadly aerosol spray for a brief high. Joe had become addicted. It was his way of temporarily escaping the demons racing through his thoughts and getting some sleep.

When Joe was released from the hospital, the problems returned. In October 2005, the situation came to a head when Army officials showed up at his apartment with the aim of encouraging him to get more treatment. He responded by barricading himself in his home. El Paso police were called to the scene, and they promptly learned that Joe thought he was seeing Iraqi insurgents on the roof. He had attached a mirror to a stick and was looking out of the window so he could see them, and he fired shots from his pistol through the ceiling.

"It wasn't really a standoff—Joe thought he was helping the cops," Brian told me, "because now the enemy was coming into his house. In his mind they were on the roof, so he let a couple of rounds go through the ceiling. Matina was out of the house with neighbors. And I got a call at two or three in the morning—and I was able to talk to one of the police negotiators who was hoping to get insight into what was going on with him. I told him Joe was back from war and had PTSD. I was concerned for my brother, but as a cop I also knew that this was a dangerous situation for my law enforcement brothers. My concern was for all—and I urged them to be cautious. All that time, Joe was actually talking to the police, letting them know where he thought the bad guys were located." Joe eventually came out and was taken to a hospital in Beaumont, Texas for psychiatric treatment.

Listening to Brian's account, I felt the similarity to my own skewed perception of reality after I'd surfaced from undercover—thinking I heard voices and saw potential intruders when I tried to sleep at night, jumping into stairwells at courthouses where I later testified, fearing my life was in imminent danger. At that time, the helicopter I saw wasn't flying low near my home to spray for mosquitoes—it was there to attack me and my family. This is what Joe was experiencing. It was very real to him. The enemy *was* on the roof. And his reactions are common to people suffering from PTSD.

During his hospitalization, an important revelation came to light. Joe acknowledged that he had been less than candid in filling out a military questionnaire given to soldiers following their active duty. He did not indicate that he'd been bothered by what he had experienced in combat. He was simply anxious to complete the form quickly so he could return home as fast as possible. And he didn't want to do anything that might jeopardize his dream of joining the family business—law enforcement.

Like many soldiers, Joe knew that mental or emotional problems can carry a stigma, and he didn't want to take the risk. This is a common attitude. During my visits to Iraq, in my many late-night conversations with soldiers, they talked about how filling out the questionnaire was like having the answers to the test ahead of time: they knew what to write on the form so they didn't end up stalling the process of returning home. And Chris could understand Joe's actions, too. He'd completed the questionnaire himself.

"You've been away from your family for a long time and you've seen hell," he said. "You're going to mislead them in your answers because you just want to get home—to some place you feel safe again."

Being the oldest brother, Brian had a close relationship with Joe and often checked in with him to see how he was doing. Before the war, they'd had many personal conversations. Weeks after Joe returned, Brian asked him to share some of his experiences, the way cops tell their glory-day war stories. But Joe's stories were *really* about war. "I still looked at him like he was my twelve-year-old brother, but here he was a combat medic. So I asked him, 'You had to patch up tons of people—how many people do you think you treated?' And he said to me, 'I really don't know. What I do remember are the ones I couldn't save.' Those are the people who stayed with him. When I heard him say that, I was like, 'Why did I even open my mouth?' I could see him turning his head, probably thinking of who died in front of him."

Joe and Matina moved to Pinehurst, North Carolina, in January 2006, and two months later he received his discharge papers. The couple lived off his disability income. Life took a nice turn when daughter Meagan was born in May. But inside, Joe was still being tormented by memories of warfare—of the soldiers and civilians he *couldn't* help—that were seared into his brain. In 2007, his problems were bad enough for Matina to take Meagan and move in with her parents—fearful, in part, because Joe had purchased an assault rifle.

That July—four years after being welcomed home in a back-yard bagpipe celebration—Joe agreed to check into a program near his family's home in New York, the Northport Veterans Affairs Medical Center. He stayed for half a year, and there were signs of progress. But ultimately the program did little for him, besides weighing him down with a heavy regimen of medication.

"My father likened it to a pharmaceutical lobotomy," Brian said.

"To see him on some of the medications, it just killed you. You look at him and he was just a shell. There was no quick wit, no involvement in conversation. He would just sit there and never interject. It was like he wasn't there. It was scary. He had his medication changed quite a few times—and a lot of it was very addicting."

Matina had moved back with Meagan into the couple's North Carolina home, hoping life together as a family would improve. But when Joe returned from his stay in Northport, his behavior began to unravel once again. The Dwyers thought it was best for Matina and Meagan to move out, and they did so. Joe, meanwhile, seemed more and more disconnected from reality—still thinking Saddam Hussein's soldiers were shadowing him, still haunted by brutal, bloody memories of desert battles. He kept knives around the house for protection against an enemy intrusion. Yet even amid all of that, he told Brian and his parents he wanted to do another tour, that his problems would fade if only he could go back into combat. This is a classic example of what veterans with PTSD experience. The battlefield becomes their norm, and everyday life becomes uncomfortable for them.

All the while, Joe inhaled Dust-Off that he purchased easily at local stores, one can after another. By one account, a local cab driver called police to report that she had been driving him for months to purchase the inhalant. Joe had told her that he needed to take a cab because he'd wrecked his car veering to avoid what he thought was a roadside bomb.

"He had grown continually frustrated with the medication he'd been given, so this was his way of self-medicating," Brian explained.

Pinehurst police had been to his house on previous occasions to check on reports of trouble, but Joe had always responded in a helpful manner. The police left each time without incident. But on June 28, 2008, Joe made a desperate call to a cab driver to take him to the emergency room.

"The driver arrived and knocked, and could see through the door that Joe was on the floor, yelling for help—he just couldn't move," Brian said.

Officers rushed to the scene and kicked the door down. They found Joe lying nearly motionless on the floor, eyes glazed from the inhalant and barely speaking.

"He was just asking them for help, saying, 'Don't let me die. I don't want to die,'" Brian recalled.

Paramedics lifted him into an ambulance. But as it sped to the hospital, sirens blaring and red lights flashing, Joe was gone—far removed from the battlefield, one more casualty of war.

"Some people say it was suicide, but it wasn't," Brian said. "It was an attempt to break out of the pain. He didn't want to die."

● ● ●

Joe's death left his family and friends grieving for a man who went off to war fully embracing life and returned home struggling to maintain his grip on it. He was thrust into becoming a symbol of hope for a country at war, then found himself hopelessly lost in the memories of a war that raged in his mind.

The pain of his passing was felt keenly by another person—someone who knew him only briefly. This man received the shocking news in a harshly worded message sent by a stranger, a North Carolina woman who had located his email address and accused him of having played a role in the tragedy. Photographer Warren Zinn, whose camera lens had captured Joe's heroic act for the world to see, felt dazed as he drove home to his Miami apartment, trying his best to process the stunning development.

In many respects, he felt forever linked with Joe by that battle-field photo, hanging a framed copy of the *USA Today* front page proudly in his home. Warren kept in touch by email for several years after Joe returned from Iraq in June 2003, but he wasn't aware of any problems until he saw a newspaper account of the 2005 barricade incident with police. And now Joe was dead. The accusatory email had stung him, but Warren's thoughts were of the Dwyer family and of a fundamental injustice: that a soldier could come home a hero and then sink to a painful, lonely death in the quicksand of PTSD.

"It was definitely shocking when I found out—it rocked me quite a bit," he said. "It felt strange that the thing that I was most proud of, one of my greatest photographic achievements, was sud-denly part of something so sad."

I had read a powerful 2008 essay Warren wrote for the *Washington Post* about the famous photo and his memories of Joe. After a few phone calls, I was able to track Warren down. I learned that Warren, who retired as a photojournalist after two tours of duty in Iraq for the *Army Times*, went to law school and now works as a criminal defense attorney in South Florida. We spoke directly about that fateful day by the banks of the Euphrates River. Other than Joe, nobody else had a clearer view of the fleeting moment in history, March 25, 2003, that saved a little boy's life—and changed the course of their own. Warren was glad to offer his perspective.

"The unit I was embedded with was the 7th Cavalry Regiment—with the Cavalry essentially acting as the scouts," Warren explained. "They were part of the tip of the spear, as the military calls it, and were out there on their own. The 7th Cav had a pretty aggressive battle plan from the first day—they were going to be taking on a couple of Republican Guard Divisions by themselves until the rest of the Army and Marines could get there. They were going to lead the charge for the 3rd Infantry Division into Iraq."

The 7th Cavalry Regiment was out of Georgia and needed a medical unit for the invasion—and that led to Joe's unit from Texas being attached to it. "The interesting thing is that Joe wasn't even supposed to go," Warren said. "He volunteered. That's how he came to join them."

On March 24, the regiment had rolled into a village, expecting a warm welcome, based on intelligence reports. Instead, the Cavalry was shelled, fighting its way out in a bloody battle. The large convoy of vehicles eventually pushed past the village by nightfall, with Warren in the back of a Bradley armored fighting vehicle monitoring radio reports, fearing the regiment might be sitting ducks for another attack as the regiment struggled to find its bearings. Unable to take pictures in darkness, he curled up and dozed off rather than worry about the ominous possibilities he couldn't control.

It might sound strange that Warren could sleep under such adverse conditions, but I've heard from soldiers on the front line that this is typical. I even experienced it myself in 2009 after being embedded with the 25th Infantry Division in Mosul. Hearing bombs in the distance during those first few days had me jumping out of bed. But by the end of the visit, I barely noticed the daily soundtrack of war.

Warren awoke in the early morning to bombs dropped by U.S. fighter jets pounding the earth outside the tanks, part of an air strike to help the regiment fend off a new attack. Eventually, the eardrum-rattling sounds of explosions ceased, and the column of vehicles stopped. Warren donned his helmet and Kevlar vest and poked his head out of the back hatch of the Bradley, surprised that the endless sea of desert sand had given way to the lush greenery of the Euphrates River Valley. But the sight was far from pastoral. Many of the palm trees lining the banks were afire, the result of the bombing.

The predawn trouble had started when the convoy headed north on a two-lane road, alongside mud homes and rice paddies that sat directly in front of the river.

"What happened was that these fighters had been coming across the Euphrates River in boats and attacking us from behind those homes," Warren said. "So an air strike was called in that hit along the river—and that's what woke me up."

Warren remembers the vivid orange hue in the sky from the sunrise, as he left the tank with his camera while Cavalry commanders huddled to plan their next move. That's when he looked off in the distance and saw a man dressed in black garb running up a dirt path that led from his home to the road and waving a white flag. After being stopped and searched, the man explained through a translator that many people had been injured back in the village. The commander, fearing an ambush, told him he would need to bring the injured civilians to the road and the unit would treat them there.

"The man went back to the village, and a few minutes later, he starts running up the road with this child naked from the waist down in his arms—with his badly injured left leg wrapped in a bloody scarf. I'm taking pictures of the guy running up the road, thinking it's a great photo. And all of a sudden, and out of the corner of my eye, I see a soldier running toward the guy. This soldier scoops the boy out of the man's arms, and comes running back up the road toward where the medics were setting up to treat him. As soon as I took the picture, I knew instantly that picture was going to go *everywhere*. I was just hoping I had the focus and exposure right."

He did indeed. And one day after Warren transmitted the photo, the world wanted to know all about that soldier—PFC Joe Dwyer—and his decision to put personal safety aside for the sake of a severely wounded child. He was summoned to the command center, where an officer told him, "You're an American icon right now." *Good Morning America* was waiting to beam him live onto the airwaves, and other media outlets were lined up for their turns.

"First, I put Joe on the satellite phone with his family, and then all the media that wanted to speak to him—we spent four or five hours together doing that," Warren said. "He was just such a nice, humble guy—and he was very articulate in saying, 'Hey, I'm just doing my job out here, and there's nothing special that I did. This is what everybody out here does.' After we were done with the interviews, he went back to his duties—and I didn't see him for the rest of the time I was in Iraq."

But they kept in touch with occasional emails after Joe returned to his base in Texas following his tour of duty. Joe's words never hinted at the turmoil that was swirling inside his mind, although he did wonder about the fate of the little boy, Ali Sattar, whom he had carried to safety. In one exchange, he wrote:

Hey Warren it's Joseph Dwyer the kid you made famous. Hope you're doing well and staying safe. I'm writing you to see if you have any pictures from that day in Iraq with the ambushes and if so if I could get copies from you. Let me know if you do…Also I'm wondering if you ever heard anything else about the kid. Enjoy your holidays and be safe.

In fact, Warren had visited Ali on his second tour in Iraq and learned that his leg had not healed well. The child had received inadequate care when an Iraqi ambulance whisked him away after his rescue. That prevented him from being airlifted to a U.S. medical facility, where he would have received more skilled care— something that bothered Joe when Warren told him about it.

In a later correspondence, Joe congratulated Warren for his good work photographing honest images of combat and wished him well in his decision to "give up the war business" for a new career in law. Joe seemed to be doing his best to keep up the facade that he was doing well—perhaps because he wanted so badly to feel that way.

I'm doing fine out here in Ft. Bliss T.X. 1 year and I'm gone. When I first got back I didn't really want to talk about being over there to anyone. Now looking back its one of the greatest things I've ever done. I hope you feel the same about what you have done. I truly believe you played an important role in this war. You told every one's story. Enough with the mushy stuff though it's great to hear from you…You take care dude I'll talk to you soon.

Only two months later, Joe was surrounded by El Paso police after shooting up his apartment, convinced that Iraqi insurgents were closing in on him. Warren was stunned to read a newspaper account of the incident and Joe's increasing troubles with PTSD.

Then came the news that stopped Warren cold in June 2008. He tried to contact Joe's parents to express his sympathy and condolences. A week later, he received a call from Joe's mother. She wanted to make sure Warren knew that some publicized reports claiming that Joe hated the photo were wrong. She told Warren that Joe loved the picture and was proud of it but simply didn't feel comfortable with all the praise heaped on him because countless soldiers did everything he did, every day, in total anonymity. Knowing Joe's feelings about the photo made Warren feel better about having taken it.

He couldn't help but think of how Joe had helped preserve the Iraqi boy's life but in the end couldn't preserve his own. Yet another thought has since occurred to him: the photo, in its first incarnation, was an important and timely symbol of hope—representing the actions not just of one brave soldier but of all the U.S. troops engaged in this new war, and of America as a whole. Today, in the aftermath of Joe's death, the photo has a new meaning of hope: it is a rallying cry to support vets suffering from PTSD.

"I think some good can come from what happened—and has come," Warren said. "The photo took on a whole new meaning when Joe died. It also made me realize that the only reason people knew about Joe's story was because he happened to be the subject of my photo. Unfortunately, what happened to Joe has happened and is happening to other soldiers every day. Their stories don't get the same attention, because there wasn't a picture of them on the front page of *USA Today*."

But thanks to the image Warren captured, nobody will forget *this* soldier.

• • •

Days after his death, Joe was buried with military honors—and his story would soon fuel one man's mission: a desire to set the record straight about the fun-loving guy who'd rushed off to enlist in the wake of America's 9/11 nightmare.

In the eyes of Chris Delaney, the system let Joe down, and he hopes that spreading the word of Joe Dwyer's story will bring about change.

"Joe went into the military one hundred percent healthy, but yet he got released and he was far from healthy," Chris said. "And there are so many other guys in the same situation. I don't want to blame people. But there has to be a change. So if you have some-body who's experiencing things like Joe—and the authorities knew he was because they were giving him medication for it—why are they letting them out? Why are they allowing them to leave the brotherhood, the camaraderie, where they would be able to talk to soldiers who've been through things similar to them?

"They could share with people who could say, 'Hey, I've also seen people die. I also know what it's like to shoot somebody with a fifty-caliber weapon. I saw the devastation it would cause.' They took Joe from a war, and flew him back home in twenty-four hours. Then he starts to build up PTSD, and now this guy has to deal with it at home with his wife and his daughter. In Joe's situation—and with other soldiers—who do they talk to? In law enforcement, you're on the job for twenty years, and you always have that partner and somebody to share with. But in the military, once you're done, you're out the door.

"That's why I say we let Joe down as a country. We failed him because he went in as a dedicated, patriotic, strong guy—so how can we let him and all the others come out without making sure they're close to being who they were before they went to war?"

The answer may lie in helping people understand that PTSD sufferers have the condition for a lifetime. They require care long after leaving the battlefield, or leaving whatever traumatic experi-ence they have encountered.

I understand that part of it because there were so many times I sought out a place from the past—whether it was at my parents' home or with my friends—only to find that I wanted to leave a short time after being there. When I was in the throes of PTSD, like Joe was, no person or place could provide that inner peace. I did not find it until peer-to-peer therapy came into my life. It seems as if the system in place for Joe was geared more toward providing piecemeal treatments, toward focusing on dealing with symptoms, and toward adjusting medications rather than approaching PTSD as a long-term affliction.

Perhaps a lesson to be learned from Joe's story is that we need to identify problems early and treat them continuously. And one of the most effective steps is to make sure that returning vets have the chance to share experiences with others who have lived through a similar trauma, talking about their fear and grief, their sense of shock and loss. That process can provide a solid foundation for weathering the emotional storms that lie ahead.

There was an encouraging development after Joe's passing. The state of North Carolina officially listed PTSD as the cause of death on his death certificate. And the Army—after much paperwork and help from Joe's military family and friends—classified his death as in the line of duty. Yet to Chris Delaney, that doesn't change a fundamental problem.

"Too many soldiers are coming home dealing with PTSD and finding themselves in a downward spiral, made worse by this country's economic crisis," Chris said. "Now they're back, just trying to survive. And then they're in the same boat that Joe was in. That's why we have an ongoing epidemic in this country."

And that's why Chris runs, carrying the memory of a fallen soldier he never knew—and a message for all of us. We all know someone who needs help or is hurting, yet many times we hesitate to get involved. Not Chris. He felt the pain and anguish of a courageous young PFC. With relentless determination, he's shined a light on a tragedy and forever changed the way Joe Dwyer will be remembered. It's a valuable lesson about empowering ourselves to find a path toward healing.

Defining Moment, *the painting by artist Angelo Marino of PFC Joe Dwyer, based on photographer Warren Zinn's famous photo.*

CHAPTER TEN

Twenty-First-Century Therapies

"Although the world is full of suffering, it is also full of overcoming it."

—Helen Keller

We've certainly come a long way since 1943 in our awareness of Post-Traumatic Stress and the seriousness of this very real disorder. That was the year the legendary World War II field commander General George S. Patton put his decorated career in jeopardy by slapping a soldier he regarded as a coward for being hospitalized with "battle fatigue"—a term we now know by the name of PTSD.

Although many years have gone by, I believe we are still in the infant stages of understanding Post-Traumatic Stress Disorder; we are still battling misconceptions and a lingering stigma surrounding the condition while seeking effective ways to treat it.

The good news is that a number of innovative and impressive programs have taken root around the United States to help individuals suffering from the effects of trauma. They are all pieces of a complicated puzzle, yet together they create a whole image that offers hope and encouragement in the fight against the devastating condition.

You can find important work being done all across the PTSD horizon—from a farm in Tampa that specializes in equine therapy to help soldiers reeling from traumatic wartime injuries and experiences to a long-distance bicycling-based rehabilitation program for Wounded Warriors; to and an intensive retreat in California for law enforcement, firefighters, and first responders; to confidential online psychological and peer support system for veterans who aren't ready to step forward for critical help; to an operation that brings injured vets back to visit Iraq as part of the healing process.

And there is much more in between. For example, ancient Greek playwright Sophocles dealt with themes related to the horrors of battle and the mental trauma that would later be known as PTSD. As a means of therapy, many groups of military personnel have attended readings of two Sophocles plays—one of them, *Ajax*, tells the story of a warrior who grapples with depression and is talked out of suicide by his wife and friend; another, *Philoctetes*, is about a Greek soldier reeling from emotional turmoil who distrusts his Army and refuses medical treatment. The performances are followed by discussions among veterans in the audience of how the plays relate to their PTSD struggles, creating healing dialogues prompted by 2,500-year-old classical dramas.

Many new and innovative programs like this are being developed today. In this chapter, you will learn about a handful of programs engaged in an array of inspiring efforts—and meet the people behind them.

Therapy options for PTSD need to be creative. I've found that hero leadership—looking for someone else to provide the answer or solution for you—does not often work. We need to empower ourselves. Every successful movement has done that, and you should follow the same road of empowerment as you look for answers to PTSD.

• • •

Quantum Leap Farm

Deep in the peaceful, wooded countryside north of Tampa, Florida, you can find a place of reassurance and renewal for soldiers and everyday folks dealing with a multitude of mental and physical challenges.

It seems fitting that the primary route to Quantum Leap Farm is on Veteran's Expressway: the busy thoroughfare leading to this pastoral, twelve-acre stretch in rural Odessa is a route to potential breakthroughs for so many members of the military suffering from PTSD, among other serious conditions. But the primary mode of movement once you arrive at the farm is with horses. This is a place where amazing and uplifting results are achieved through the art of equine therapy—a place where horses help clients shaken by trauma (or dealing with a range of disabilities) to regain confidence and move forward in life.

Dr. Edie Dopking founded the Quantum Leap Farm in 2000.

After a career as a nuclear medicine technologist at St. Anthony's Hospital in nearby St. Petersburg, Florida. She then shifted into private business in the field of magnetic resonance imaging. Edie also began volunteering at an equestrian therapy center for children, where she worked with a former Navy SEAL. He had dreamed of starting a similar program for veterans, but didn't have the time or resources. Instead, he suggested to Edie that she could create a program on some property she and her then husband owned in Odessa. That planted a seed in her mind. After selling the MRI business—and beginning work on her doctorate in aging studies research at the University of South Florida—she decided the time had come to change career course and start an equine therapy center for people who could benefit from interacting in various ways with the calming presence of horses.

The endeavor began modestly, with three horses Edie owned, and one friend assisting her three days a week. Today, Quantum Leap Farm is a bustling nonprofit operation with a large and talented staff that works closely with the Tampa-based James Haley Veterans Hospital and Bay Pines in Seminole, Florida—the first and fourth busiest VA hospitals in the nation, respectively. And it has earned the stamp of approval from General David H. Petraeus, commander of the U.S. Central Command, who wrote in a certificate of commendation: "I wish to express my heartfelt appreciation to Quantum Leap Farm for their Warriors in Transition Workshops and Wounded Warrior Programs. These equine assisted therapy programs facilitate successful returns, reunions, and reintegration for service personnel and their families."

One such program at Quantum Leap draws its inspiration

directly from military terminology. It is called At E.A.S.E.—
Equine-Assisted Self-Exploration. The program—created and
directed by farm staff member, behavior health counselor, and
trauma specialist Carla Staats—uses a trained mental health counselor and horse specialist to lead ailing veterans through a range
of activities that embrace problem solving, coping strategies, and
relationship and team building.

Carla had an interesting experience joining Quantum Leap. She
had just moved to the area in 2007 after marrying longtime Tampa
Bay Rays baseball broadcaster Dewayne Staats. She had earned a
license three years earlier from the Equine-Assisted Growth and
Learning Association (EAGALA) and was seeking a way to use her
extensive mental health experience in a setting that incorporated
her therapeutic expertise with horses. Carla called Quantum Leap
one day in 2008, hoping to introduce herself to Dr. Dopking, but
the owner was out of town. The next day, Carla flew to Utah to
make a presentation on equine therapy with veterans at a national
conference. In the audience, listening to Carla, was Edie Dopking.

"It was wild," Edie told me. "I'm sitting there, and Carla is talking about exactly what I wanted to do at Quantum Leap. I couldn't
believe it. Finally when she got to the Q and A segment, I raised
my hand and asked, 'Where are you doing this?' She said, 'Tampa.'
And I said, 'We need to talk!'"

Jenna Miller—an equestrian enthusiast with experience as
instructor, competitor, and trainer—was also at the conference.
She was in the midst of obtaining her master's degree in mental
health counseling at Tampa's Argosy University and dreamed of a
career combining her love of horses with counseling.

"I met Carla in Utah, and we immediately hit it off," Jenna recalled. "I really believe everything aligned on this for a reason."

She and Carla soon teamed up with Edie to help start At E.A.S.E. In short order, they got the program up and running, while establishing a strong relationship with the medical staffs at the area's two VA hospitals. Now both Haley and Bay Pines assess patients and send them on a regular basis to Quantum Leap.

At the heart of the partnership between Edie, Carla, and Jenna is a shared passion for horses, whose value is enormous for people facing physical or psychological challenges.

"I can't tell you how often somebody who is in a wheelchair or has a walker tells us, 'You know, for that hour I'm on the horse, nobody knows I have a disability," Edie said. "I look just like anybody else.' I remember the first time I got on a horse as a child, it was something magical for me. And I think, 'How empowering for someone with a disability and with limited access—all of a sudden, they have legs. How *good* is that for their psyche?"

But there's another reason that horses have a natural therapeutic touch, she explains: "We exploit the horse's movement to benefit the rider—and there are two things that make it therapeutic. One is rhythm. You've got that one-two-three-four—and there are some studies lately on a device called an interactive metronome. It's about doing things to a rhythm, and the conclusion is that this helps organize cognition and coordination with Traumatic Brain Injury patients involved in the therapy. We think there's a parallel with horseback riding.

"The other thing is that a horse's movement models the normal human gait. In fact, we had a woman who was a quadruple amputee who lost both hands and both feet. She was injured in an IED explosion. She got up one of our horses and the craziest expression came over her face. We said, 'Are you OK?' And she said, 'I haven't walked in eight months. This feels so much like walking. I can barely contain myself.' We walked with her for an hour, and she loved it."

Carla told me about another injured vet, a Marine who had suffered a traumatic brain injury in battle. He was transported in a van from Haley Veterans Hospital, seated in a wheelchair, with a look that conveyed a sense of disconnection to his surroundings.

"We wheeled him onto a ramp that was at ground level, and we have this old horse named Rocky—the oldest on the property—and he has a thing for people in wheelchairs," she said. "He walked right up to the Marine and nuzzled him on the face. And this guy just started laughing. He couldn't talk, but he could laugh like crazy, and that was great to see. Rocky made him seem like an entirely different person."

"Horses are some of the best therapists," Jenna added.

The overlap with individuals dealing with PTSD is substantial. For one thing, anyone who has suffered a catastrophic injury has no doubt experienced some level of the disorder. But there's also a subtle, metaphoric factor at play that helps those afflicted with the condition.

"Think of the horse as the ultimate prey animal—they are herbivores, not predators—and they're gorgeous, big, and meaty creatures," Carla explained. "Humans, on the other hand, are the ultimate predator. Metaphorically, a soldier is the prey and the predator; they're big and strong, yet vulnerable. So there's a subconscious connection there."

She continued: "In addition, horses have so much to teach us about living in the moment. They don't carry yesterday into today and they're not worried about tomorrow. You might be getting into my hay and I'll deal with you right now, and then let's all return to grazing. We have this wonderful saying here: 'Deal with it—and *return to grazing*.' It's teaching people how to stay in the moment and try not to dwell on things you have no control over."

Edie sees another direct parallel between horses and people coping with PTSD, one based on certain innate equine characteristics. "Horses have very complex social relationships with the members of their herd—like members of a combat team, or members of a family, too. They can be very herd dependent. They have hyperexaggerated startle reflexes like PTSD patients do. Horses are somewhat geared to be looking for predators all the time, so they're easy to spook. All horses have a very strong flight instinct, and they're very good at reading body language. And so soldiers with PTSD can relate to equine behavior. The thing is, horses deal with the problems better than the humans do, so there's a lot to learn from them."

Quantum Leap counselors know the value of equine therapy early in the process following a traumatic event, which could lead to full-blown PTSD if left untreated. It's similar to my belief that creating peer-to-peer dialogue, in the wake of the experience, can prevent Post-Traumatic Stress from developing further.

"You have to have the symptoms of Acute Distress Disorder longer than a month before getting a PTSD diagnosis," Carla said. "There's so much focus on the diagnosis. But what if everyone who returned from combat just went through a natural decompression program, like with one of our workshops, and maybe wouldn't wind up having the full PTSD diagnosis? We've had veterans say to us, 'I wish it was like the old days when you came back on a ship, because at least you had the time to decompress.' So attacking this head-on, early in the game, is very important."

That underlined the conversations I've had with World War II veterans. The time they had together while returning home allowed for them to share inner thoughts; in essence, they were doing peer-to-peer therapy. Today's soldiers may be in Iraq or Afghanistan on Monday and be back on Main Street USA by Wednesday. There is simply no time to process all they've experienced.

Success stories abound at Quantum Leap Farm. One involves a Vietnam vet who suffered multiple injuries during the war. He was making great strides, although he talked constantly about his bitterness toward the VA. He arrived for regularly scheduled therapy the day after Edie had hired the company Big Ass Fans to install three of the aptly named, huge blades on the ceiling of the large, open riding arena to offset the hot Florida temperatures. He froze at the sight of the giant blades and adamantly refused to go inside. Edie, Carla, and Jenna persisted, even though they were not sure what had caused his reaction. They took it one step at a time and coaxed him inside the arena. Ultimately, their professional, caring manner allowed the man to let the air out of his balloon—part of the metaphoric process I spoke of earlier in this book. He shared with them that he had been involved in a helicopter crash during his time in Vietnam. And it was clear to them that the oversized, whirring fan blades had triggered a flashback to his crash in the jungle.

It was another example of how there is no finish line with PTSD. Here was a trigger to an event that took place some forty years earlier. That's why awareness of your triggers is important, so you understand the internal reaction. The Quantum Leap therapists, knowing the cause of that reaction, furthered the discussion with a simple question. What would the horses do? They reminded him to be like a horse and just focus on the here and now.

Jenna recalled another case with a soldier who had just returned from Iraq and feared riding the horses because they reminded him of the camels he had encountered during combat in the desert. But as he became comfortable with the horses, he simultaneously talked through and got past his negative associations with camels from the battlefield. "That's one of the things our horses do— they provide an outlet that people can project their feelings onto," she said.

The learning process at Quantum Leap occasionally incorporates designed activities, geared toward encouraging enhanced communication with others. One particularly docile, well-grounded horse allows participants at the farm to actually paint messages and designs on it—a way of promoting self-expression. That reminded me of Dr. Gordon's therapy exercise incorporating drawing and dance as ways of sharing inner thoughts before actually verbalizing them.

There's also a designed activity called Life's Little Obstacles. Participants in the activity help build an obstacle that the horse has to go around and name it after different challenges in their lives, such as financial problems, family stress, drugs, or alcohol.

"The goal is to get past the obstacle without touching the horse or talking to it—and without talking to each other," Carla said. "This exercise provides a learning tool for empathetic communication and its importance in the healing process."

She recalled one particular day working with a group of Marines and their family members. They broke into small groups for the exercise, all assigned a different horse. The veterans and family members came to see each horse as their own Marine—one that didn't want to be led, talked to, or helped in any way in circumventing an obstacle. The *actual* Marines had to do their best in communicating positively to tackle the problem, which allowed them to see what their family members and friends go through when they try to help. At the same time, the Marines said they also identified with the horses, which were resistant in getting past obstacles in their path. And their parents and family members experienced their own realization: the challenge mirrored what they had been feeling in trying to help a son or daughter, home from the war, deal with a traumatic event. In the end, everyone had gained insights from the horse by putting themselves in someone else's shoes.

It was a revelation and healing moment for vets and families and typical of the excellent work done on a little horse farm getting big results on the PTSD front.

To learn more about Quantum Leap Farm, visit http.quantum leapfarm.org or call (813) 920-9250 for additional information.

(left to right) Me, Dr. Edie Dopking, Jenna Miller, Dave Scheiber, and Carla Staats at the Quantum Leap Farm.

• • •

Ride 2 Recovery

They sat around a long conference table inside the towering Bethesda Naval Hospital—nearly a dozen uniformed men and women listening intently to a pivotal presentation. The speaker in this closed-door meeting wasn't an admiral or chief surgeon; he was a lanky civilian whose casual demeanor contrasted sharply with the formal atmosphere. But the man and the medical team were speaking the same language—one of hope and possibilities for veterans who paid dearly on the battlefields of Iraq and Afghanistan.

John Wordin had come to talk bicycles on this summer morning, and the gears of the military establishment were turning with every word.

It was a command performance—one I witnessed from the far end of the table. John and I had gotten to know each other through our work with the troops, and he'd invited me to sit in on the session.

A former world-class competitor and ex-coach of one of the most dominant American cycling teams in history, John was outlining a project that has spun countless success stories for struggling vets since its inception in 2008. With a name that describes the mission well, Ride 2 Recovery, the program helps individuals who have lost limbs—or lost their way with PTSD or Traumatic Brain Injury— find their footing again in life by pedaling.

Three months after that meeting in Bethesda where John met with such officers as Rear Admiral Cindy Dullea, Key Watkins, commander of Navy Safe Harbor, and Captain Anne Swap, commander of administration at the world-famous medical facility, a new partnership was officially announced. The U.S. Navy formally embraced John's cycling therapy efforts, inspiring a new Bethesda Naval rehabilitation program that he will help oversee: Project HERO (Hospital Exercise Rehabilitation Opportunity).

The Navy and other branches of the armed forces have recognized the enormous personal payoff that vets have enjoyed from the long-distance, confidence-building bicycle events that John has been leading around the United States in Ride 2 Recovery.

With bikes he personally customizes for each rider—some with two wheels, others with three or four, depending on the rider's physical limitations—he and his staff have taken large groups along

450 miles of California coastline. They have rolled 350 miles from Tampa Bay through the Florida Panhandle. And they've trekked 500 miles from Walter Reed Army Medical Center in Washington, D.C., to the site of the Coca-Cola 600 NASCAR race in Charlotte, North Carolina.

Project HERO takes a modified approach geared toward hospital patients. As soon as they are physically ready, the patients are put through the paces in smaller increments—sixty to ninety minutes on a bike for three to four days a week. But John is hopeful that many will catch the cycling bug and one day join him and his ever-increasing armada of veterans on one of his weeklong Ride 2 Recovery tours.

"The one thing that's cool about cycling is that you look at six days and fifty miles a day and think, 'That's going to be *tough*,' but they really figure out they can do it," he said. "First, cycling is low impact, and that's good. But over time, instead of getting weaker, you actually get stronger. The first couple of days, the riders struggle—and the last few days, they flourish. So they always end on a high note. You get stronger and stronger every day."

Another factor that propels the veterans—some without arms or hands, some without legs below or above the knee, and so many nursing deep-seated emotional wounds—is the sense of camaraderie. John instills it not only with the special model bikes he has created, all under the slick military moniker of *Stealth*, but also with a credo from the battlefield: "Nobody gets left behind. When we ride, it's a brotherhood. There's not necessarily one person dedicated to helping cyclists who fall behind or have trouble along the route. Riders make friends. The whole idea of

Ride 2 Recovery is to travel in groups—whether you're a fast group, slow group, or medium group. That way, all the riders have somebody to look after them—just like they did when they were in Iraq or Afghanistan, when they were on patrol."

John continued: "That allows them to develop the same sort of *esprit de corps* they shared in combat. When they came back, they were isolated in their hospital beds because of injuries. And now, with this program, they have other buddies again, and it rekindles the feeling of brotherhood, which is one of the magical elements of the ride."

John didn't start out on a bicycle course in life. In college, he was a burly six-foot-five, 260-pound defensive end at Cal State–Northridge in the 1980s. But injuries to a knee and ankle in his senior year ended his football career. "The whole reason I got into cycling is that the team doctor said if I didn't, then I'd have a hard time walking when I was forty," he recounted. "And when you're twenty-two years old, you don't want to hear that. I'd seen all the 260-pounds guys come back at 320, and I vowed I wasn't going to be like that."

His brother and a good friend had taken up the sport, and they talked John into giving it a try. He enjoyed the aerobic, physically challenging side of cycling from the start and became hooked after riding from Orange County to San Diego with a group of buddies. The weight began to fall off his frame, and in short order, John was competing in races at 177 pounds, with barely any body fat on him. He became a standout pro cyclist, then became a rider, coach, and director of the Los Angeles area's Mercury Cycling Team in the mid-1990s—guiding the squad of international veterans to the pinnacle of the sport. The group competed at the Tour de France and won the title as North American Team of the Year an unprecedented seven years in a row.

"That's never been duplicated," he said. "We were the Lakers of cycling, the winningest team in the world during our era, from 1998 to 2002." When John shared this with me, I joked with him that it's all point of reference. He's a West Coast guy. If he was from the East Coast, it would be the *Celtics* of cycling.

After retiring on top as a competitive cyclist in 2004, John tried his hand at some other ventures that tapped his fitness expertise. One was an organization he began in 2004 called the Fitness Challenge Foundation, which worked with obese youngsters. He was good at what he did and won awards for his contributions, including an award from California Governor Arnold Schwarzenegger. But John knew he hadn't yet found what he was looking for in life.

His stellar reputation from the racing world opened an unexpected door in 2007. A therapist and cycling enthusiast at the Veterans Administration in Palo Alto, California, contacted John and asked whether he would help start a bicycling rehabilitation program for PTSD patients at the VA. He met with Palo Alto VA officials, did some riding with them, and afterward laid out his vision for Ride 2 Recovery—a comprehensive cycling program involving long-distance challenge rides, open to any vet with an injury, seen or unseen.

"We're one of the few programs open to anyone to participate, whether you have a mental injury or a physical one," he explained. "There are other veterans service organizations that will not work with you if you don't have a physical injury—and some insist on the injury being a visible physical injury. We're diametrically opposed to that philosophy. If you're injured, you're injured. It doesn't matter to us."

One of John's first moves after starting the Palo Alto program was to fly to D.C., where he visited the secretary of the Veterans Administration and presented his plans. He left with the assurance that the national VA wanted to become involved. As he continued with his planning, John was contacted by an official at Walter Reed's rehabilitation center—the Army facility wanted in on the program, too.

"So our first-ever Ride 2 Recovery event took place in March 2008—we did a ninety-minute bike ride at Walter Reed and took about five or six patients out to do a ride in Rock Creek Park," he said. "One of the young vets who came along had been through about fifty surgeries. We basically hoisted him onto a borrowed bike, and he took off riding. He had the absolute time of his life, and we knew we were on to something."

John quickly began to expand the scope of his fledgling program, planning several ambitious long-distance events. The first was the seven-day ride from Walter Reed to Charlotte, drawing fifty-seven participants, with John funding the whole excursion—bikes, food, and accommodations along the route—out of his own pocket.

"Within the first and second days, you could already see how much had changed in the faces of the warriors who were taking part," he said. "We had vets with different injuries—one with TBI, some PTSD, several amputees. We could see how much the ride affected each one of them."

The next big step was an October 2008 ride in California along the Pacific Coast. By that point, word of the rides had gotten out and John found himself inundated with requests to take part. He took along some forty-five veterans—including about seventeen who were fresh out of the hospital and had never ridden before, some with physical injuries and some suffering psychologically. One of the participants was a young man who had been shot in combat and had been thought dead. He survived but returned to the States dealing with severe PTSD.

"He was trying to figure out whether he was going to 'off' himself or get on with life—he was very much at a crossroads," John recalled. "To see his transformation, and to have everybody else see it, was magical. Everyone was watching this kid over time. And at one of the postrace dinners, he asked if he could speak. He got up in front of about two hundred people and just brought the house down talking about what this ride meant to him—how it changed his life and how he'd use the experience as a springboard to get past some fears he had. It was so emotional and amazing."

If there was an early turning point for the program, that was it. The riders returned home, spread the message to their friends on various bases, and Ride 2 Recovery was rolling.

The new challenge that arose was to develop specially equipped bicycles to accommodate the individual needs of every rider. The manufacturers John had been working with weren't interested in building adapted bikes. Fortunately, John had the knowledge and training to create them himself—making one for a soldier with an above-the-knee amputation, one with a below-the-knee amputation, another for a vet missing an arm, and so forth. "It just took a little research and some MacGyver-ing and we started coming up with solutions," he said.

One such bike was built for an Air Force quad amputee named Delvin McMillian. Delvin was told that it was impossible for him to ride a bike of any kind, much less a regular upright bike. After hearing about the Florida event from a United Health Care employee who had taken part, Delvin was determined to make riding part of his life. He contacted Ride 2 Recovery to see if that was possible. John took it from there, calling people he knew at Walter Reed and Brooke Army Medical Center to see if any quad amputees had ever ridden before and to get their recommendations. The response wasn't encouraging: no, it wasn't possible for Delvin to ride an upright bike. But the words just served as a new challenge for John. Working with his equipment director, the former Mercury Cycling team mechanic Scott Moro, they built a custom Stealth upright bike with special electronic controls that Delvin has now ridden in three Ride 2 Recovery Challenge events.

The program continued to grow in 2009 through word of mouth among veterans. But John's endeavor got another boost when the head of the Army's Wounded Warrior Transition Command, General Gary Cheek, came along for a ride that year. "When he was done, he told me, 'This is the best program we could be involved in,'" John said. "That's when the military command started to take notice." Then, in the final event of that year, Chief of Naval Operations Admiral Gary Roughhead took part and became an instant fan, thus paving the way for John's summer meeting at Bethesda Naval Hospital.

"That was a planning meeting for how we were going to roll out the Bethesda program," John said. "All the hospital administrators were there, and we figured out how the program would be implemented. After that meeting, medical staff from Bethesda joined us for the California ride that October and another group took part in the Florida ride in December."

Following those events, Admiral Roughhead and the Bethesda Naval Hospital commander, Rear Admiral Matthew Nathan, announced the creation of Project HERO: an ongoing physical and mental rehabilitation program in conjunction with John's Ride 2 Recovery program.

"Essentially, the staff and patients will participate in daily and weekly cycling rides as part of their recovery—as a way of restoring hope," John explained. "It's a really big deal, because it will become the centerpiece of our program going forward. The Department of Navy would like to integrate the program into all of their military hospitals in the country—including their big ones in Bethesda, San Antonio, San Diego, Portsmouth, and Jacksonville."

But John still wants to focus on other military hospitals and VA facilities, like the Palo Alto center where the program first took root. "We started out as an ongoing mental and physical rehab program—and the events were a big motivator for the vets, because they all want to go out and have fun," John said. "The ones who have the most success in the program ride year-round now, and basically can ride for the rest of their lives."

Ride 2 Recovery's long-distance events will continue around the country, now drawing some two hundred participants per event from all military branches. I marveled at the growth curve of John's program, expanding from two events and fifty-five total riders in the first year to six events and five hundred riders in the second year, and steady growth for the future. Along the way, Ride 2 Recovery has been featured on *NBC Nightly News with Brian Williams*—and it even made a splash on ABC's hit reality show *Extreme Makeover Home Edition*, starring host Ty Pennington.

The show, which aired in February 2011, focused on U.S. Army Staff Sergeant Patrick Ziegler, who was shot in his left leg and seriously injured during the Fort Hood massacre and was suffering from Traumatic Brain Injury. I knew of Patrick from my own work at Fort Hood following the shootings, and John had gotten to know him when he built a specially equipped bike so Patrick could participate in the one-year anniversary memorial events of the Fort Hood tragedy.

By chance, *Extreme Makeover* producers were planning a show tied to Patrick's challenges in life since the shootings, and they heard of the custom bike John had built for Patrick. The show had even bigger plans: to build a dazzling new home for Patrick and his wife. And producers enlisted John's help in creating a state-of-the-art rehabilitation room. He rose to the occasion, creating a space-age cycling simulator as the focal point.

"The segment revolves around this indoor bike simulator that we created for Patrick," John said. "It was similar to one I wanted to include for Project HERO. You get on it and the experience is identical to riding on the road, in terms of the feel. It's all computer generated, so if you're going up a five-percent grade on the road, you're going up a five-percent grade on the simulator."

Working in conjunction with a software firm, John built the

simulator for two, so Patrick's wife can ride at the same time. "It engages the family, which is another element of our Ride 2 Recovery program that's proven to be very successful," John said. "In addition, if Patrick goes for a ride outside, we've equipped his outdoor bike with a GPS unit that allows him to map routes. Then when he gets back home, he can hook the GPS up to his computer, download the routes, put them in the simulator—and then ride the exact same route with a three-dimensional computer image. You can even race a computer-generated rider, or you can compete against your buddy."

In addition, the simulator allows Patrick to visually track the physical output in both his legs, so he can focus on strengthening his injured one. As John described the project, I listened in amazement—truly appreciating how much difference one dedicated person can make in the life of another, and how so many, including the folks at *Extreme Makeover*, are making meaningful contributions to enhancing the lives of vets in need.

"Staff Sergeant Ziegler went through hell during the Fort Hood shootings, and it didn't end when the gunfire stopped," Ty Pennington related to me. "PTSD darkened his life for a long time, but he was helped through it by his wife and family at Fort Hood and is in a position to help others with PTSD experience the joy and love he now feels. It was an extreme honor to work with a true American hero and to witness firsthand the happiness that is created from being part of a community."

John has high hopes for his cycling simulator in widespread applications with the military. In the meantime, he has some big plans for a ride tied to the tenth anniversary of 9/11—starting at Ground Zero, then continuing to Shanksville, Pennsylvania, where passengers forced hijackers to crash the plane into a field, and ending at the Pentagon, where the third catastrophic attack took place.

"What a tremendous idea," I thought. And before he was done laying out all the details, I jumped in with a spontaneous decision: "John, just tell me where to sign up. I lost friends on 9/11. I don't know how I'll hold up with all that cycling, but my wife, Billie, is a marathoner—so count us in."

John told me the rides are open to the general public—with their entry fees going back into the organization to help pay for other veterans. The trips average about $3,000 per rider for the bike, food, and lodging along the routes. Fortunately, the formidable costs have been picked up by corporate donations, and John offsets other costs through nonstop fund-raising.

Seven races are planned for 2011, with John's staff doubling from six to twelve to accommodate the increasing number of participants. And guiding the ride is that overriding philosophy: nobody gets left behind.

"Even if you're tired or you're having a problem, there's someone there to push you, or there's a support car to pick you up," he said. "Some folks are physically injured to the point they can't make it every mile. And maybe they only make it half or two-thirds. But everybody goes into it with a goal. For some, that goal is riding an hour a day. But what happens is, whatever their goal was after the first day—it's out the window because they realize that they undersold themselves. And they end up doing more than they ever thought possible."

Just like John Wordin—a man whose passion for cycling has led so many on a ride to recovery.

For more information on Ride 2 Recovery, visit www.ride2recovery.com.

A Wounded Warrior taking part in one of John Wordin's Ride 2 Recovery events.

• • •

West Coast Post-trauma Retreat Inc.

West Coast Post-trauma Retreat is a confidential safe haven for those who put their lives on the line in the most harrowing of circumstances—an intense, one-of-a-kind therapy program in a secluded nook of Northern California, a place for hardened first responders across America to face head-on the anguish that has overcome them and to heal emotional wounds from the job.

WCPR, as it is called, moves to the dynamic beat of its tough, relentlessly driven founder—former West Coast cop Mike Pool, a bear of a man with a big heart to match. His deep compassion doesn't mean that he coddles the male and female cops, firefighters, and paramedics who attend one of the twelve-week-long sessions each year. On the contrary, he and his staff of experienced peer counselors and certified psychological clinicians work tirelessly to make the participants pour themselves into the painful memories from which they've been running. Sometimes they are haunted by grisly murder cases and accident scenes, sometimes by memories rooted in their own childhood traumas that they never dealt with. But all are dealing with PTSD, very often multiple layers of it, and breaking down the self-protective barriers they have built up over the years is one of the primary challenges for Mike and his team. At times that leads to intense confrontation, bordering on physical.

"I can't tell you how many times I've almost come to blows while we're putting this program on, because you can tell when some of the people coming in aren't being truthful with whatever is going on with them. They're not giving it up. So more than once, I've had them out on the deck, and we've squared off, and I thought we were going to go at it. I put my finger in their chest. I told them to go home and said, 'You're wasting your time, you're wasting your family's time, your kid's time. You're lying.'

"But you know what? A cop can take that from a cop. A doc can't do that. A spouse can't do that. My goal is to open the door. You have to establish the trust, and that's not always easy. You have to be willing to put yourself out there, too. So I share my story, and I've got no qualms getting out there and crying with them. When I'm talking to these people, in a lot of cases, I'm seeing what I saw in my mirror ten years ago."

Mike's police experiences in the 1990s, during his thirty years in municipal law enforcement, ultimately led him to found a program that today has a perpetual waiting list through word-of-mouth referrals. The catalyst was a cop Mike worked with in 1993, who became obsessed with finding the killer of a little girl brutally murdered inside a church. "One thing led to another, and he was doing interviews with the suspect," Mike recalled. "He got through with the interview, and I found him in the bathroom throwing up and really in bad shape. As time went on, this guy became obsessive-compulsive with his cases and he wouldn't put them away—cases with no suspects, no leads and no way to proceed. But he would keep piling the reports on his desks."

The cop continued immersing himself in dead-end cases that offered no promise of a resolution. Not long after that, the man was discovered sitting at his desk with a gun in his mouth.

Mike explained, "He was taken off duty and the organization was told, 'Do not talk to him'—and everyone was told he was on leave with a hiatal hernia injury. Well, lo and behold, what happened not long after that was he jumped off a bridge and killed himself. Nothing was done for the organization. It *destroyed* our department, and we never really recovered from that."

Meanwhile, Mike began experiencing his own troubles later in the 1990s. He had been a hard-nosed street cop who always looked for the biggest, meanest troublemaker to take down, then was an undercover street agent busting drug dealers, and a SWAT team member for twenty years. He had a reputation as a good cop and one nobody messed with, in part because of his imposing six-foot-one, 250-pound frame and passion for power lifting. But away from the job, personal problems mounted—he found himself with his life on the rocks, experiencing suicidal thoughts.

Fortunately, his best friend, his soon-to-be-wife, and two other close friends staged an intervention. "I thought I was going to dinner with them in San Francisco, but my best friend and the couple that was with us instead took me to the airport—and I wound up having *my* dinner on a United Airlines flight by myself heading east," he remembers. "It turns out they'd signed me up for a one-week therapy program in Massachusetts called the On Site Academy. Basically, they handed me my luggage and told me I needed to get my act together. At work, I was put off on a stress leave and my organization was told, 'Do not talk to Mike'—the same screwed-up treatment they gave my friend years earlier."

Mike immersed himself in the program, regained his sense of personal balance, and returned west, promising himself to make a difference with others. "I would do all I could to make sure nobody ever experienced what my buddy went through or what I went through."

Shortly after his return, Mike met with the county district attorney, a good friend of his, and spoke with her about an idea to help cops and other first responders grappling with destructive issues. Her husband, he learned, was a psychologist, and that opened more doors. Meanwhile, a law enforcement colleague of Mike's in another department was on the verge of earning his PhD in psychology.

"We started pulling all these people together, had two years' worth of meetings, and then flew out the people from the On Site Academy in Massachusetts to put on our first program in 2001. In our second session, we only brought a few of their people out and we started it from there. And we've been running it on our own ever since."

I first heard about WCPR from a federal agent friend. I reached out to Mike soon after and arranged to take part in a program, gladly accepting his offer to serve as one of the many peer counselors for the small group of clients: generally from five to seven for each session. I was impressed by the ratio—at least four peers for every participant. And my job, like the other counselors, would be to offer insight and emotional support from our similar experiences dealing with traumatic situations. We'd be working alongside a group of trained clinicians, including two licensed psychologists, to provide those attending the program with the best of both worlds: fellow first responders they could learn to trust and on-site mental health experts to infuse the intensive therapy with their professional training and techniques.

"Our program is peer based and clinically guided," Mike said. "Very often, the people who go through the program as clients come back and work as peer counselors. What happens with the peers is that we're able to confront and talk to people in a way that doctors and clinicians would never be able to. And, of course, clinicians can provide extremely helpful input."

After landing in San Francisco, a friend drove me for more than an hour into the wooded, hilly terrain north of the city. I lost cell phone reception the further we traveled—a reminder I was leaving the outside world behind, much as the WCPR participants would.

Finally, we arrived at the unmarked entrance and drove up a long, steep driveway. I grabbed my bag and walked onto a wooden deck that served as the front entryway to the multilevel retreat house. I would later find out that deck was more than a front entrance: it was a meeting place during breaks, a place for one-on-one comforting sessions, and a site for intense confrontations.

I was welcomed by Mike Pool. We shook hands, and he introduced me to members of his staff and other peer counselors, including a cop named Nick Turkovich. Nick, the new peer coordinator for this session, held an orientation meeting with all the peer counselors. He went over our responsibilities and had of each us sign confidentiality forms to protect the privacy of the clients.

Confidentiality, Mike explained, is the cornerstone on which WCPR operates—without it, precious few first responders would be willing to take part. "Initially, we were underground, because *nobody* was going to tell their department that they were coming to us. It was just not happening. God forbid anyone would find out about it. We kept growing through word of mouth, and today we have a mix—some people don't want *anybody* to know they're here, and we have departments that send people to us. I also might get a call from a highway patrol officer who wants to come to the program and asks if I would call their association. I tell them that I have a person whose name I don't want to give up, but will you foot the bill? They have no problem with that. Other departments will send people to us just for training—nobody else in the organization knows that they're coming to our program."

The clients began arriving Sunday afternoon, mingling with us on the deck—and on the surface it reminded me of so many casual get-togethers I'd been part of. But I knew that this was the start of a weeklong therapy session that none of us would ever forget.

The work began immediately in a large open dining area off that main deck, which serves as a classroom as well as a breakfast, lunch, and dinner location. The initial goal was to break down the self-protective walls participants had constructed over time. It started with introductions and background of why the clients were here. I could immediately sense the apprehension and uncomfortable feelings among the group.

Then came the first of many group meals—with an abundance of food served throughout the week as a way of promoting relaxed interaction and giving participants a break from the growing intensity. Like the around-the-kitchen-table dinners I had as a kid, a family atmosphere was starting to develop.

An ice-breaking exercise followed: Each client interviewed another client, and introduced that interviewee to the group. That's when Mike stepped in.

"Usually I ask, 'OK, based upon your fifteen years in law enforcement, what has that left you with?' I answer for them—'I'm pissed off. Maybe I'm drinking. I treat my kids badly. My marriage is in the dumper.' Then when we go around the room and ask each person the same question, most of the time they all say the same thing. So right off the bat, they realize they're not alone—and they're all faced with the same issues. That has a huge impact."

The days were long and grueling, often lasting from 8 a.m. to 10 p.m. Monday featured a PowerPoint presentation of Emergency Responder Syndrome. Mike and the staff made sure that there was participation from the group and insisted that everyone discuss the symptoms they'd been exhibiting. I was acutely aware that nobody was going be able to hide in this group.

"That's when we get into first-responder personalities—and we find out that they have similar personality traits," Mike said. "Based upon what we've learned, for some the job found us—we didn't find the job. There are a percentage of first responders who fit a certain profile. We may say something that has to do with their parents, their childhood, their need for approval and attention. They look at us and say, 'How the hell did you know?' I would say in the vast majority of the cases that we see, we just hit it on the head. If you're a kid, and your dad never says he's proud of you, you may try to get that feeling and adrenaline rush from somewhere else. This is all part of looking inside ourselves as to why we became first responders."

Then Mike led each participant through a grueling, blow-by-blow dissection of his or her worst incident on the job. The participants were anxious, and their stories sad and gut wrenching. These were men and women who had seen unsettling and terrifying things that most never do, and the accumulation of daily traumas had taken a toll on their psyches. You could sense the tension, the withdrawal, the feeling that they did not want to be there.

"We take whatever incident they think caused them to be here and we debrief it. And we do this over a three-day period. We talk about the facts of the incident and I'll say, 'OK, I want you to walk me through it step by step by step—tell me what I see. Tell me what I smell, what I hear, what I taste. It's like working out. The more you do it, the stronger you get. At first, they're like, 'I don't want to talk about it.' But we just keep going over it. I had this one cop take me through the worst crime scene you could imagine, involving multiple ax murders and a decapitation. It took him an hour and a half to do it. This kid went from throwing up on day one just thinking about it to being able to walk me through it on day four as if it was just a matter-of-fact police report. You build up a callus around the raw memory."

I marveled at how Mike worked—shifting as the situation required between the roles of big brother, father figure, tough old uncle, vulnerable friend, and fellow first responder. He was both a leader and someone willing to be led. But whatever role he played, his goal was to get people to face—and gain a better understanding—of their personal demons.

"What I tell them is, 'You're going to dance with the devil today, but this time you're going to lead,'" Mike said. "Once they get out of their debriefing, they could very well hate me, because of the kind of questions I've asked and because I forced them to talk. And then they get to go out and interact with other participants—and the 'good guys'—the peers."

Near the end of the week, Mike led them through a debriefing of a significant relationship in their life. "It's to try and make them understand what got them to this point. In my case, it was an abusive alcoholic father. I wasn't an alcoholic. But I did rage. I did get pissed off. I never talked to anybody—well, my old man was that way. So it's all part of gaining a better understanding of who you are."

Throughout the session, Mike and his staff spent their breaks analyzing the behavior and progress—or lack of it—of each participant. They noted how participants were sitting, the expressions on their faces, and whether they were getting involved in the give-and-take. Friday morning, Mike reviewed everything he and the leaders observed during the week, conducted a WCPR graduation, and then got ready to do it all over again several weeks later.

Graduates of the program aren't simply sent back to their jobs and left to fend on their own, however. There's a ninety-day follow-up period in which peer counselors keep in regular touch by phone and email with those who have gone through the program to make sure they're progressing well, and they gradually cut back on the contact as the ninety-day period comes to a close. But for Mike, the relationships are often ongoing.

"I still have people call me years later. And I get calls at all hours. I had a guy call me—he was a first responder at the Oklahoma City Federal Building bombing in 1995. It was about four in the morning, and he said, 'Mike, I had a nightmare about the bombing.' Now, I've always told people, if you have a nightmare at three in the morning, that's when I want the phone call. I don't want you to wait until eight in the morning, because I know what it's like to wait those extra five hours until you can talk.

"When this guy called at four, I said, 'I'm so sorry to hear that.' But he went, 'No, you don't understand. It was just a fricking nightmare. I can go back to bed now. Thanks.' The point is— you'll never get rid of those nightmares. But we give people the tools to put the nightmares in their place."

For Mike, helping first responders is more than a job; it's a ministry. Many of the first responders return to work feeling an enormous load off their shoulders, and they start talking openly to colleagues about the value of the therapy they received in the program— continuing a cycle of healing through peer-to-peer interaction.

All the while, WCPR succeeds on the strength of Mike's broad shoulders, in-your-face approach, and endless willpower. He gets no salary—none of the all-volunteer staff does. He knows he can't do this forever, and he plans at some point down the road to delegate more of his responsibilities. He'd also like to share the program and have it in place throughout the United States.

"I never imagined that what we created would grow to what it is today—a lot of departments around the country have tried to replicate the program but haven't been able to do so yet. What we have is unique—it's like the Big Bang theory; we just happened to hit at the right time. But we'd love to have fifty of these programs all over the country. That's part of our mission statement. We will give this program to anyone who wants it, but they'll have to do it our way. It's peer-to-peer—and it's confrontation. Because that's what works."

To learn more about West Coast Post-trauma Retreat Inc., visit http.wcpr2001.com or call (415) 721-9789.

Mike Pool is a retired cop making a difference as one of the founders of West Coast Post-trauma Retreat.

•••

Vets Prevail

One of the biggest hurdles on the road to recovery is taking that first step—getting past the initial fear of coming forward even when you know something doesn't feel right. The reluctance to face the societal stigma that still hovers over PTSD remains an issue for an untold number of veterans, derailing them from obtaining support that could change—and perhaps even save—their lives. But vital assistance is only a click away thanks to a new organization called Vets Prevail, a growing, Chicago-based online service that allows veterans to get crucial help and training in a confidential atmosphere, while they are sitting in front of a computer in the privacy of their homes.

The operation is the brainchild of two former MBA students at the University of Chicago—Rich Gengler, an Iraq War veteran and aircraft carrier pilot, and Roger Sweis, who brings a background steeped in mental health care to the project. They have since added a third key member to the team, Justin Savage, a former combat cameraman who has chronicled the pain, courage, and sacrifice on the battlefields of the Middle East. He oversees the multimedia and technical elements of the interactive Web operation.

"The tools that we provide online are completely confidential and anonymous, and that makes it easy for veterans to take part," Roger told me. "Second, we're not part of the government—the Department of Defense or the Veterans Administration. We're a veteran-owned and operated organization. Primarily, we employ

other veterans. So we know what it's like—and that really reso-
nates. Third, we're trying to make methods of seeking help and
care a little more engaging and user-friendly. Usually, the first
way doctors want to examine you is very clinical—and that can be
tough, to go right from 'You have a problem' to 'Let me bring you
into my office and examine you.' That's a big gap. And what we're
doing is filling in that gap."

They do that by offering privacy in the outreach with soldiers,
and then providing social support by encouraging the soldiers to
connect, when they are ready, with peers in the Vets Prevail online
network. Free online re-integration training is offered on the site,
as well as live chat sessions with fellow veterans. In addition, the
site provides detailed feedback—via an interactive assessment
tool—that serves as a gauge for PTSD and depression. I wondered
how they get the veterans to respond online as part of the process,
especially when so many might be reluctant to answer probing
questions about their mental state.

"We let them know on our site, 'Hey, we're just getting to know
you and trying to understand you a little better so we can deliver
services more effectively for you,'" Roger replied. "If somebody is
in crisis, we make sure we get them appropriate crisis support. If
someone is suffering from a severe, diagnosable case of depression
or PTSD, we route them to doctors we work with. If needed, we
could provide a seamless transition to a VA program or provide
hotline numbers. There are many resources out there, but they're
just not connecting with these folks. And that's one big way we
can help."

The Vets Prevail website also offers financial incentives—in the form of redeemable certificates and prizes—for veterans who accumulate a certain number of points while participating in the assessment and evaluation process. We all like playing games, and winning free stuff makes it even better. If it motivates reluctant soldiers to take a step forward and seek the help they need, why not?

I was fascinated with the story of how Vets Prevail came to be—a fateful convergence of individuals with the training, sense of mission, and passion to make a difference in the lives of others.

Rich had been part of the 2003 invasion of Iraq, flying numerous combat missions as an aircraft carrier fighter pilot. "When I came back in 2003, it was at the front end of PTSD awareness, and there wasn't a lot of acceptance of the problem," he said. "There wasn't a lot of attention paid to it." Rich was not personally afflicted with the condition, but he grew increasingly aware of many veterans who were.

Following a stint as a test pilot in California, he decided to move to Chicago in 2006 to obtain his master's degree in business. That's where he met Roger. They attended the same entrepreneurial classes and, during the course of their studies, met a university doctor, Benjamin Van Voorhees, involved with online treatments for depression targeting teens from Chicago's South Side.

Roger came from a family with deep roots in the mental health field, operating clinics on the South Side that served inner-city families and the chronically mentally ill. Listening to Dr. Van Voorhees, a Navy veteran, gave Roger and Rich an idea. They knew there was a major issue with veterans returning from war grappling with trauma-related problems.

"We knew that many would not seek any care due to the stigma surrounding PTSD," Rich said. "We thought we could create a great first step in providing preventative care to this group. We just jumped right into doing it."

"Literally within weeks of meeting Dr. Van Voorhees, we knew this was what we were going to do," Roger added. "It just made sense on a really deep level. In addition to offering anonymity, it's easily accessible, is an important first step toward care—and also offers participating vets a chance to serve as peers for others."

There were growing pains in the beginning. "Rich and I would travel from coffee shop to coffee shop, anywhere to find free access to the Internet, so we could brainstorm," Roger recalled. "We were literally making cold calls to the top mental health researchers in the country, military mental health experts, people at the top of the Veterans Health Administration's technology and Web development department. With the business background we had, we knew that if you want to help people, it's got to be realistic and fit in the existing system."

After several months, they ran into a friend who made available some office space for their fledgling operation. Soon after, they landed the support of the National Science Foundation and the local Veterans Administration, and they received the blessing of a scientific advisory board. Then, with a grant from the McCormick Foundation, through its Welcome Back Veterans Initiative, they launched their dream project in 2009—appropriately, on Veterans Day.

Justin, following ten combined years of service in the Army and National Guard, came on board to help with the look and operation of the Vets Prevail website. He had photographed and filmed many heart-wrenching sights during his 2004 tour of duty in Iraq. "We documented everything alongside all the infantry squads, whether it was a night raid or a morning search or memorial services. We captured imagery of soldiers kneeling at the dog tags of another fallen soldier, so families back home could see that level of sacrifice, compassion, and those internal aspects of the combat experience. I was exposed to a little of everything in that year."

After returning to the States, Justin spent time with the National Guard helping train troops preparing for combat in Iraq. He worked with the VA to help soldiers transition to the next phase of their lives in employment and education. He also worked with various doctors in the Chicago VA, which put him on a direct path to meeting Rich and Roger. "Given my experience in multimedia, helping soldiers and all military members transition through difficult situations, we all thought it was a great fit," Justin said.

From his work at the VA, Justin was able to translate and simplify technically worded writing about mental health support, making it easy to digest for anyone logging on to Vets Prevail. "I was able to do it in a more convenient and less stigmatized means through the Internet," he said. "That became the product service we provide."

In less than a year, Vets Prevail had registered more than two thousand veterans and had provided services and treatment for half of them. The numbers are an encouraging start to a tremendously valuable endeavor, although Rich, Roger, and Justin know all too well that it's only a fraction of the returning veterans who need support. Recent studies have indicated that the number of vets suffering with mental health issues fall somewhere between three hundred thousand and eight hundred thousand. Suicide has risen to crisis levels. The shocking statistics underscore in my mind the need for a coordinated network to link groups such as Vets Prevail to so many initiatives that exist to combat PTSD.

"There's no silver bullet to this problem," Roger said. "But at least working together, we could exponentially multiply our efforts and do what we can to help."

Vets Prevail has tapped into the online social networking generation and created an Internet community that embraces thousands of vets dealing with personal issues related to war. In speaking with them, I was immediately struck by how none of this was possible for previous eras of veterans—and how immensely valuable a tool it is for this young, tech-savvy wave of returning warriors.

Growing up in northern New Jersey, I was immersed in a variety of cultures—visiting my grandmother in Little Dublin or the grandparents of my friends in Little Italy, Little Poland, or other enclaves. By becoming more aware of the differences in each culture, I discovered that we are more alike than not. I've also come to understand generations in a cultural context. And the culture of the *younger* generation obviously embraces technology—tweeting, texting, Skyping, and all manner of social media that serve as an intrinsic way of everyday communication.

Rich, Roger, and Justin have turned that cultural reality into a vital support system. They've created a modern operation that offers an important comfort level for young soldiers in need of assistance, and they have extended a technological lifeline—one designed to help vets prevail.

To learn more about Vets Prevail, visit www.vetsprevail.com or send an email to team@vetsprevail.com for additional information.

(left to right) Justin Savage and Rich Gengler of Vets Prevail.

•••

Operation Proper Exit

The quiet missions continue above Iraq's desert landscape as two Blackhawk helicopters hover, dip, and sometimes circle back for a closer look at a strategically predetermined patch of earth that holds the power of healing.

Inside the military chopper, a handful of returning U.S. combat veterans peer intently at the familiar ground where their lives were forever changed. One by one, they connect to memories of anguish that have haunted their thoughts—and they experience a powerful sense of closure in the process.

This is Operation Proper Exit, a program designed to help give wounded Iraq War veterans a profound emotional and psychological experience by revisiting the site of their trauma. The ambitious undertaking is a major initiative of the Troops First Foundation, launched in 2008 by Maryland resident and retired businessman Rick Kell.

Rick never served in the armed forces—a medical deferment because of a problem with his peripheral vision kept him from going to Vietnam in 1971. But he's felt a driving passion to support the troops, especially those who returned from war missing limbs or battling the less visible wounds of PTSD and Traumatic Brain Injury.

That commitment and dedication led him to fight his own battle against skeptics in the Pentagon who initially rejected his unique program—and then go on to win the full-fledged support of the top U.S. commanders in Iraq. They immediately embraced Rick's concept of bringing wounded veterans back to the combat zones where they fought; doing so allowed the veterans to see that their sacrifices were not in vain, and it empowered them by returning to the locations of their devastating injuries.

Operation Proper Exit has flourished since the first trip in 2009, directed by Rick and buoyed by the support of former PGA and European golf-tour professional David Feherty. In the first year alone, Rick coordinated eight visits to Iraq that involved more than fifty Wounded Warriors. He has accompanied the veterans on each journey, witnessing personal transformations that have fueled his resolve to keep the program going, as well as expanding the Troops First Foundation outreach in new areas.

"Without exception, I saw them all change within the course of the week we were there," Rick told me. "Soldiers who were squared away in marriage and business and were doing well wanted to go back to see the positive changes they had in the country that had taken place. Even they experienced some life-altering moments when they returned to Iraq. I like to say that we will take you back and show you the progress that you helped bring about in the country. But as far as closure and what it means to you personally, all we do is provide the opportunity for you to figure that out."

For safety, that opportunity requires flying aboard a Blackhawk—rather than risk driving "outside the wire," or away from the safe confines of the military base. "We're able to get coordinates and get air-space clearance from the Iraqis, because they control that now," Rick explained. "On a recent trip, we took one of the guys to the bridge in Fallujah where he was injured in an IED explosion. We were able to do about three or four loops in the Blackhawk, and he could videotape the whole scene on the ground. Once again, he saw the changes and the place where his life had changed dramatically. In so many ways, they come to terms with that and they're able to move forward at a different pace."

I liked the way Rick put that—"to move forward at a different pace." And it struck me: while this will help these brave vets to make steady, deliberate progress on their continued path to recovery, that same concept of striving to move at a different pace holds true for all PTSD sufferers.

I also wondered about Rick's path and what had led him to devote so much time and energy to a cause that has become the

guiding mission in his life. As it turns out, the catalyst in the creation of Troops First happened to be something I'm quite familiar
with: the game of basketball.

Rick had run a small advertising agency for thirty years, with
clients in Maryland, Virginia, and Washington, D.C. His work
brought him in contact with the college basketball program at the
University of Maryland and Terrapins head coach Gary Williams—
Rick produced his television and radio show. Along the way, he
also got to know renowned coach Bobby Cremens, who had led
Georgia Tech to impressive heights, and Mike Jarvis, who made a
mark in the D.C. area coaching George Washington University's
hoops teams in the 1990s.

"One of the last things I did for the agency was go to a Maryland
basketball game in December 2004, and they honored some troops
who were doing rehab at Walter Reed," he recalled. "I leaned over
to a buddy of mine and said, 'This is powerful stuff. We should get
some of the coaches together and take them over to Iraq and do a
March Madness kind of event, where they could coach teams made
up of soldiers.'"

Rick had made a career of coordinating projects and getting
things done, and this was no different. He worked with the
Department of Defense and the United Service Organizations—
better known as the USO—raised the necessary funds; enlisted
the help of Coaches Williams, Cremens, Jarvis, and Kelvin
Sampson; and brought the first Operation Hardwood to Camp
Arifjan in Kuwait.

As Rick described that first event, I had to smile: I'd officiated
a basketball game in that very same facility during my 2009 visit

to Kuwait and Iraq, and I told Rick that I remembered seeing Operation Hardwood Classic banners and photos hanging all over the gym. Amazingly, I even knew all of those college coaches. I've been with Gary Williams and Mike Jarvis when they come for Dick Vitale's annual gala to benefit the V Foundation in Sarasota, Florida. Kelvin Sampson is an NBA coach. And I've known Bobby Cremens for decades through family connections dating back to my childhood in Paterson, New Jersey. Father Mario DiLella—the uncle of my best friend, Jimmy—served as a chaplain in the U.S. Air Force, and he went on to become the chaplain at Georgia Tech, where he became a fixture on the bench at every one of Bobby Cremens's games. It was a true six-degrees-of-separation moment for Rick and me.

"That's how *all* of this has been for me," he said when I told him about the connections. "There seems to be a higher power at work here," he responded with a laugh. "I got back home after that trip and quite candidly thought I'd be one-and-done. I was finishing up my ad business and was getting ready to do some consulting."

But Rick's cousin was a sergeant major with the Special Operations Care Coalition and worked at Walter Reed Army Medical Center helping injured special-ops soldiers and their families. "He said to me, 'Look, if you're going to do these basketball events over there, you need to come to Walter Reed and meet some of my guys,'" Rick recollected. "The short story is, I took him up on his invitation—and the journey began."

The USO was impressed by Rick's work with Operation Hardwood and asked him if he'd stage several more sports events for them. He obliged, earning a small consulting fee that became the start-up funds for the Troops First Foundation. In addition, Rick built on the success of his basketball trips and created Operation Links, bringing PGA tour players to Iraq at Thanksgiving. The first group went over in November 2006, with Jerry Kelly, Frank Lickliter, and several others, and followed in 2007 with an A-list trip featuring Tom Watson, Butch Harmon, Tom Lehman, and David Feherty.

"Feherty and I became attached at the hip," Rick said. "And he is probably the most passionate man I've ever met for doing things for the troops and their families. He's given so much in a short period of time that nobody will ever know about, beyond the scope of the foundation."

Rick and David began teeing up ideas about different ways to help troops—programs that weren't already being done by other organizations. "In other words, we didn't want to go out and raise scholarship money for children of warriors who were killed in action—there are many organizations that do that very well," Rick said. "We looked where we could bring our collective resources to bear and make a difference."

Rick wasn't immediately sure what form that would take, but he spent many hours at Walter Reed in the presence of wounded veterans, a core group he looked to as mentors. "And every day, they would say, 'I want to go back to Iraq'—and that would inevitably come up in conversations at dinner, going to the movies, whatever we were doing," Rick remembered.

"That's a common sentiment I hear from recently wounded soldiers—they're distressed to have left the team and their guys behind, like they let them down. But one day at lunch, I said to these guys, 'Look, you can't go back and kick down doors.' And they said, 'That's not what we're talking about. We just want to go back and see it.' They wanted to validate their experience—to see if their sacrifices and the sacrifices of those who didn't make it back have had some value and meaning and made a difference."

The conversation resonated with Rick, so he went to work—once again—tapping the contacts he had made from his first trip. But an obstacle stood in his path.

"I started knocking on doors at the Pentagon, but it was slow going—I guess they viewed what I was proposing as pretty radical thinking," he said. "Their perspective was, 'Why would we want to take soldiers who were injured back to an active theater?' All I could tell them was, 'I'm not in their shoes and can't speak for them, but I can tell you that if I know one hundred wounded veterans, one hundred of them want to go back. If I know five hundred, five hundred want to go back.' But quite candidly, the medical community at the Pentagon was not ready to endorse this—and didn't want it to happen."

But Rick was undeterred, and as he related what happened next, we suddenly discovered another six-degrees-of-separation bond.

One of the people he frequently briefed was Troops First Foundation advisory board member Tony Odierno, a retired Army captain who lost his arm to a grenade in Iraq and the son of General Ray Odierno. I had talked many times with Tony and, as you'll recall from the opening pages of this book, had met and spoken about peer-to-peer therapy with his father—the top-ranking commander in Iraq—during my visit to his Al-Faw Palace office.

"Just before Ray went back to Iraq to become the commanding general in August 2008, Tony, Ray, and I played a round of golf," Rick said. "And I handed Tony a packet of information I'd been working on with David Feherty about the foundation. Ray looked over the material—and he took particular interest in the part about Operation Proper Exit."

Nothing happened at that moment. But seven months later, as the window of opportunity at the Pentagon was closing, Rick decided to reach out directly to General Odierno.

"I emailed Ray and said, 'I've been around the military enough to know that if the CG in Iraq says he will support this initiative, it at least gives me an opportunity to go back to the Pentagon and try again. But it turned out that I didn't have to do that."

General "O" had paved the way and enlisted the support of Sergeant Major of the Army Ken Preston. Some three weeks after Rick sent his email, the Army's Surgeon General, Vice Chief, and Judge Advocate General Corps had all signed off on the program. Just over two months later, the first Operation Proper Exit took place—and it has been going strong ever since.

To be selected, participants must be thriving in their recovery and stand to benefit from a return trip to Iraq. "This isn't a program to take someone who is struggling, throw them in a situation, and see if it fixes them," he said. But for those who do go on the therapeutic trips, tales of personal renewal abound.

"In eight trips, I've taken fifty-five guys who have fifty-five different sets of expectations—and the stories are endless," Rick said. He tells one of former Army Sergeant Kenny Butler, who was hit by an EFP (explosive formed projectile) that entered underneath his arm, went through his chest on the left side, and exited on the right side, taking off his right arm.

"Kenny's now attending Norwich University and hopes to be a high school history professor," Rick explained. "He's athletic. He rides bikes in competitions. And you look at him and know that he's embraced the next phase of his life.

"But when Kenny went over, he came to me one night and said, 'I've got to tell you something. I've never been able to speak about this because I didn't understand it. But there's been a voice in my head since I went home with my injury that kept telling me I was defeated. It has been haunting me, even though I learned how to live with it. But on this trip, I was able to confront it—and I can absolutely tell you it's not there anymore.'"

What happened to Kenny was powerful on many levels. He had a visible wound that we could see and empathize with. However, he had an unseen wound that tormented him. And because of this opportunity—the chance to confront that voice in his head—he was able peel away another layer of his Post-Traumatic Stress.

One particularly significant segment of each trip takes place when the veterans meet with Iraqi military leaders, an experience that the U.S. command has initiated. "When our warriors can hear from members of Iraqi leadership, it always makes a difference," Rick said. "Their message is: 'Your blood is in our soil. You are our brothers. Iraq is your second country. We welcome you here, we want you here, and we will protect you.'"

Those aren't the only impactful words the veterans hear during their visit. They also meet in person with the top U.S. leaders, such as Generals Odierno, Robert Cone, Bob Brown, Robert Caslen, and others. Still, perhaps the most meaningful words of the entire trip are spoken by the Wounded Warriors themselves—in the form of insight and inspiration that they share with active-duty troops.

"That's an aspect of the program I never thought of," Rick said. "When I was trying to get this launched, I really only thought of the veterans I was taking to Iraq. However, in General Odierno's first email back to me, he wrote that this wouldn't only be good for the warriors you're bringing back; it would be extremely powerful for troops here on the ground."

That interaction has proved immensely beneficial indeed. In the first eight Operation Proper Exit trips, more than forty town-hall meetings took place between the visiting vets and military personnel, as well as countless smaller sessions and one-on-ones, a perfect example of peer-to-peer support in action.

"I can't think of a more effective motivational visit from anybody than these warriors who go back," Rick said. "They absolutely captivate—there's such a brotherhood that exists between the wounded vets and the troops who listen to them talk. Many of the questions asked are about family, about support for family, what they've gone through—a lot of it really is 'but for the grace of God, there go I.' And they want to know, if something happens to them or their best buddy, what takes place? How are you treated? And the warriors are able to answer all those questions."

But they do more than answer questions, according to Rick. They provide direction: "There have been many statements from our warriors in these town hall meetings with the message, 'It's OK to get help. You need to be aware of yourself if you're experiencing change that you can recognize, or something is just different. You need to talk about what you're experiencing, and it's OK to talk with your chain of command and get some help.' The words of encouragement are very forceful, very meaningful, and extremely valuable."

That message is what I share when giving presentations, whether in Mosul, at the Federal Law Enforcement Training Center, or at Fort Hood—I tell people in the audience that by the very nature of what you do, you're always concerned with taking care of others. But there are times when you have to get a little selfish; it's OK to take care of yourself, and it's OK to ask for help.

Rick isn't only focused on Operation Proper Exit logistics these days. He's revamped the PGA outreach program; it's now called Operation Fore Thanksgiving. He takes golfers to Iraq through his foundation and has been particularly impressed with the commitment of Tom Watson. "He's bought in uncondition-ally," Rick said. "The summer he almost won the British Open on the cusp of his sixtieth birthday, I was getting emails from Wounded Warriors who Tom had played golf with and hunted with. I'm forwarding them to him—and he's answering them before he even tees off!"

Rick has staged a golf tournament at the exclusive Chevy Chase Club in Maryland, featuring teams of three Wounded Warriors and one pro—dubbing the event "The IED of Golf." "All the guys at Walter Reed love that—they think it's pretty cool because here, IED stands for Improvised Explosive *Day*," rather than Device, he said. "And Chevy Chase has hosted our IED of Golf for Walter Reed the last three years. Tom Watson and many pros fly in on their own expense—nobody is compensated."

The work never ceases for the man on a mission. He wants to create an Operation Proper Exit for Afghanistan. And his next major undertaking is to help wounded veterans with housing in the United States; he hopes to raise millions to allow them to fend off foreclosure or buy affordable homes.

"One of the programs we want to launch in 2011 and we hope to fund by 2012 is a housing grant program," he said. "It's really meant to provide a down payment or get somebody at risk of losing their home out of a bad mortgage and get them refinanced. It's not to give away a home but to shrink a mortgage payment comfortably within a monthly disability check—so it's affordable and sustainable."

His goal: to raise $2.5 million a year to provide fifty $50,000 housing grants per year.

"Unfortunately, that's not even the tip of the iceberg when it comes to what a lot of these young veterans will need. You know about the Vietnam-era homeless guys. But there are already more than seven thousand homeless veterans from Operation Enduring Freedom in Afghanistan and Operation Iraqi Freedom. That's the number accounted for, so you know there are more than that.

"It's an embarrassment—we can't let this go unaddressed. And a lot of these guys have PTSD and TBI. The amputees, because it's physical, get a lot of attention—and they deserve every bit of it. But so do the other vets whose injuries aren't visible."

All of them are fortunate to have an advocate like Rick Kell, a man who never stops thinking of ways—as his foundation suggests—to put the troops first. I understand his devotion to the cause. I've been around some of the greatest athletes in the world—Michael Jordan,

Magic Johnson, Larry Bird, Julius Erving, Kareem Abdul-Jabbar, LeBron James, Kobe Bryant, and Shaquille O'Neal. The list goes on and on. But being around our troops is the most rewarding and inspiring experience I've ever been a part of.

When I said this to Rick, he told me I was preaching to the choir. "I've been blessed to be able to do this," he said. "Knowing the journey these kids have been on, it makes working with them so easy."

To learn more about the Troops First Foundation and Operation Proper Exit, visit www.troopsfirstfoundation.org.

The first Operation Proper Exit group at Hero's Highway in Balad, Iraq.

• • •

You've read about some unique therapy options in this chapter, and one of them may be right for you or a person you know. That is why there are thirty-one flavors of ice cream—we all have our preferences. It's been said that the most important thing about having a goal is precisely that—having one. Take the step and reach out to learn more about these types of programs and how they can help. If you or someone you care about is dealing with PTSD, finding the right therapy may be one of the greatest gifts you can give.

CHAPTER ELEVEN

On the Front Lines

"Nobody can go back and start a new beginning, but anyone can start today and make a new ending."

—Maria Robinson

It was a brutally hot July afternoon, and doubt was swirling in my head like the sandstorm that suddenly swept over the twisting, makeshift roads. I was outside Camp Arifjan—smack in the middle of the Kuwaiti desert.

Despite the difference in terrain and temperature, the blinding sand reminded me of snowstorms during my childhood in the Northeast, or the kind of Rocky Mountain blizzard I once experienced as an NBA referee, trapped for three days during Christmas week after working a game in Denver. There I was, in the summer of 2009, a passenger in one of several SUVs protected by a security detail, barreling through the desert at speeds that rivaled my days as a young New Jersey State Trooper in the 1970s. Sheets of fine, flying particles blocked the sun and whipped against the windshield as we made our way to Ali Al Salem Air Base an hour away. And the whole time, I kept returning to one thought:

"There's no way we can fly in this."

The sand I knew best was on the beaches near my home in West Central Florida, where I had been only a few days before. But this was a completely different world, far from the life I knew as a veteran NBA official, preparing for a goodwill tour to visit U.S. troops in Iraq. I was holding a Kevlar vest and helmet I'd been issued and was keenly aware that the gear was meant to protect the body's "kill area." The reality that we were entering a war zone in northern Iraq—unsure of what lay ahead—increased with every passing mile. The more the sand pounded our path to Ali Al Salem, where we would board a C-130 for the flight to a base in Mosul, the more my concerns mounted. Did I make the right decision to come here—to accept the invitation of San Francisco-based sports-radio personality Ron Barr and join him on his annual trek to visit the troops? Would we be safe? Why was I putting Billie and the rest of my family through this? I reminded myself that I had faced fear and the unknown before and that my anxiety was a natural reaction to the situation I was in.

The storm was still raging when we finally arrived at Ali Al Salem and made our way into a holding area. Inside a large building, hundreds of troops were waiting to be transported to the combat zone or returning to it from their fifteen-day leaves. The mood was somber, almost like Sunday-morning church before the sermon. A large American flag hung on the front wall alongside a big-screen television showing a boxing match on HBO. Soldiers in full military gear—camouflage uniforms, desert-tan combat boots, and weapons of every kind—conversed quietly or sat in silence. Some reclined in black sleeper-lounge chairs, trying to calm their nerves. They were going to Baghdad, Mosul, or other places unknown to most of us. As I moved around the room, I could feel the powerful undercurrent of emotion. There was so much to take in, so many stories in the faces of the soldiers. I had an urge to reach out to the military personnel in this room. But I still felt like a stranger among them.

I placed my Kevlar vest, helmet, and gear on a chair and continued to circulate, wearing my gray NBA T-shirt, long dark pants, and running shoes. I wanted to stand out with my attire, to signal that I was part of the Sports Byline on the Frontline in 2009 mission, to offer moral support and encouragement. I tried to project confidence and calm in hopes of striking up a conversation with some of the soldiers. Inside, though, my pulse was racing like water rapids though my veins—*quick blood* was the term we used in my days as a Jersey trooper.

A cloud of tension hung in the air as I looked around, reading concern in the eyes of the soldiers, male and female. I knew about fear from my own life and knew it was nothing to be ashamed of. I could see it, smell it, sense it in this room. The fact is, it would be abnormal for them not to be experiencing fear now. And I was caught in its grip as well—even though I was only going to be spending one week in the war zone before flying to Germany for a three-day visit with wounded troops.

I noticed a table in the back of the room where soldiers picked up Bibles and other religious materials, a stark reminder of the gravity of the situation—that many wanted to make themselves right with their Maker before stepping into battle. I couldn't help but observe the wedding rings that many of the men and women wore in the hall, and I thought of the ripple effect that war has on families.

In a far corner, I saw a thirtysomething soldier sitting with one leg over the arm of a chair. He had what looked like burn scars on his arms, face, and ears, and he seemed unable to fully extend his fingers. As I worked my way toward him, I wondered whether an IED blast had caused his disfigurement and what other unseen wounds might have scarred his spirit, possibly sowing the seeds of a long-term problem I knew well—Post-Traumatic Stress Disorder.

The seat next to him was empty—then it was mine. I waited a while, looked over, and nodded. And I realized there was not going to be any right time to start this conversation. So I said in a steady, self-assured voice, "Hi, I'm Bob Delaney." The soldier acknowledged me, continuing to stare at the boxing match unfolding on the big screen. What seemed like several minutes passed and I tried again. "I'm heading to Mosul, Camp Marez," I offered, hoping to start a give-and-take. The soldier turned and looked at me with no reply, but I pressed on, explaining that I was an NBA referee on tour to visit troops. He remained silent, so I tried a different tack. "Where you headed?" I asked.

"Tikrit," came the slow, monotone response.

"How long you been in the Army?"

"My third tour," the soldier said matter-of-factly, turning his head back to the TV, clearly wanting no part of my cocktail-party conversation. And then he added, in a dismissive tone, "I got a job to do."

He had a job to do. His words abruptly ended our conversation but triggered a dialogue in my head, making my own uncertainties and worries shrink in comparison. This soldier had seen things most people can't even imagine; he had put his life on the line twice, and it was his job to face death again. I wished him well and didn't push further.

Finally, after several hours, the sandstorm subsided enough for us to fly. Our assigned group was called to the front of the room and Social Security numbers were yelled out to match our names. We put on our Kevlar vests and helmets and formed two side-by-side lines, then headed out of the building to several awaiting buses.

The wind and sand were still blowing, but what got my attention when we stepped outside was the blast of intense heat, 120 degrees, which felt even hotter with our protective gear on. And I was sweating profusely—partly because of the heat, partly the nerves. The bus ride to where the C-130s were lined up took fifteen minutes, but it felt like an hour, and inside you could hear a pin drop.

After passing through the final of multiple security checkpoints, we were given orders to exit the bus and again form two lines. The short-sleeved NBA shirt I wore beneath my vest didn't protect my arms from the wall of heat generated by the aircraft's burning fuel, so it was a mild relief when we boarded minutes later. Inside, my tour mates and I quickly took our seats while the soldiers sat back to back in four long, adjoining rows. We strapped in, shoulder to shoulder, knees to knees, and hip to hip.

The plane rumbled down the runway and lifted off for the hour-long flight deep into Iraq, bucking its way through the gusting wind and making creaky, unsettling sounds I'd never heard before on a takeoff back in the States.

The loud, mechanical rattling continued even at cruising altitude, which made it impossible to converse—and the earplugs we had to wear would have made it difficult to hear anyway. Ron Barr knew the routine well from many previous trips and had talked his way into the cockpit before departure. Once we leveled off, Ron invited me up front to say hello to the pilot, a man with a shaved head who simply went by Captain Kojak, after the old detective on TV.

Following a few minutes of small talk, I returned to my seat. And it didn't take long, sitting in nervous silence, for my thoughts to start wandering. As a veteran ref, corporate and law enforcement consultant, and author, I have traveled all over the country, grabbing flights at all hours to get to the next city. Now I was totally aware that when we landed, it would be in a place that I knew only from the nightly news and morning paper. A strange feeling of separation came over me. I had left my family behind—my wife, my kids, and my grandchildren—and I realized how tough it is for soldiers to say good-bye to their loved ones and know they may never make it back.

Suddenly, I was yanked from my reflections as the C-130 went into a steep dive. I had a strange and frightening sensation of lightheadedness, and there was a strong gravitational pull that is never good news when you're on a commercial flight. Instinctively, I wondered whether we might have mechanical trouble or, worse, be facing enemy fire. But in the next moment, a soldier who obviously saw the fear in my eyes yelled out and motioned that this was a military-style descent, one used for landing in combat zones to avoid enemy fire.

Minutes later, we touched down in Mosul and taxied to a stop. I instantly began focusing on what might lay head on this journey. At the same time, I couldn't help but think that this was the same flight Sergeant James Gallagher had taken at some point, and I thought of the fears he had endured; the same fears that all of these soldiers—Marines, Air Force, Army, and Navy men and women—experience.

When we landed at Camp Marez, members of the 25th Infantry Division, CP North, welcomed us. We were escorted in vehicles along dirt roads that took us straight to the mess hall, where we had dinner and began meeting and mingling with the troops. We later received a briefing from General Bob Brown, one of the top commanders in Iraq.

It didn't take long to learn a whole new language, phrases such as "outside the wire" (being off the military base), "in country" (being in Iraq), "in theater" (the war zone), "down range" (referring to the war zone), "d-fac" (the dining facility, better known as the mess hall).

But that wasn't the only thing I learned in a hurry. I discovered that no one really sleeps in a war zone. At any time, I could walk outside my CHU (contained housing unit) and find soldiers engaged in conversation. There were rows upon rows of CHUs—consisting of two beds inside a room less than twenty feet wide and ten feet long—forming "streets." They were identified by letters, such as M row or C row, and protected by T-walls, which were essentially large concrete barriers to help contain the blasts of possible "incoming." That's a word that means so much more when you are *living* in a war zone. I'll say this, though: I never felt safer in my life, because of the security details assigned to us throughout our visit. They were true pros.

We visited FOBs (forward operating bases) throughout northern Iraq. And everywhere I went, I'd share my undercover story from *Covert*—and how I suffered and dealt with PTSD—as a way of encouraging soldiers to reflect on and discuss their own experiences. I gave away hundreds of donated books for the trip, and that allowed me to do daily book signings as an additional way of connecting with the troops and engaging them in dialogue.

I savored the opportunity to speak to the troops and get a feel for what they were experiencing in the line of duty. One night, maybe at three or four in the morning, I was headed to the latrine at the end of my street and ran into four soldiers socializing—holding bottles of water and smoking cigarettes. I joined the conversation— they were discussing which body parts they would be willing to live without. It was an amazingly candid back-and-forth about the real results of war. The soldiers said that the improved body armor to protect the kill areas—coupled with the fast response to get injured personnel off the battlefield, the state-of-the-art medical equipment at the front line, and the expertise of the medical teams and first responder units—made them confident that they would survive a devastating injury. But with what intact? The body armor may protect the kill area but not the limbs. So they talked as if they were discussing sports or the weather, with a matter-of-fact tone devoid of emotion or fear. Would they be OK losing one leg? Two legs? One leg and an arm? I listened to the dialogue, the entire time asking myself, "Am I really hearing what I'm hearing?" And it dawned on me that this is the mind-set of modern warfare.

One member of the group of soldiers had been with me earlier that night at a book signing. As the conversation among the others continued, the young man asked to speak to me in private. We walked off by ourselves and he shared something with me.

"Sir, I thought I was going to go to my knees when you were signing books in the d-fac tonight," he said. "I got a cold sweat and felt sick to my stomach—when the flashbulbs were going off as photos were being taken. It reminded me of six months earlier when I was in Mosul and an IED exploded, killing two of our soldiers. The flash took me back there."

I listened to his words, knowing exactly what caused his reaction—a trigger. I told him that they can occur anytime, anywhere, even in the most secure places and everyday situations. I thought about how many soldiers experience the same sensation at weddings and parties with cameras flashing but hide their true feelings. I thought about a story I'd heard about a wounded female soldier whose commanding officer had invited her to an outdoor celebration. She declined, thanking him for thinking of her and her family but explaining she could not attend. "Why not?" asked the officer. She replied, "Sir, you said there was going to be fireworks, and I can't know how I will respond. The last time I was at an event and fireworks went off, I dove under a table. I would not want to put my family through that—to scare them or those around me. Maybe in time I will be able to attend."

I'll never forget the troops I met on this trip, how they didn't think twice about placing themselves in harm's way to do their jobs. The word they use—*job*—doesn't really explain it, especially when I recall a sergeant who told me that soldiers do their best soldiering when they're not afraid of dying.

I was glad I had the chance to speak to so many of them—in groups and one-on-one—encouraging them not to bottle up the fear and anxieties they were pushing down to get through each day. I was fully aware that my standing as an NBA official gave me a way of connecting with them, creating a doorway to communication. And my experience infiltrating the Mafia thirty years earlier gave me another way of getting their attention; it gave me credibility in their eyes and was a way to break down barriers to a topic that needs to be out in the open. I hope I demonstrated to them the power and value of admitting that it's OK to be scared. And I know they taught me something about courage and the spirit of sacrifice.

When we left Iraq after a week, returned to Kuwait, and then flew to Landstuhl, Germany, to speak with troops there, the experience was no different. We spent three days touring the hospital where wounded soldiers are flown in from the distant battlefields of Iraq and Afghanistan. One person, in particular, stands out in my mind. I was sitting inside a building called the Warrior Center, doing another book signing, when a soldier in civilian clothing approached me. I could tell he wanted to talk, so I broke away and found a place that offered some privacy. The man—an Army captain—told me that he was going through PTSD therapy. He explained that while he was in Iraq, he could tell that something going on inside him was "not right"—feelings of being disconnected, depressed, and unable to concentrate. It took him some time to acknowledge his growing turmoil, but finally he approached his commanding officer and told him he needed to take himself out of the fight. I remember how he put it: "I had to take a knee."

It was an image packed with meaning for me. In football, the guy who takes a knee fielding the kickoff in the end zone gives his team the ball at the twenty-yard line rather than taking a chance of running the ball out for potentially better field position. It's a decision the player makes for the good of the team rather than an attempt at personal glory. The captain knew what was good for the team by taking himself out of the war zone. He knew he needed to get help in the way of therapy, to get back on track, and then return to the battlefield. I asked him how long he realized something was wrong before he made the brave move to seek help. "About five weeks," he said. I told him he was strong and courageous—the kind of person we need to recognize as a true leader who cared for his troops and was honest with himself. I shared with him that many times we sense things are not right. It's a gut feeling, yet we allow our minds and hearts to overrule the realization, and we talk ourselves out of it.

I tell the story of the captain, who eventually returned to active duty, as an example of the way we should encourage the PTSD bar to be moved: recognize a problem within, seek help, work at recovery or make a particular adjustment, and return to doing what you do well, often with new insight and perspective.

• • •

In the weeks after I returned from Iraq and Germany, I couldn't stop thinking about the many soldiers, officers, and medical personnel I had befriended on the trip. It was an emotionally intense experience, and it deepened my resolve to do anything I could to bring greater awareness to the topic of PTSD. I was particularly honored to have gotten to know and to have built a relationship with General Brown, a basketball star at Army who played for Duke University coaching legend Mike Krzyzewski. It felt truly gratifying when General Brown remarked that he wanted to bring me back to Iraq, as well as Afghanistan, so I could speak about PTSD to more soldiers in the field. The General also brought my work with the troops to the attention of other U.S. Army officers. And less than four months later, I was engaged in a serious phone call with one of them.

On November 5, 2005, an Army psychiatrist allegedly had opened fire at Ford Hood in Texas, killing thirteen people and wounding thirty. It was one of the worst mass shootings at a U.S. base ever, and the face of the tragedy in the massive international news coverage was that of Fort Hood's Commanding General Robert W. Cone. He was the one who stood before the television crews and reporters at the press conferences in the wake of the massacre, answering a deluge of media questions and explaining that the alleged gunman, Major Nidal Malik Hasan, had been wounded and captured alive.

I thought about the traumatic shock waves that would be rippling through the base and wished there was something I could do to help. Barely ten days later, my cell phone rang while I was traveling through New York en route to Philadelphia to officiate a 76ers contest. It was General Cone. He wanted me to come to Fort Hood and address base personnel, many of whom had been emotionally devastated by the rampage.

We pinpointed three days in early December that worked for General Cone and didn't conflict with my NBA schedule. Several hundred copies of *Covert* were shipped to the base—again, something I could use as an icebreaker with the soldiers and base staff I would meet, a way to establish a connection and create a dialogue about the traumatic event they had experienced, either firsthand or indirectly. I flew into Killeen, Texas, and was met by my escort for the three days, Lieutenant Colonel Tom Meyer. Everywhere I went, Tom was there to keep things running with clockwork precision.

Our first stop was at a Fort Hood leadership gathering in the III Corps Headquarters conference room, where I addressed generals and high-ranking officers, civilians, and various family members to share the message of peer-to-peer therapy as a first line of defense to Post-Traumatic Stress.

I presented that same message the next day to two large audiences, one in the morning and one in the afternoon. General Cone had arranged for soldiers and civilians to attend the sessions, which were held in a base auditorium. I was delighted that the room was filled to capacity for each talk, only because it increased the chances that my message would reach—and hopefully help—more people. I could see in the faces of some of the soldiers in attendance that they didn't know who in the world I was, and they clearly didn't want to be there. The first audience also included a large number of first responders and people who worked at the location of the shooting. The largest group was from the 20th Engineer Battalion, which saw four of its own killed and eleven more wounded—more than any other unit. The batallion's commander, Lieutenant Colonel Pete Andrysiak, was there with his surviving unit members, only four days after holding a memorial service for their fallen colleagues in the same auditorium. Many attending, according to Tom, had already served one tour in Iraq or Afghanistan and had taken part in the surge of 2007, when violence reached a peak.

A portion of the questions in the Q&A session that followed dealt with busting the Mob and what life was like officiating games with players from Michael Jordan to Shaq to Kobe. I knew that once the give-and-take began, it would open the door to the sharing of more difficult and honest feelings. And that is exactly what followed. A number of others in the audience stood up and openly talked about their struggles in coming to terms with the trauma from the shooting and their time on the battlefield.

A book signing followed each session, and it gave me a chance to speak directly to members of the audience. One soldier asked me to sign his book to four different people, and I gladly obliged. The quiet, withdrawn young man lingered to talk with me, and it didn't take long to figure out that the four names I inscribed were to his buddies who had been killed in combat.

Two female civilians also approached me during the signing. They had been inside the room at the site of the shooting and had witnessed the carnage. They wanted to talk, and I could see how much the experience had shaken them to their core. I underlined the process of peer-to-peer therapy and encouraged them to be their own initial support system.

The next day, I had breakfast in the mess hall with Lieutenant Colonel Andrysiak and some of his soldiers. I shared with them how they would need one another to work through the complex emotions as they prepared to deploy to Afghanistan, and the more layers of trauma that awaited them.

I learned about everything being done at Fort Hood to help soldiers suffering from PTSD well before that terrible incident. During a tour of the base, I was taken to the Resiliency Campus, which included a chapel, fitness center, reflection pond and garden, and several counseling services available to soldiers and their families 24/7. I met with several behavioral health specialists and later visited an important new endeavor at Fort Hood—the Warrior Combat Stress Reset Program—designed to help military personnel returning from combat with PTSD. The intensive, three-week treatment program focuses on reducing hyperarousal and reactivity and on providing tools to help prevent future trauma. The program incorporates group counseling; biofeedback; individual counseling; movement exercises; and alternative therapies, such as massage, acupuncture, and yoga. The initiatives were recognition of the enormous cost of war to the human psyche. I realized that the program would also assist those dealing with the torment caused by a senseless, inhuman act perpetrated on safe ground, far from the battlefield.

In addition, General Cone, supported by Deputy Commanding General William Grimsley and their staff members, has increased Fort Hood's proactive approach in mental health care as a result of the shootings. He directed a review of the overall approach to behavioral health programs and instituted a plan that ensured all those affected—military and civilians—would be identified, tracked, and cared for over the long haul. Following that review, he made certain that Fort Hood had enough resources to handle the demand for behavioral health services. His bottom-line message: care is awaiting everyone who needs it, and nobody should be ashamed to seek it.

As the healing process continues, a permanent reminder of pain and resiliency stands today at Fort Hood—a six-foot-tall granite block etched with these words:

"Death leaves a heartache no one can heal. Love leaves a memory no one can steal."

General Bob Brown and I walking across the
tarmac after landing in Mosul, Iraq, 2009.

CHAPTER TWELVE

"Are You Robert?"

"As we are liberated from our own fear, our presence automatically liberates others."

—Nelson Mandela

I t was a rainy, rainy morning, and I had been warned not to be late for work because it would cost me an hour of annual leave time. It was still dark outside because it was so early. I thought I saw the bus coming, so I had to hurry to make my way across the street. All I remember after that is seeing everything turning upside down. I don't remember anything else."

The man speaking those words, in a slow and strained delivery, sat across from me on a couch in a small, modestly decorated apartment. The apartment was part of a large assisted-living complex in Rockville, Maryland, for seniors and people with special needs.

People such as Robert.

I first met Robert in 2008 when he came along with his family to a book-signing event I was doing for *Covert* in the Washington, D.C., area. I was immediately struck by his engaging personality and his eagerness to discuss the details of the book with me.

I could also see there was something a little different about him—his short and stocky five-foot frame, his somewhat awkward gait, and the deliberate delivery of his words. Later I learned that he was born with Williams syndrome—a genetic condition marked by learning disabilities, mild retardation, and a cluster of medical problems. But the condition also brought defining personality traits: a gregarious manner, passion for music, and good language skills, which in Robert's case was a natural eloquence.

Flash-forward to the summer of 2010. By then I knew more about his personal history from talking with his family. And with their blessing, I visited Robert one afternoon at his home in Rockville. I wanted to see how he was doing and speak to him about the catastrophic moment that had taken place one year earlier—a moment that had forever changed his life.

Yet there was so much more I would find out about Robert in our time together. I came away seeing how much a thoughtful, developmentally disabled man in his early fifties can teach us all about facing and overcoming the ravages of Post-Traumatic Stress.

This is the value and power of Robert's story. It is a story that underscores the importance family and friends play in the healing process, as well as the critical role of peer-to-peer therapy.

More than anything, his story illustrates how an individual can persevere through unbearable pain and survive with a greater sense of self-awareness and a renewed purpose in life. It is a simple but strong message of overcoming and moving forward, one deliberate step at a time, Robert-style. Society might consider his voice an unlikely source for such a vital lesson, but it is one that can speak volumes—straight from the heart—to anyone seeking a way out of the shadows of Post-Traumatic Stress.

An aluminum walker, several feet from the couch on which Robert sat, provided a visual clue of the recent suffering he had endured that fateful morning of April 15, 2009. At that time, he was living semi-independently only one block away from where we sat—just a short walk up Montrose Road, a busy thorough-fare with vehicles barreling along two lanes in each direction. His former home was a comfortable two-bedroom apartment in a towering complex, where Robert was a familiar and friendly presence—always exchanging a hearty welcome with the staff at the front desk.

A nonprofit agency, the Jubilee Association of Maryland, pro-vided a few hours of assistance each week in managing his daily tasks. In addition, his parents met a graduate student, Keith Austin, who was studying vocational special education, and Keith came into Robert's life, moving into an extra room in the apartment and becoming a close friend and trusted counselor.

All the while, Robert relied heavily on the love and support of his parents—well into their eighties but still very active—and three older siblings. His world was filled with the challenges pre-sented by his substantial disability. But he had carved out a life that gave him a sense of independence, dignity, and achievement during his nearly thirty years as a clerk in the U.S. Government Printing Office.

Having Williams syndrome had left Robert with certain motor-skill impairments that prevented him from driving. But he learned how to get around town just fine. In addition to using public transportation to go to work, he took cabs to do his own weekly grocery shopping or to hit the mall, where he could peruse CDs and T-shirts, go to the movies, or buy himself dinner. Sometimes, he would even ride the subway to downtown D.C. for a classic rock concert. He'd sit alone amid a sellout crowd in some upper-level cheap seat, soaking up the tunes of Billy Joel, Bonnie Raitt, or other performers whose songs touched his soul. Growing up, fueled by his love of music, he had learned to drum on a set in his parents' basement and to play by ear—in his own style—the familiar melodies of his favorite rockers on a piano in their living room.

No artists were higher on his list than Bruce Springsteen and the E Street Band. And I couldn't argue with Robert's taste—I share the same feeling about my fellow Jersey boy and his group. Before the accident, Robert had saved money from work to buy a ticket for Bruce and the band's May concert at the Verizon Center in downtown D.C. As the date neared, he talked constantly to family and friends about going to see the Boss for the first time. It was Robert's birthday treat to himself—the concert fell only four days before his fifty-second birthday on May 22.

Meanwhile, every day he rose at 5 a.m. and got dressed; filled his duffel bag with snacks, sodas, and magazines; and crossed busy Montrose Road to wait for the bus that would take him on the first leg of his hour-long daily commute. Robert would then switch to the subway, take it to Union Station near the U.S.

Capitol Building, make his way through the jostling crowds of commuters, and walk several hilly blocks to the massive GPO building. There, he'd show his badge to the security guard and go about his duties—sorting mail, making copies of blueprints, and filing papers. In the late afternoon, he would retrace his steps to the subway, bus, and home.

Robert's slow pace often irritated his first supervisor. He began timing him as he completed his daily duties—only adding to the feeling of pressure and worry that shadowed Robert. He'd get reprimanded for making mistakes and occasionally was the target of mean-spirited comments. But a coworker, Margo Shiffert, always rose to his defense over the years, and fortunately the department heads who followed that first boss were all understanding and supportive.

Of course, Robert's physical limitations sometimes caused him to be late for work. That had prompted the warning about docking his pay—the reason he was in such a hurry to catch the bus that morning in April. A steady rain fell and visibility was poor as Robert hurried to the curb, waiting for a break in traffic. He thought he could see the bus rumbling up Montrose toward its stop and decided to cross the street quickly as a wave of cars passed. He stepped off the curb. After that, all he recalls is the nightmare image of whirling upside-down through the air.

What Robert doesn't remember—and never saw—was the car that seemed to come out of nowhere and hit him full force in a thirty-five-mile-per-hour zone. The impact knocked him through the air, and he landed headfirst on the concrete edge of the curb.

Robert was rushed to nearby Suburban Hospital with a serious head injury, two shattered legs, a torn lung, broken ribs, and a punctured bladder—and an uncertain prognosis for survival. When he finally broke through the haze of semiconsciousness two weeks later, Robert lay shocked and confused in his hospital bed—and in the tightening clutch of Post-Traumatic Stress.

• • •

As I sat and talked with Robert in his assisted-living apartment, I wondered whether it was hard on him residing in such close proximity to the accident scene, thinking that the site on a regular basis could trigger memories of the trauma.

I was glad to hear his answer—he wanted to live where he did now because it was comfortable and familiar. He wasn't going to let what happened deter him from being in a neighborhood that still felt like home.

I was also glad Robert's oldest sister, Susie, had decided to stop by his apartment for my visit. He frequently looked in her direction while answering questions, as if he was in need of some reassurance from a trusted source. Her presence had a calming effect on him, and she helped elicit more elaboration from Robert when it was needed.

As Robert told me more of his story, it didn't take long for me to realize that he'd suffered from Post-Traumatic Stress well before the accident.

I asked Robert about his childhood and he told me about his experiences during the early years of special education in the 1960s and early 1970s. Children with all manner of conditions—retardation, autism, hyperactivity, and emotional disturbances—were all grouped together in the same classes. In the upper elementary grades, groups in special education broke down along two lines: the bullies and the victims. And unfortunately, Robert's short stature, unusual appearance, and gentle, innocent nature often made him an easy target for the bullies. On any given day, he was teased and beaten up, then threatened with frightening retribution if he told what happened.

"I hid things from my family that nobody should have to hide," Robert said to me. "I was told that if they found out I had told on them for what they were doing, they would find me and kill me."

His voice was creaky and short of breath, the result of the lung injury from his accident and the lingering effects of the breathing tube that had been placed in his throat for weeks. I've transcribed many tapes during my years in law enforcement, giving me a heightened awareness and sensitivity to not only what is being said, but also *how* it is being said. And I know that if you focused only on the typed words, you would miss the meaning behind them. Robert's words were remarkably well chosen—but they came out of his mouth with difficulty, and were coated with emotion.

"They kicked me…They punched me…They slapped me… They undid my clothing…And they broke my glasses and called me fat lips or bubble butt. I didn't know why my body was shaped the way that it was. It was just driving me *crazy*."

The taunts, constant mocking, and humiliation continued in middle and high school. His parents had worked hard to help Robert through school, meeting with school officials and teachers to discuss his problems and strengths and to find programs that met his needs. There was no structure in place for children like Robert at that time; the first legislation requiring appropriate education for people with disabilities was passed in 1975, when Robert was eighteen. Then as now, individual parents and teachers did their best to help disabled children succeed. But good programs were few and far between.

At the same time, there were bright spots. Robert's parents arranged for him to have a "big brother" to take him on outings. They enrolled him in a Saturday duckpin bowling league, where Robert did surprisingly well and despite his motor-skill difficulties won a shelf full of trophies.

But despite the fun time, he lived with the shadows of bullying. And as is often the case, the bullying he suffered was below everyone's radar—parents, teachers, and friends. He was too scared to bring it to anyone's attention.

"I even thought about suicide," Robert said softly.

I echoed Robert's quiet tone and asked, "What kept you from doing it?"

He paused before answering: "I didn't know how."

"The idea of holding a gun scared me to death, and I couldn't figure out how to run into harm's way," he continued haltingly. "And I knew my family loved me. I thought that not everybody I'll come in contact with during my life could ever be so cold or cruel. I thought that if I just waited and held on to my spirituality, I would be OK."

Robert eventually found a safe haven in high school in his senior year—as manager of the football and baseball teams. The head coach of both teams, a tough but compassionate man named Jack Freeman, noticed Robert's plight and put him on the squads to hand out towels and keep track of the equipment. The players always looked out for Robert and, for the most part, kept his tormentors at bay.

"They served as a protective shield of brothers for me," Robert recalled. "They gave me a sense of hope and safety."

I was moved by what that coach and his team did, and I reminded Robert that I knew something about bad guys from my years undercover.

"Robert, I know you read *Covert*," I told him. "The criminals I investigated were bullies, too—and bullies are very weak people. You are strong. The reason I did my job was because there are bad people in this world who prey on other people. As a cop, that's what was important to me—*stopping* those people."

Robert nodded, then shared something else I could relate to from my experience with the Mob. Just as I had gotten informal therapy after surfacing from my undercover work—helping me recognize that I had experienced PTSD—Robert benefited from speaking to a therapist, Crystal Marcus. She helped him put the bullies and mean kids who had hurt him in perspective.

"I realized that I had survived; I never knew what happened to those other guys, but I survived," he said. "But all through the years and even now, I have nightmares."

"I do, too," I assured Robert. "I still have similar dreams. Even though I know a lot of the mobsters I helped arrest have died, there's still part of it that stays with you. That's normal. And talking about it is therapeutic."

For Robert, another potent kind of therapy awaited—a form of the peer-to-peer approach that can be life changing.

• • •

In 1994, his parents heard a National Public Radio report about a relatively unknown condition at the time—Williams syndrome. The NPR segment described traits that matched Robert to a tee and mentioned a special music camp held each summer in Lenox, Massachusetts.

It was a revelation for Robert, then thirty-seven, and his parents. And in no time he found himself face-to-face with young adults, teens, and children who looked very much like him and shared the same outgoing personality, verbal abilities, and love of music. It was the first time Robert had a sense of who he was and why he was that way. It was the first time he had a true sense of wholeness. He was among peers, many of whom had similar experiences growing up, dealing with bullies, or being stared at in public. Learning that there was a Williams syndrome community—being embraced fully by it— transformed him and suddenly gave him a new perspective on his life.

"Discovering I had Williams syndrome was like a dream come true," Robert said. "Until then, I didn't know why my brain didn't function in a normal way—or what people say is normal. And I didn't know why I wasn't smart enough. But now I understood. And it made all the difference to me."

That didn't mean that after finding his place in the world with the Williams syndrome community, Robert's life was worry-free— not by a long shot. In 1997, he suffered the first of two small strokes—most likely stemming from the high blood pressure and heart problems that are common to many born with the syndrome. But he made a good recovery, with the only lingering sign being a slight slur in his speech.

Robert pushed through. He even became a featured panelist at Williams Syndrome Association events around the country, giving talks to encourage others to have confidence in their ability to lead productive lives and how much it meant to him to be part of the Williams syndrome family. He was emerging as a mature voice and a respected member of the Williams syndrome community.

He was proud of that and proud of working for the Government Printing Office. The job boosted his morale and self-esteem, and even more important, it won him friends. He gained a sense that he had achieved something on a par with his three siblings, all of whom had gone on to rewarding careers. By 2009, he was less than a year away from his thirtieth anniversary with the government and known throughout the GPO building for his friendly ways.

And so every workday before dawn, he would set off with his duffle in the darkness. He completed the journey year after year—until that rainy April morning when his life changed in a blur of glaring headlights and screeching tires.

• • •

His family kept a daily vigil around his hospital bed in the weeks after he'd been rushed to the emergency room with life-threatening injuries. The doctors were unsure whether he would live. Emergency surgeons mended his injured bladder and put together the shattered, jigsaw-puzzle pieces of his broken right leg—far worse than the break in his left. For the following two weeks, he drifted just beneath consciousness, hooked to monitors, unable to swallow or breathe on his own. He didn't talk, but a squeeze of the hand let family members know that he heard them.

The day after the accident, his niece Jenny brought Robert an iPod loaded with some of his favorite tunes—including an album of Bruce Springsteen's greatest hits, which seemed fitting, considering the concert he had planned to attend. His brother noticed that the familiar tunes seemed to have an effect, quickening the pace of the beeps on his heart monitor especially when his favorite song, "Born to Run," blared through the tiny iPod speaker. But the nurse on duty thought it might be getting Robert overly stimulated in his fragile state, so the volume had to be turned down.

Gradually, over the next few weeks, Robert began awakening from his fog. His first words—to the surprise and relief of everyone—were to request a soda.

But as he made physical progress, his emotional state was another story. The enormity of what had happened to him began to sink in and triggered constant waves of tears, anger, and confusion. Just as he had been hurled upside down by a car, his entire world had been turned on its head. He wanted to return home, to life the way it had been before the accident, but the heavy casts on his legs and the wires surrounding his hospital bed were a constant reminder that his life would never be the same.

After three weeks, Robert was transferred to a nearby rehabilitation center, where specialists worked with his legs and helped him become mobile again with a daily regimen of painful exercises. He lay in a bed covered with a mesh tent to keep him from falling out, and his spirits were low—despite the best efforts of family members who stayed by his side each day, despite cards that flooded in from relatives, friends, and all his new brothers and sisters from the Williams syndrome network.

Five weeks after the accident, Robert was making slow and steady improvement. He was becoming more alert every day, enough for his family to plan a small birthday celebration in his rehab center room. His brother, a newspaper writer, had on several occasions interviewed legendary Springsteen saxophonist Clarence Clemons. The D.C. tour stop with the Boss and the E Street Band had come and gone several days earlier, much to Robert's sorrow. But his brother had an idea. Without mentioning it to Robert, he made a call to a Tampa Bay-area music promoter close to Clemons—Johnny Green—and asked if he could get a message to the "Big Man." Green instantly obliged. He called Clemons in the city where he was performing, telling him about Robert's plight and his deep disappointment about missing the concert of his dreams.

Late in the afternoon of Robert's birthday, his rehab center room was filled with balloons and cards wishing him well. In the midst of conversation and laughter, the phone rang. Susie picked up the receiver and remembers precisely what the deep, gentle voice on the other end said. "Hello, this is Clarence Clemons. I'd like to speak to Robert."

Smiling broadly, she handed her brother the phone. His eyes lit up as he realized who was calling him: the rock star whose memorable sax solo put the pedal to the metal in "Born to Run," the song that connected with Robert even while unconscious. The conversation between the Big Man and the Little Man took about three minutes, but it had a lasting impact.

Clemons first wished Robert a happy birthday. Then he shared that he had once been in a near-fatal car accident on the way to try out as a free agent with the Cleveland Browns in 1966. After leaving the hospital, bruised and cut, he decided to give up his dream of playing in the National Football League and devote himself to another passion—playing his sax. That eventually put him on the road to the music clubs of Asbury Park, where he crossed paths on the boardwalk with a young performer named Bruce Springsteen.

"The rest is rock-and-roll history," said Robert. "That story gave me hope. I felt that he had gone through something similar to what I went through—and then went on to something even better. When the Big Man called me, I felt like I was part of the band. He said to me, 'You are my brother.' And I said to him, 'You are part of *me*.' That was a big moment in my life."

I listened in amazement as Robert related the conversation to me. And it wasn't just because of the truly generous gesture by Clarence. His caring voice was another example of the immeasurable value derived from personal connections—from those who understand what it means to suffer trauma in their own lives. That is the essence of peer-to-peer support and the therapy it offers.

It turns out, that call meant something special to Clarence as well.

"I knew exactly where Robert was coming from," the heralded E Street rocker would later reflect. "And I knew he was on the verge—you get this depression that develops, and you can either give up or you can keep going. And if somebody says something to you that strikes home, something that you can relate to, it can help you understand things better and move forward knowing that you're not alone. Giving a little hope is what it's all about. I was glad it helped Robert and it was good for me, too. We felt a definite connection—and I'll always have him in my heart and mind."

What Clarence did in offering his words of encouragement—and also sharing the experience of his own car accident—gave Robert that important assurance he was not alone. Robert could talk to somebody who understood what *he* was going through and come away feeling that he could make it through this dark period. And maybe something even better was waiting for him on his path in life.

In fact, something *was* about to happen.

• • •

Fourteen months after his accident, Robert flew to St. Louis for the Williams Syndrome Association national conference. As awareness of Williams syndrome has grown, so has the event—drawing some 1,500 parents, children, and family members. Normally, he attended the conference with his parents, Barbara and Walt, but the trip was difficult for them to make at eighty-eight years old, so he was accompanied instead by his sisters, Susie and Miriam.

Throughout the first two days, Robert—moving with the help of his walker—was greeted by countless well-wishers who were thrilled to see what a strong recovery he had made. Many also had noticed that he was on the program to address the entire conference. Robert was excited by the invitation to speak, to open his heart to his Williams syndrome family, but he struggled, too, with the challenge of revealing the emotional pain that he had lived with.

When longtime Williams Syndrome Association executive director Terry Monkaba introduced Robert that morning, Susie turned to him and asked whether he needed help getting to the stage. But he said no. He needed to get there on his own. Then he made his way slowly from his seat in the front of the auditorium up the stairs to the podium.

As someone who does a lot of public speaking—and knows that it's natural to get some jitters before a speech—I asked him whether he was nervous as he looked out at a packed house.

"I was a little bit nervous, but I thought, 'I've *got* to do this; I have to make this speech that's been hiding deep inside of me— I've got to come through and give these people a message of hope,'" Robert declared.

He was a natural. He talked about his accident, and then moved on to a larger theme drawn from the lessons of his life—his strained but steady voice booming out over the crowd.

"I want you in my WSA family to have a *vision* for yourselves, even if you don't feel good about yourselves. Because I've had to struggle through this. And I know you've also had to struggle through a lot of things. And you will struggle through a lot of things as your lives progress—things like teasing and pointing and other things that don't make you feel very good. But I want you to have resolve. I want you to have a vision of *hope*."

As Robert described what he had endured, he began to cry. His sisters held their breath, watching him work to regain his composure. Then, his voice returned, steady and sure. As he walked off the stage, the room erupted in a thunderous standing ovation. The keynote speaker Dr. Ray Guarendi—a clinical psychologist, syndicated-radio parenting expert, and author—knew he had a tough act to follow. He drew laughs seconds later by announcing that he planned to take Robert on the road with him.

Looking back, there was one line Robert spoke—describing his accident—that stands out in my mind, a phrase that can serve almost as a mantra for PTSD sufferers: "I almost didn't make it out alive," he told the crowd. "But *I am here.*"

Those three words say so much about what people coping with PTSD can aspire to: "I am here." It is a simple goal but such an important one. No matter what trauma you endure, no matter how much the foundation of your life has been shaken, those words mean that you are making your stand. You are finding your way. You are moving forward.

You are here.

There was something else I realized. Robert's speech was true peer-to-peer therapy. He was speaking to people just like him, who had endured their own hardships and felt uplifted by his words. And Robert was learning something about himself from his peers—in the same way Dr. Jim Gordon speaks of the group leader's learning from therapy participants.

"When I cried, I was releasing years of pain and sorrow, anger, and fury," he said to me. "And when I was done, I felt like a different person. I felt like they had given *me* hope."

In a way, Robert's speech was a release from a lifetime of multiple layers of PTSD—from the bullying he endured as a child to his accident a year earlier. And the healing he felt came from *talking* about it—whether in his personal therapy sessions over the years or to a group of people with similar life experiences.

For the next two days of the conference, Robert couldn't take more than a few steps without someone approaching him and thanking him for his words. One parent of a child with Williams syndrome stopped him to say she felt as if God had spoken through him. He basked in the kind of spotlight he had never imagined possible. Ironically, it resulted from a terrible accident that nearly took his life. But just like Clarence Clemons, Robert has lifted himself up and is ready to rock and roll.

• • •

By the way, I did neglect to provide one detail in Robert's tale: his older brother is Dave Scheiber, my coauthor.

I didn't want to color your reading of the story by telling you that on the front end. But knowing it brings home an important point: we all may know somebody in the grips of PTSD—a family member, a friend, a coworker. And it is so important to reach out to them. Because, as Robert Scheiber's story illustrates, there are many people ready to help. And, in his own words, there is hope.

What Robert means to his Williams syndrome peers was captured one day at the conference, when a small child with Williams syndrome recognized him in the lobby. The little boy stared up at him excitedly, as if he were looking at Michael Jordan.

"Are you Robert?" he asked with a high-pitched voice.

It was a moment to savor, another two-way connection that touched Robert and the young child. Robert had survived taunts, bullying, illness and physical traumas, and had found his inner strength; now he was giving a new generation a sense of its power. His spirits had once sunk to the depths, but that moment held pride and hope for his future.

This is the goal we can strive for in overcoming trauma—a message for everyone struggling in the darkness of PTSD. He was telling the little boy and all others that there is strength within you to overcome, to find your way, to be yourself. And this is the message of a man named Robert.

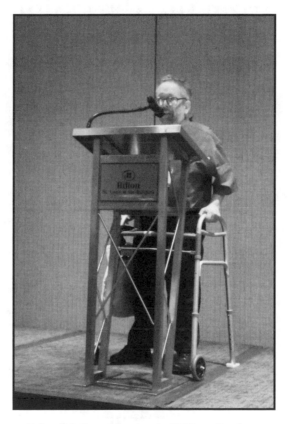

*Robert Scheiber addressing the Williams Syndrome
Association conference in St. Louis.*

From the Dark Side
to the Light Side

"Hope is like the sun, which, as we journey toward it, casts the shadow of our burden behind us."

—Samuel Smiles

I t was a typically warm July morning in Washington, D.C., when I descended a steep escalator to catch a red-line Metro train. I rode the crowded, rush-hour subway car in silence as it traveled the tracks beneath the nation's capital and the waters of the Potomac River—one small part of a journey that had begun for me many years earlier. I was lost in thought as the train emerged from the darkened tunnel and whisked me into the sunlit landscape of Northern Virginia—soon gliding to a stop at a bustling city unto itself: the Pentagon.

I had gazed at the sprawling landmark during countless landings and takeoffs at Reagan National Airport during my NBA career but never set foot inside. Now, as my work with troops deepened on the PTSD front, I had begun making contacts and friends throughout the upper echelon of the military. And that ultimately led to an invitation I was thrilled to accept: a tour of our country's strategic command headquarters. I looked forward to getting a clear visual image of the place where the Department of Defense makes critical decisions in the world.

Of all the sights I saw during my two-hour tour that day, one scene stands out in my mind—the section of the Pentagon that was demolished on 9/11, when terrorists commandeered American Airlines Flight 77 and crashed into the building. All 59 passengers and crew members on board were killed, and another 125 people inside the Pentagon died as the Boeing jetliner plowed through three inner rings on the building's west side, igniting an inferno.

Standing in Corridor 4 where the crash occurred, I thought about the men and women who died that day. A framed, color-coded desk chart depicted where employees had been on that terrible morning. Each color denoted whether staff members had been killed, injured, or uninjured—or whether, by a twist of fate, their lives had been spared because they had been absent from work or were simply away from their desks at the moment of the attack. The chart underscored the random nature of trau-matic events and how our lives can change in a millisecond—something I'd learned all too well during the early years of my law enforcement career.

Yet the illustration also drove home another stark aspect of PTSD—the ripple effect that the condition has on trauma survi-vors. The people who were away from their desks when the plane struck have their own painful connection to the horror of that morning, as do family members and friends who lost loved ones.

When I speak to people about PTSD, I liken its ripple effect to an earthquake. We often focus on the epicenter, where the most damage occurs. But the aftershocks take place for hours, days, weeks, and months later. People at that epicenter may feel the ground shake the hardest, but folks further away feel tremors, too. And they have a story to tell that is no less important, although they may minimize their experience, feeling that others have dealt with a much more serious trauma.

This is something to remember in dealing with PTSD: we tend to judge or even dismiss our own pain and distress as somehow not as valid as the harm to someone in the midst of a violent event. But being affected by a ripple from a traumatic event can be as serious as being in the middle of it, and the emotional impact needs to be recognized and brought out into the open. Repressing it may cause another layer of traumatic stress to develop within.

It was impressive to see how much care and sensitivity had been put into memorializing victims of the Pentagon catastrophe, as well as in providing a way for people affected by the disaster to find a measure of comfort. A small indoor chapel has been built where the plane struck, which gives anyone a chance to pray for or remember those who lost their lives that day. There is another value to this kind of remembrance. It allows people touched in some way by the tragedy the opportunity to meet, console one another, share feelings—all immensely helpful in the processing of traumatic events and another form of peer-to-peer therapy.

Looking through a window, I could see a beautiful and serene outdoor memorial—open twenty-hour hours a day, seven days a week. It honors the lives of the 184 combined victims of Flight 77 and the Pentagon workers killed that day, with 184 separate benches, one dedicated to each victim. It reminded me that, when we think of 9/11, our tendency is to dwell on New York City and the collapse of the twin towers. We may not focus on the loss that is forever part of the grounds here and on the hallowed field in Shanksville, Pennsylvania.

As I left the Pentagon, I again thought of all the people who carry trauma with them following a life-changing incident. I'd thought the same thing after visiting Ground Zero, the Pearl Harbor Memorial, the devastated Federal Building in Oklahoma City, Columbine High School in Colorado, and so many other scenes of horrific events.

Later that day, I visited the Vietnam Veterans Memorial—with its stunningly long marble wall bearing so many small, etched names of those who served and died in the jungles of Southeast Asia.

On a nearby hillside, several large bronze statues of U.S. soldiers appear to be looking at the wall—as if observing the crowds of people searching for names they remember. Those statues capture the anguish and loneliness so many Vietnam vets felt upon returning home in the grip of PTSD—their brutal experiences overlooked and unappreciated by many Americans at that time because of the immense unpopularity of the war.

I followed a path across the solemn grounds and arrived at the vastly different National World War II Memorial, with its large fountains and towering columns representing each state—a majestic tribute reflective of a war our country embraced. I felt proud looking at the column dedicated to New Jersey's brave troops, knowing that my Dad had served in the Pacific as a member of the U.S. Navy. I also felt a tinge of sadness knowing that I'd never be able to walk these grounds with him, perhaps hearing stories I've never heard before. My father is in the advanced stages of Alzheimer's now and will never make that trip. But I thanked him quietly as I stood there amid the crowds of tourists.

The words of General Douglas MacArthur were etched overhead for all to see: "Today the guns are silent. A great tragedy has ended. A great victory has been won. The skies no longer rain death—the seas bear only commerce—men everywhere walk upright in the sunlight."

I understood the motivational tone of General MacArthur's words following such a turning point in world history and a momentous achievement for our country and the Allies. But I know that everyone who served did not walk upright from warfare, and many would return home bearing the emotional scars of combat that so few understood—preferring not to talk about what they had experienced, suffering from a condition that had no name or diagnosis then.

Today there's an ever-increasing awareness of PTSD and its crippling effects. Two extended wars have increased the problem significantly. Many Americans have volunteered to serve, and as a result of their efforts, thousands of them will carry a mental and emotional burden for years to come. And because their injuries are invisible—unlike the obvious physical injuries of Wounded Warriors—they can go unnoticed even though the damage may be just as serious. I also think it's important for us to understand that, when identifying Wounded Warriors, we don't overlook the potential for *their* invisible wounds.

As we are reminded all too often, anyone who puts on a uniform to serve and protect is at a heightened risk for experiencing trauma and those invisible wounds. On January 25, 2011, two members of the St. Petersburg Police Department in Florida—Sergeant Thomas Baitinger and Officer Jeffrey Yaslowitz—were slain in the line of duty while attempting to serve a warrant on a fugitive who opened fire on them with an automatic weapon from the attic in which he had been hiding. The tragedy was the latest in an alarming pattern of law enforcement murders, following the shooting deaths of two Miami police officers earlier in the same month; two Tampa policemen who were killed while making a traffic stop the previous July; and four Seattle cops who were gunned down in late 2009 while sitting inside a coffee shop.

I was honored to speak before members of the Tampa Police Force and Hillsborough County Sheriffs Department six months after the loss of their brave colleagues, Jeffrey Kocab and David Curtis. I never imagined that only three weeks after that presentation, I would be standing before a packed auditorium at the St. Petersburg Police Training Academy, reaching out to members of law enforcement still reeling from the lingering shock of losing two of their own in Sergeant Baitinger and Officer Yaslowitz. An air of sorrow and raw emotion hung over the room as a I spoke to the gathering, which included veteran officers, cadets, and emergency service workers. I often invoke humor to break through to those listening, but this was not the place for that—the pain was too fresh, and I could feel it deeply. As always, I related my personal journey into Post-Traumatic Stress and underlined how important it was for them to share their feelings with peers, slowly allowing the healing process to begin.

Unfortunately, what happened in St. Petersburg, as well as the terrible incidents in Miami, Tampa, Seattle, Oakland, Fort Hood, and elsewhere, is part of a growing wave of violence rooted in the use of automatic weaponry by criminals. That increased firepower, coupled with a pervasive lack of respect for human life and authority, adds another layer of danger for those on the front line. The damage caused by the random, rapid-fire spray of bullets is devastating, and sadly, it can put anyone of us at risk—as we learned all too well from the rampage in Tucson, Arizona, on January 8, 2011.

A deranged man with an automatic weapon turned a simple town-hall-style event outside a grocery store into a scene of mayhem and a national tragedy. In moments, Congresswoman Gabrielle Giffords was critically wounded with a bullet in her head, and eighteen people were shot—six of them fatally, including a federal judge, John Roll, who was heroically saving another's life, and a bright-eyed nine-year-old girl, Christina-Taylor Green, eager to see government in action. Instantly, new seeds of psychological trauma—impacting victims, families, friends, law enforcement, and first responders—had been sown.

The harsh reality is that we can't stop these horrific incidents from happening, but we can help those affected find ways to cope and heal. As you have read in these pages, there is much good work being done to address PTSD. And there are many stories of brave individuals finding ways to persevere and make significant steps forward, in spite of enormous loss or ongoing pain.

But even with the strides we are making, there is still much work to be done. And the words of a friend of mine—a man who had a vision and passion for life—illuminate a path I intend to follow in helping others move beyond the shadows.

• • •

I still listen to his speech two or three times a month. The inspiring message was delivered by championship college basketball coach Jimmy Valvano at the first annual ESPY Awards on March 4, 1993—an event that has become an ESPN fixture honoring the greatest moments and achievements in sports each year. Jimmy was dying from inoperable cancer when he was assisted to the podium and presented with the Arthur Ashe Courage and Humanitarian Award.

His talk was a testament to his passion for life and determination to make a difference in the world. He spoke with his trademark humor and wisdom, culminating the speech with an announcement—he would be starting the Jimmy V Foundation for Cancer Research, with ESPN's support. The words people recall most from that evening revolve around the motto Jimmy coined for the foundation: "Don't give up; don't ever give up." He added, "That's what I'm going to try to do every minute that I have left. I will thank God for the day and the moment I have."

But I have discovered new meaning in another passage from that speech:

> It's so important to know where you are. I know where I am right now. How do you go from where you are to where you want to be? I think you have to have an

enthusiasm for life. You have to have a dream, a goal. You have to be willing to work for it.

Jimmy could just as easily have been directing his message to people suffering from PTSD. It is so important to focus on the things in life worth living for—your family, your friends, *yourself.* And you need to reach for an important goal: to let others know about the torment you may have bottled up inside, to talk about your private hell. And then you have to do the work involved in reaching that goal. You can start by finding a person or people who have gone through similar experiences and with whom you can share the burdens you've been carrying alone. You'll be amazed by the many doors that can open to put you on a path toward recovery.

Jimmy had his own dream, a dream to beat cancer. And he worked for it by assembling an all-star team of friends and fellow basketball peers—most notably the basketball Hall of Famer and ESPN college hoops broadcasting great Dick Vitale, ESPN commentator John Saunders, and Duke University coach Mike Krzyzewski, as well as doctors, researchers, and financial experts committed to carrying on his mission. He died a month after his memorable call to action, but I like to say that Jimmy—who coached North Carolina State to the 1983 NCAA championship against the odds—is doing his best coaching job ever now with the V Foundation. He's put together the team, has developed a game plan to beat cancer, and has created many success stories along the way. I've been honored to serve in recent years as the V Foundation's national cochair for the Blow the Whistle on Cancer Campaign. And I've seen the organization grow, under the guidance of Jimmy's brother and V Foundation's chief executive officer, Nick Valvano, into a major player in cancer research, prevention, and fund-raising.

When Nick speaks at various V Foundation events around the country, he often asks cancer survivors in the room to stand up. And scores of people do, every time. The disease was often synonymous with a death sentence. Today, through the efforts of countless dedicated people, the term *cancer survivor* is part of our daily vocabulary.

That is my vision for PTSD sufferers. My hope is that the day will come when we can ask audience members who have faced and overcome PTSD to stand—and that many who have regained control of their lives will be proud to do so, standing up to a stigma that has lingered over mental health issues for so long.

I also share the vision that lies behind the V Foundation's mission and believe we need a similar organization, dedicated to PTSD research, education, and therapeutic services. As I wrote earlier in this book, I believe we are still in the early stages of understanding this disorder, with new ideas and exciting programs making progress on a multitude of fronts. Chapter Ten describes some of these outstanding efforts. In many cases, such programs are separate entities, doing noble and vital work on their own, without any connection to others striving for the same ends. My goal is to help unite these efforts into a vast network to provide information and support for people unsure of where to turn. As a first step in reaching this goal, we need to coordinate existing efforts and organize options for PTSD sufferers.

It will take cooperation on multiple fronts. This reminds me of words I read while earning my master's degree in leadership at

St. Mary's College of California. The theorist Joseph Rost wrote that leadership is "an influence relationship between leaders and collaborators, who intend real changes that reflect their mutual purposes." Leaders and collaborators have been effecting change in many important social arenas for decades.

The global war on terror, which involves multiple levels of leadership among international law enforcement groups, enhanced intelligence sharing between nations, and ongoing military endeavors, has allowed us to carry on our daily routines with an increased awareness since the wave of fear from 9/11.

John Walsh made a major impact after the tragic 1981 abduction and murder of his young son, Adam. In enlisting the help of law enforcement, politicians, and community leaders, the result was the creation of the Center for Missing and Exploited Children. Walsh empowered himself and others to become an engine for investigation and pressure for important changes. The result has been legislative reform that has created tougher penalties for sex offenders and expanded victims' rights, as well as a higher level of coordinated law enforcement response.

We've made huge strides as a nation in other areas, such as raising awareness about the dangers of smoking and drunk driving. Others are lifting their voices for important mental health causes such as depression, a symptom of PTSD. Actor Joey Pantoliano of the HBO hit series *The Sopranos* has started the NKM2 Foundation—short for No Kidding, Me Too, and dedicated to erasing the social stigma surrounding depression. Los Angeles Lakers star Ron Artest raffled off his 2010 NBA championship ring to promote awareness of the issue and raise funds for his Xcel University charity, generating more than $650,000 for youths at high risk for developing mental health problems. These are valuable developments in sending a message about people dealing with PTSD and other mental health issues—that they are experiencing normal reactions to abnormal situations.

We need to create peer-to-peer programs early on, so that a new generation sees them as a first option when dealing with traumatic events rather than suppressing emotions and letting them fester. We need to educate and raise awareness of the importance for intervention so that layers of turmoil do not build up over time and lead to aggression. If unresolved, as we've seen, the anger and frustration of PTSD *will* come out—many times in the form of violence to others or to oneself.

We can follow the lead of so many other notable movements—and create our own for PTSD.

• • •

I've gained an invaluable education during my journey into Post-Traumatic Stress, and the learning process never stops.

Earlier in this book, for instance, I made mention of World War II General George Patton's slapping a soldier suffering from battle fatigue—accusing him of being a coward when the man was grappling with what we now refer to as PTSD. There were, in fact, two well-publicized incidents of Patton's belittling and striking a soldier inside an evacuation hospital. One incident occurred on August 3, 1943, although medics determined that the Army private in question was suffering from malaria and dysentery; the other episode took place a week later, with another private exhibiting symptoms of PTSD. The 1970 movie *Patton*, starring the late George C. Scott, combined those two incidents into one—with the target of the General's ire portrayed by veteran actor Tim Considine, whose numerous screen credits include such television classics as *The Hardy Boys* and *My Three Sons*.

When the opportunity arose to speak with Tim, I jumped at the chance. I wanted to know how he prepared for the role and the humiliation that Scott's raging portrayal of Patton in the famous film scene subjected him to. Perhaps it would provide a window to the way PTSD sufferers felt in another era.

"I wish I could say that I deeply researched the role," Tim said. "The part was offered to me very late, and within days of accepting the offer I was on a plane from New York to Madrid to begin filming."

As it turned out, Considine did find a way into the heart of the soldier he portrayed. It's a revealing story. Tim turned the role down several times. He wasn't interested in what sounded like a brief and hardly memorable appearance on screen. But the executive in charge of casting—a contemporary of his filmmaking father, John Considine Jr.—prevailed on Tim to take the part. Then a chance phone call with his cousin, the late, great journalist Bob Considine, made him realize the small role was a substantial one.

"I was telling him that I was on my way to Madrid to be in a movie and he asked, 'What movie?'—and I said, '*Patton*'—and there was a pause," Tim recounted. "Then he said, 'Don't tell me you're going to play the soldier he slapped?' This was the first moment I understood that this might be something important, and much heavier than I realized."

Tim didn't want to meet George C. Scott before doing the scene, and Scott felt the same. When they were introduced on the set, each looked away. They wanted to feel the intense emotions of their characters without being influenced by any real-life fraternizing prior to filming.

"I researched the role as much as I could after I arrived, and when it came time to shoot the scene, the director, Franklin Schaffner, literally took all day—filming from every possible angle," Tim said. "After every take, George would pass by me without looking at me and quietly say, 'You OK?' and I'd go, 'Yeah,' and that was it. We didn't want to know each other.

"I just wanted to focus on what I was feeling—what that soldier was feeling. I went into the scene thinking of the expression 'shell-shock.' I saw my character as extremely confused about what his feelings were and truly battling himself. He didn't understand his problems—*was* he a coward? All he knew was that his heart raced and he got weak and hysterical when thinking about things that happened in combat. My take on it was this: I didn't know what was wrong with me, but it was something physical and mental—and then this very imposing authority figure was berating me. And I couldn't explain *anything* to him. It was awful."

Tim's portrayal of that soldier struck the essence of PTSD: confusion, conflicting emotions, numbness, and a physiological response. Four decades later, he remains proud that the role he almost rejected has become a cultural marker in the timeline of PTSD awareness.

• • •

I've encountered many other important markers in that timeline—a combination of noteworthy programs, people, and developments furthering the fight against PTSD.

I won't forget meeting John Phelps, an accomplished Wyoming artist whose son—Marine Lance Corporal Chance Phelps—was killed fighting in Iraq in 2004. The story of how Chance's body was flown back to the United States, accompanied by Lieutenant Colonel Michael Strobl, was brought to life in the stirring HBO movie *Taking Chance*, with Kevin Bacon playing the part of Strobl. Chance's death also inspired his family to honor his memory by offering help to others. John takes veterans struggling with physical and mental injuries on hunting trips in Wyoming. And Chance's mother, Gretchen Mack, established the Chance Phelps Foundation to assist veterans and their families facing hardships and to provide support for wounded men and women returning from war.

In addition to staging a 1,500-mile walk to heighten awareness and raise funds, the foundation began expanding its scope in 2008. A ranch-retreat in Wyoming was opened—on land and facilities donated to the foundation—as a place where veterans and their families from around the country can come to relax, reflect, and rebuild their morale.

I thought of Carol Paukner and all the many brave first responders at the World Trade Center when the U.S. Senate voted in favor of the 9/11 Health and Compensation Act, overcoming disappointing partisan objections that caused the bill to be reduced from $7.4 billion over ten years to $4.2 billion over five years. Yet even the smaller package should make a difference, creating the World Trade Center Health Program—a permanent operation designed to screen, monitor, and care for first responders and survivors dealing with serious maladies stemming from the attacks on the twin towers. The bill passed at the eleventh hour of the 111th Congress, when a consortium of supporters on both sides of the aisle helped derail a possible filibuster that would have killed the vital legislation. And many, from New York City mayor Michael Bloomberg to the NYC Firefighter Brotherhood Foundation, credit the comedian and *Daily Show* host Jon Stewart with making the ultimate difference—after Stewart devoted an entire program to the issue and chastised the opposition for "an outrageous abdication of our responsibility to those who were most heroic on 9/11." A *New York Times* article even drew comparisons between Stewart and broadcast news legends Edwin R. Murrow and Walter Cronkite for his advocacy.

I was also moved by the sight of the striking flight crew memorial in Grapevine, Texas, titled *Valor Commitment Dedication*, featuring bronze statues of a pilot, first officer, male and female flight attendants, and a young passenger. The sculpture, eighteen feet tall, honors the 33 flight crew members who died along with 213 passengers—a group representing twenty-two states and seven countries—when terrorists hijacked and crashed the four planes on 9/11. I couldn't help but think of all the crews I've interacted with over the years, flying from one city to the next, and how it's so easy to take their hard work for granted. I thought of the fear those who lost their lives on 9/11 felt and the bravery they exhibited, as well as the daily pain from the trauma their families have endured. It underscored the reality that Post-Traumatic Stress can take place in all walks of life.

I'm grateful for the opportunity to have spoken with Matina Dwyer, widow of Private Joe Dwyer. After she read the "Defining Moment" chapter, she relayed a message through her brother-in-law Brian for me to call her. I spoke with her on Christmas Eve, as she and Joe's parents wrapped daughter Meagan's presents. She sounded good and full of life, although I have learned that what the rest of us want to call closure never truly comes for those who suffer such a great loss. As we talked, Matina reflected about how, when he returned from Iraq, Joe didn't feel comfortable speaking with people who hadn't been through what he'd experienced. "And I'm not a person he could talk to, because *I* didn't understand what he went through," she told me. There was no way Matina could fill that role, nor should she or any combat spouse in her position feel guilty for not being able to be part of the peer-to-peer therapy process. I told Matina I was honored that the tale of Joe's courage could be included in *Surviving the Shadows,* and I know that in the future I will be sharing more time with her and Meagan.

And I'm grateful for a phone call I received from Mary Gallagher ten months after paying a visit to her Long Island home and learning more about her life with Jim. Mary, it turned out, had just received a letter from the Marine Corps dated March 1, 2007. Somehow, the correspondence hadn't been mailed or had been lost in the bureaucratic shuffle before it finally showed up in her mailbox three years later. She read through the official, one-page letter quickly—her thoughts racing, trying to make sense of a message arriving so long after Jim's suicide. The letter seemed only to be restating facts about his death she knew all too well, but the summary at the end left her breathless:

"It has been determined that Gunnery Sergeant Gallagher's death was in the Line of Duty. We extend our continued condolences and support to the Gallagher family as we mourn the loss of a good Marine."

It was a bittersweet moment. The words couldn't change the reality of her terrible loss, but the acknowledgment that the U.S. Marines viewed Jim's death as *in the line of duty*— not by his own hand—was a stunning revelation. So was the fact they had made the determination *three* years earlier. The fact is that government errors are made, and at least in this case, the message was the right one.

Mary's decision to get involved with Hope for the Warriors was spurred by a desire to help veterans suffering from PTSD and other injuries, and to change attitudes about suicide. The job put her on a path that has made a difference in the lives of many veterans and has been a force for healing her own life as well. Mary has been honored with a Hope & Courage Award, presented by Hope for the Warriors. TV and film star Gary Sinise—known for his role as Lieutenant Dan in the movie *Forrest Gump* and highly active in veterans affairs—presented Mary with the award.

"These honorees represent outstanding examples of selfless acts of service to our nation," said Hope for the Warriors' president Robin Kelleher. "They have demonstrated extraordinary courage in the face of extraordinary circumstances."

Mary was overcome by emotion and a wave of stage fright as she stepped to the podium to receive the honor. Her heart pounded as she thought about Jim and what the award meant to her. Amid the blur of activity, she accepted the award to thunderous applause.

And it wasn't until later that she wished she could have that moment back, because she had wanted so badly to single out and thank her three children for being strong, and helping her heal. "Their resilience and love gave me strength," she told me later. "That award wasn't just for me. It was also for them. It's a moment I still regret, that I didn't say something about my kids."

I assured Mary that her children were well aware of what was in her heart. I was proud of her for the recognition she received and felt a mixture of emotions for Jim's posthumous recognition by the Marines—glad to know his service to country was not being overshadowed by the circumstances of his death but still saddened by his loss.

The decision to classify his death as in the line of duty—just as the Army did for Joe Dwyer—is an encouraging sign. Hopefully, the bar is moving in the right direction, pointing to a shift in attitudes toward those who died with the battlefield still raging inside.

• • •

Opportunities continue to come my way to meet the great men and women who serve our country. And I was privileged to speak at a conference sponsored by Salute America's Heroes—an organization dedicated to supporting severely wounded veterans and their families—at its annual December event called Road to Recovery, at the Walt Disney World Resort near Orlando, Florida. More than one hundred injured veterans, dealing with the physical and emotional scars of wars in Iraq and Afghanistan, came from all over the country with their spouses and children to attend the weeklong event.

It was a chance for them to enjoy greatly needed family time in the land of the Magic Kingdom and to hear presentations on PTSD and other issues. There were panels on medical problems and career development, as well as information on strengthening relationships, improving finances, and dealing with the many obstacles facing veterans as they reenter civilian life. Gary Sinise performed for the vets and families with his Lieutenant Dan Band. Tampa Bay Rays' veteran play-by-play announcer Dewayne Staats signed autographs and talked baseball with the troops. The Orlando Magic mascot cavorted with kids and adults. And I signed inscriptions on copies of *Covert* for several hours, giving me the chance to interact with and observe the many inspiring military men and women in the presence of their loving, supportive families.

I was struck first by the children and how happy they all seemed—and not just because they were getting a trip to Disney with their parents. I couldn't help but think what a difference it made for them to be around other kids whose dads or moms were missing a foot, a leg, a hand—or moving in a wheelchair. They were around other children with situations similar to their own, and that unspoken peer-to-peer dynamic was undoubtedly good for their young psyches.

I saw a group of adults craving information and hope, anything that would illuminate paths of action for dealing with baggage from the battlefield. I was reminded of a metaphor shared with me by Lieutenant Colonel Tim Karcher, who had lost both legs in Iraq and was being cared for at the Fort Sam Houston Center for the Intrepid. He likened PTSD to a diet. Some of us need to lose five to ten pounds, some fifteen to twenty, and others are morbidly obese. And we also know that, as with dieting, the most difficult pounds to lose are the last five to ten. However, there are many people who have very happy and productive lives while carrying an extra five to ten pounds. My belief is that the same thing can take place with Post-Traumatic Stress. It's not necessarily about losing all of it—it's about learning to lose enough that you can live comfortably, even if you haven't shed the condition entirely.

I was pleasantly surprised at the Road to Recovery conference to learn of an on-site, Internet-based screening test for PTSD, adapted from a successful assessment test for traumatic brain injuries developed at Mount Sinai Hospital in New York. Both tests were being made available to vets—with spouses encouraged to accompany them—in any of four private hotel rooms. Although the more time-intensive TBI test requires about forty-five minutes, the one for PTSD—designed with the help of national PTSD expert Dr. Mark Wiederhold—takes roughly fifteen minutes to complete. Vets sit down in private and answer an array of questions on a graduated scale of one to five in terms of severity of symptoms. And they leave with a printout that provides an immediate gauge of their condition, with a recommendation for treatment options.

Unfortunately, organizers told me that only a handful of veterans at the conference had taken the PTSD test, apparently wary of what it might involve. So I volunteered to take it before my speech—partly to gauge the experience and see how I fared, but mostly to encourage as many as possible to follow my lead and take the plunge.

Some sample questions were:

- Do you have repeated disturbing dreams of a stressful experience?
- Do you suddenly feel as if a stressful military experience were happening again as if you were reliving it?
- Do you feel very upset when something reminds you of a stressful military experience?

I explained to the group in the room that I would have been off the charts with my replies thirty years earlier. Now my printout indicated no signs of PTSD. "You got better," explained Dr. Wiederhold. "That's why we give the test periodically."

Dr. Wiederhold's chief contribution to the study of PTSD lies in an innovative approach to therapy—the creation of a virtual reality environment for the sufferers that carefully introduces elements that caused the initial combat trauma. He has done this over the past decade as founder and chief executive officer of the Virtual Reality Medical Center in San Diego.

"Our therapy is approved by the Institute of Medicine—it's called exposure therapy," he said. "Pretty much everybody thinks this therapy is the way to go. There are several ways of doing it, but generically it's known as cognitive behavioral therapy. We use the virtual reality approach, because what we found is that if you ask a person to imagine an event, it's hard to do after a few minutes."

That's not the case with the advanced simulation technology Dr. Wiederhold uses. He immerses participants in a complete 360-degree virtual world that forces them to stay in the moment. "The good news is that we can control what a person sees and control what I call the velocity of exposure," he added. "Some people need a little bit more, some people a little bit less. You can individualize it. And at the same time, we monitor their physiology in real time, giving us an objective measure of their response. You actually expose them to the stressful event to get them over it."

The similar virtual reenactment of the traumatic event allows the individual to experience and express emotions tied to the actual event. It made me think of Mike Pool's verbal exposure therapy at WCPR and Operation Proper Exit's practice of exposing vets to the physical locale of their trauma. And it was similar to how Mary returned to the Gallaghers' former home at Camp Pendleton after Jim's death and forced herself to confront the site of her enormous pain, and how Robert Scheiber came to terms with so much emotional torment by giving his inspiring, cathartic speech at the Williams Syndrome Association conference. Facing the pain head-on is a step toward healing.

Prior to Dr. Wiederhold's virtual reality treatment, vets are trained to build up their skill sets in preparation for handling situations presented in the virtual world. "Then we basically normalize the exposure—and get to the point where the traumatic reaction is extinct," he said. "It works very well."

Dr. Wiederhold later addressed the conference, explaining that the virtual reality therapy was used with good success on site in Iraq during the war. "What we're working on, in addition to acceptance and awareness, is expanding the treatment so we can go a little bit further —and maybe get to some of these issues before they become full-blown problems," he told the audience.

It was exciting for me to learn about yet another treatment on the spectrum—and one that might help prevent Post-Traumatic Stress from developing into PTSD. Veterans and spouses seemed equally interested in this potentially new option unveiled during a week of hope.

Not even record, subfreezing temperatures in Florida that week could chill the uplifting atmosphere. And the unseasonably frigid weather brought to mind a fable—one I learned from Arthur Wunderlich, father of my fellow NBA referee Mark Wunderlich. The wind and sun were having a discussion one day that led to a bet. At stake was which force of nature could get a man to remove his coat. The wind went first, blowing harder and harder to no avail. It then added a drop in temperature. The man responded by raising his collar and pulling his coat tighter around him, refusing to let go no matter how hard the wind blew. Then the sun took its turn. The cold gave way to warmth as the sun shone directly on the man, who began to release his grip on the coat, and as he felt more comfortable, unbuttoned it and took it off.

We need to be more like the sun when we interact with others dealing with PTSD. The more warmth we provide, the more people will open up. That is the heart of peer-to-peer therapy.

• • •

In one way, this book is ending now. But our journey together through these pages was never about arriving at a specific destination—as I mentioned earlier, there is no finish line when it comes to PTSD.

The hope was simply for you to learn along the way, gaining new insights and knowledge as we move from the shadows into the light.

*Spending time with soldiers at Fort Hood after
sharing a PTS/PTSD presentation.*

"Take Care of Each Other"

"If you find it in your heart to care for somebody else, you will have succeeded."

—Maya Angelou

t was a call I hated to make, but there was no choice. Basketball fans had come out in force to watch a 2010 nationally televised exhibition game between Florida's two NBA teams—the Orlando Magic and the much-hyped Miami Heat.

Unfortunately, earlier that day, the maintenance crew at the Tampa arena had applied the wrong kind of polish to the hardwood, making the court nearly as slippery as the ice at the home rink of the NHL's Tampa Bay Lightning.

For the safety of the players, I recommended that the contest be canceled—knowing the move would be a big disappointment to the many thousands who'd bought tickets hoping to see stars like

Dwight Howard, LeBron James, and Dwyane Wade in action. I also knew that the scrubbed ESPN game would be a downer for a group of special guests—injured veterans from Iraq and Afghanistan. They were being hosted by the Embracing Florida's Wounded Heroes organization and were to have been honored between the first and second periods.

After the NBA decided to cancel the game, I was courtside with ESPN/ABC's broadcast team of Mike Breen, Hubie Brown, and Jeff Van Gundy. One of the injured vets in attendance— Lieutenant Bobby Woods, who had been shot only months earlier in Afghanistan—was standing several feet away, so I introduced him. I recounted Bobby's heroic personal story and brave actions on the battlefield. Then I asked him if he would remove his safety helmet—what the Wounded Warriors affectionately refer to as their brain bucket. He obliged, revealing a massive wound to his head sustained in combat. The realities of war were suddenly front and center.

I explained that Bobby was one of the wounded guests who could walk, but we had fourteen others and their families in an upper section of the arena who could not. As I pointed to them in hopes that the announcing team would wave, Van Gundy cut me off and proclaimed, "We're going!" All three headed with me and Bobby Woods through the nearly empty stands for an impromptu visit with the Wounded Warriors.

We mingled with them for an hour. And I think it meant as much to the members of the broadcast crew as it did to the veterans and family members.

Van Gundy told me and Retired General Chip Diehl, codirector of Florida's Wounded Heroes, that he would never again use the word *courage* when speaking about NBA players. "*This* is courage!" he said, standing in the midst of the honored group.

I knew exactly how he felt—it's the same reaction I have whenever I meet or spend time with the men and women who protect our country, not to mention the members of law enforcement, firefighters, and first responders who put their lives and emotional well-being on the line every day. That's one reason it was such a privilege to showcase their bravery and selflessness in *Surviving the Shadows*—to cast light on the burden of PTSD that many develop as a result of their duty and to reveal important medical approaches in the battle against this condition. Although I know that other valuable medical research and techniques are part of that fight, I wanted to share with you some of the groundbreaking work and cutting-edge therapies across the PTSD spectrum.

In the end, I hope you have come away with greater insights and understanding of how PTSD can take hold of a person—and how that person can learn to take hold of his or her life again.

The reality is that events causing PTSD to take root will always be part of our daily existence: combat, car accidents, natural or human-created disasters, assaults, even bullying. When we hear that word, we tend to think of it as a traumatic experience for kids. But it can come in many forms. You read about the terrible treatment Carol Paukner endured from her sergeant a day after her heroic efforts at the World Trade Center, and I have witnessed this kind of behavior throughout my professional life. I found it interesting that one in three adults has been at the receiving end of workplace bullying, according to a 2010 front-page

USA Today article. Bullying in all forms is another area that will continue to generate much discussion and study in the area of PTSD in the future.

As I've shared this journey with *Surviving the Shadows*, another important journey in my life is ending. This was my last season running the courts as a referee—an occupation I have been honored to have since 1987. Reflecting on all my NBA experiences— working with the most skilled officials at the highest level and with some of the greatest athletes on the planet—is best left for another time. For now, I'll just say that I'm grateful that the NBA provided me such a tremendous opportunity.

I turned to refereeing many years ago to find a sense of peace, after surfacing from my undercover operation infiltrating the mob amid the emotional turbulence of PTSD. And ultimately, my profession gave me a platform to help others seeking relief from their own PTSD turmoil.

Along the way, I know—and often share with people—that everything I've accomplished has been with the help of others.

I've been lucky in the game of life, lucky to have been blessed with great leaders and partners. The list starts with my Mom and Dad and includes family members and all the good people who took time to mentor me. They had the patience to help me understand and the willingness to share their wisdom—whether it was in everyday life, my years playing basketball and baseball, my career with the New Jersey State Police, or my quarter century in the NBA.

There have been teammates at every stop to ensure success. My good fortune has continued in the literary world, too. In 2006, I met Dave Scheiber, a talented, award-winning journalist who wrote a two-part article about my life for the *St. Petersburg Times*, titled "Courting Danger." As our relationship developed, I realized Dave would be the person with whom I would want to tell my story, and the result was *Covert*—named one of the best books of 2008 by *USA Today* and in the process of becoming a movie.

We've now completed our second book, which you hold in your hands—and have more ideas for future projects to share with you.

What started out as a newspaperman and a former Jersey trooper and NBA referee has developed into a true partnership and friendship for years to come. The word *collaboration* is used often, and I fully experience its meaning working with Dave Scheiber— another example of how lucky a guy I have been my entire life.

There are three phrases I use on a constant basis. Whenever I leave the locker room, I say to my officiating partners as we head to the NBA floor, "Take care of each other." Some of the younger referees know it's coming, and they beat me to it before I can get all the words out.

Whenever I address players in the pregame captain's meeting as crew chief, I always cap my remarks with "Stay healthy."

And in many phone conversations and emails, people who know me well are accustomed to my sign-off phrase, "Stay safe."

I offer all of those words as we continue this journey of hope into Post-Traumatic Stress.

Stay safe.

Stay healthy.

Take care of each other.

Acknowledgments

"Feeling gratitude and not expressing it is like wrapping a present and not giving it."

—William Arthur Ward

My coauthor, Dave Scheiber, and I are grateful for the help we received along the way in making *Surviving the Shadows* a reality. In that spirit, we'd like to give our acknowledgments as a gift of thanks.

First, we wish to express our appreciation to our literary agents, Uwe Stender of TriadaUS Literary Agency, and Philip Turner of Philip Turner Book Productions LLC, along with our editor Peter Lynch and all the good folks at Sourcebooks, Inc. for their fine work on our behalf throughout the process.

We thank the many individuals who allowed us into their lives—giving us a chance to get to know them, opening up about the pain they persevered through, and letting us tell their stories so others can hopefully find inspiration in how they have survived the shadows. That "thank you" extends to the gifted doctors, therapists, and program innovators who have poured their time and energy into helping people suffering from PTSD, and helping us learn more about the condition.

We'd like to recognize General Robert W. Cone and his wife, Jill, for the exemplary work they have done in the wake of the Fort Hood shootings—and the ongoing support programs that are provided. I am indebted to General Cone for his hospitality at the Al-Faw Palace and his introduction to General Ray Odierno, who has also made the mental health needs of troops a major priority. Thanks to my good friend, General Bob Brown, and his wife, Patti. He's currently the commander at Fort Benning, Georgia, and I was embedded with General Brown's unit on my first visit to Iraq. All of these military leaders have lent invaluable support to the peer-to-peer approach.

Lieutenant Colonel Tom Meyer, who worked with General Cone at Fort Hood and later joined him in Iraq, went out of his way to listen to our questions and provide consistently insightful answers and information. General Will Grimsley, Deputy Commander Fort Hood, also was an immense help during my visits there.

I thanked my former New Jersey State Police partner John Schroth in *Covert*, but he deserves another round of kudos for the no-nonsense, peer-to-peer support he gave me when I had lost my way after surfacing from my undercover assignment in the '70s. So does retired FBI agent Joe Pistone, the real-life Donnie Brasco, who did the same for me—and Dr. Hank Campbell, my former psychology professor who diagnosed me with PTSD and helped get me back on track.

I'd like to give a shout out to the entire Jersey State Police Division—I'm eternally proud to have been part of the "Outfit." I appreciate their ongoing support.

If you recall, I went straight from a Mob trial to my first trip into the war zone of Iraq—an amazing, life-enhancing experience made possible by an invitation from national broadcast personality Ron Barr and AKA Productions' Dwayne Ulloa and Jon Bullock. On those trips, I was also joined by former NFL players and great Americans Tim Dwight, Antonio Freeman, and Jim Miller.

Every book project can benefit from a strong support staff, and that was certainly the case with us. Dave and I would like to give a tip of the cap to the fine read-back, feedback efforts and morale boosts provided by Billie Delaney, Janie Scheiber, Walter Scheiber, Miriam Seidel, Shannon and Ryan Henderson, Danelle and Mike Madigan, Summer Egly, Dana and Ken Miklos, Sue and Richard Ellis, Kathy and Mark Tudyk, Jim and Kathy Gray, Laurie and Ron Coleman, Jim and Laura DiLella, Carter and Chase Egly, Valerie, Laura, Mollie, Julia, Emma, and Davey Scheiber, and also to Valerie for her skillful design contribution with our proposal. In addition, we thank Susie Spangler for her insights and input, in particular with the "Are You Robert?" chapter, and her valuable contributions as an artist/designer (http://susanspangler.com) to our book cover, and Barbara Scheiber for her invaluable perspective on Robert and excellent backup word editing of the manuscript.

Judy Goldstein and Larry Spiegel of Appledown Films provided creative insight during the research process. Retired Brigadier General

Acknowledgments

Chip Diehl became a proponent of our project early on, working tirelessly to spread the word about *Surviving the Shadows* and opening doors for the book being distributed within the military community.

Our thanks go out to a pair of leaders of the Hope for the Warriors organization, Robin Kelleher and Tina Altherall, who introduced me to Mary Gallagher—and Mary, in turn, introduced me to Chris Delaney and Brian Dwyer and the story of Private Joe Dwyer. We know there are many, many individuals and organizations doing great work on behalf of veterans, and we thank them for their efforts.

We'd like to give a nod to "The Big Man," the late Clarence Clemons, who took time out of his busy performance schedule to speak with us for the "Are You Robert?" chapter, and to St. Petersburg-based music promoter Johnny Green for paving the way.

Finally, special recognition to Matt Winick, for providing detailed research and information regarding my years in the NBA.

And thank *you* for coming on this journey. See you down the road.

About the Authors

Bob Delaney has been a distinguished referee in the National Basketball Association for the past quarter century and, in June 2011, retired from the game as one of the most respected officials in league history.

Prior to his NBA career, he spent fourteen years (1973–81) as a highly decorated New Jersey state trooper. Delaney infiltrated organized crime families along the East Coast, going undercover on a mission that ultimately led to numerous convictions of mobsters. That experience was chronicled in his 2008 book, *Covert: My Years Infiltrating the Mob*, named a best book of the year by *USA Today*.

He has received numerous awards over the course of his career, including: The President's Volunteer Service Award from President Obama, outlining Delaney's ongoing PTSD awareness and education work with the military, law enforcement, firefighters, and first responders, and the United States Army Outstanding Civilian Service Medal.

Delaney received the 2000 NBA Community Service Award and the National Association of Sports Officials Gold Whistle Award in 2003. He is in demand as a speaker at corporate meetings, sports banquets, social events, and schools throughout the country, and he has been featured on ESPN, ABC Sports, CNN, and HBO's *Real Sports*.

Dave Scheiber, a national award-winning journalist and coauthor of *Covert*, is a past first-place winner in one of the industry's most prestigious writing contests—the National Headliner Awards. He was also a member of a *St. Petersburg Times* team nominated for the Pulitzer Prize, for a series that won the National Education Writers Association first prize; a first-place winner for investigative reporting and feature writing in the Associated Press Sports Editors competition; and a recent National Institute for Health Care Management finalist for a story on military medicine.

His work has appeared in a wide variety of publications—from cover stories in *Sports Illustrated* to the *Washington Post* to Fox

Sports, where he currently covers all major professional sports in Florida as a columnist and television correspondent. Scheiber resides in St. Petersburg, Florida, where he and his wife—parents of six children—perform in a popular classic rock band in the Tampa Bay area.